Lecture Notes in Edu

MW01234988

Series Editors

Ronghuai Huang, Smart Learning Institute, Beijing Normal University, Beijing, China

Kinshuk, College of Information, University of North Texas, Denton, TX, USA

Mohamed Jemni, University of Tunis, Tunis, Tunisia

Nian-Shing Chen, National Yunlin University of Science and Technology, Douliu, Taiwan

J. Michael Spector, University of North Texas, Denton, TX, USA

The series Lecture Notes in Educational Technology (LNET), has established itself as a medium for the publication of new developments in the research and practice of educational policy, pedagogy, learning science, learning environment, learning resources etc. in information and knowledge age,—quickly, informally, and at a high level.

Abstracted/Indexed in:

Scopus, Web of Science Book Citation Index

More information about this series at http://www.springer.com/series/11777

Ronghuai Huang · Dejian Liu · Ahmed Tlili ·
Yuan Gao · Rob Koper
Editors

Current State of Open Educational Resources in the "Belt and Road" Countries

 Springer

Editors
Ronghuai Huang
Smart Learning Institute
Beijing Normal University
Beijing, China

Ahmed Tlili
Smart Learning Institute
Beijing Normal University
Beijing, China

Rob Koper
Open University of the Netherlands
Heerlen, The Netherlands

Dejian Liu
Smart Learning Institute
Beijing Normal University
Fuzhou, Fujian, China

Yuan Gao
Smart Learning Institute
Beijing Normal University
Beijing, China

ISSN 2196-4963   ISSN 2196-4971   (electronic)
Lecture Notes in Educational Technology
ISBN 978-981-15-3042-5   ISBN 978-981-15-3040-1   (eBook)
https://doi.org/10.1007/978-981-15-3040-1

© Springer Nature Singapore Pte Ltd. 2020
This work is subject to copyright. All rights are reserved by the Publisher, whether the whole or part of the material is concerned, specifically the rights of translation, reprinting, reuse of illustrations, recitation, broadcasting, reproduction on microfilms or in any other physical way, and transmission or information storage and retrieval, electronic adaptation, computer software, or by similar or dissimilar methodology now known or hereafter developed.
The use of general descriptive names, registered names, trademarks, service marks, etc. in this publication does not imply, even in the absence of a specific statement, that such names are exempt from the relevant protective laws and regulations and therefore free for general use.
The publisher, the authors and the editors are safe to assume that the advice and information in this book are believed to be true and accurate at the date of publication. Neither the publisher nor the authors or the editors give a warranty, expressed or implied, with respect to the material contained herein or for any errors or omissions that may have been made. The publisher remains neutral with regard to jurisdictional claims in published maps and institutional affiliations.

This Springer imprint is published by the registered company Springer Nature Singapore Pte Ltd.
The registered company address is: 152 Beach Road, #21-01/04 Gateway East, Singapore 189721, Singapore

Foreword

Increasing access to educational materials has been a matter of concern for teachers and educational policymakers. While the open educational resource (OER) movement is normally traced back only to the late 1990s and early 2000s, the seeds of improving access to educational materials is enshrined in the constitution of UNESCO adopted in 1945, which as part of its function states that UNESCO will "Maintain, increase and diffuse knowledge" … "by initiating methods of international cooperation calculated to give the people of all countries access to the printed and published materials produced by any of them." This further received a major boost when the United Nations General Assembly adopted the Universal Declaration of Human Rights in 1948. Article 26 (1) and 27 (2) focused on the rights to education for all and the rights of the creator of knowledge, which is at the heart of the OER movement. However, the understanding and practice of universal access to learning resources remain depressingly low. A UNESCO policy paper in 2016 reported that in 2012, there was only 1 reading textbook for 12 students and only 1 mathematics textbook for 14 students in grade 2 in Cameroon. This report highlighted that in many countries students lack access to books due to their high cost "Without textbooks, children can spend many of their school hours copying content from the blackboard, which severely reduces time for engaged learning."[1] Studies commissioned by Commonwealth of Learning (COL) shows that on average higher education students in Bangladesh spend BDT 1850 per year on books and supplies,[2] and in Malaysia 76.4% of learners decide not to buy textbooks due to high costs.[3] In the United States by 2016, the cost of textbooks increased 181% since 1998 in comparison to 48%

---

[1] https://unesdoc.unesco.org/ark:/48223/pf0000243321.
[2] http://oasis.col.org/handle/11599/2740.
[3] http://oasis.col.org/handle/11599/2739.

increase in the general consumer price index.[4] Students in US spend about USD 1,200 per year on textbooks, and 94% of the learners who had foregone purchase of the books due to high cost are concerned that it would impact their grades.[5]

Since 2002, when the OER term was coined in a UNESCO meeting, there have been several efforts to improve access to educational materials at all levels of education. In 2012, COL and UNESCO organized the first World OER Congress that called upon governments to release educational materials developed with public funds to release with an open license.[6] The OER global report 2017[7] prepared by COL highlights some of the major issues: only 41 countries indicated some kinds of policy support for OER; urgent need for capacity building both in the government sector as well as among teachers to find, use, and create OER; lack of awareness among stakeholders about over 100 existing repositories; and there is wide variation on the status of OER in different parts of the world. The Ljubljana OER Action plan[8] released at the second World OER Congress organized by UNESCO and Government of Slovenia highlighted five key areas of action to mainstream OER for achieving Sustainable Development Goal 4: (1) the capacity of users to find, reuse, create, and share OER; (2) language and cultural issues; (3) ensuring inclusive and equitable access to quality OER; (4) changing sustainability models; (5) developing supportive policy environments. Taking note of this, UNESCO has taken steps to adopt a recommendation to enhance international collaboration to mainstream OER.

The editors of this book have made a comprehensive attempt to bring together several initiatives in a number of countries to highlight the status of OER focusing on a geopolitical group of "Belt and Road" countries. Mainly it covers some of the countries in Africa, Asia, Europe, and Middle East documenting and highlighting little-known facts and developments in the field of OER. Using a template-driven approach, each of the chapters in the book provides key information on the status of OER activities, policies, infrastructure, outcomes, and impact. It is important to note that integration of OER in teaching and learning has impacted the educational landscape in different countries differently: from increasing access through repositories to the adoption of open educational practices, blended learning and offer of massive open online courses. Where policies are not clear, the community is taking action to release learning resources with open licenses. The case studies covered also highlight the existence of several training activities on OER and highlight the need for additional capacity building to effectively integrate and use OER in teaching and learning. Overall, the case studies also indicate the overlapping and

---

[4]https://www.aei.org/carpe-diem/chart-of-the-day-the-astronomical-rise-in-college-textbook-prices-vs-consumer-prices-and-recreational-books/.

[5]https://uspirg.org/sites/pirg/files/reports/NATIONAL%20Fixing%20Broken%20Textbooks%20Report1.pdf.

[6]http://www.unesco.org/new/fileadmin/MULTIMEDIA/HQ/CI/CI/pdf/Events/English_Paris_OER_Declaration.pdf.

[7]http://oasis.col.org/handle/11599/2788.

[8]https://en.unesco.org/sites/default/files/ljubljana_oer_action_plan_2017.pdf.

interdependence nature of OER with other related areas such as open learning, open access, open data, and how OER are integrated into the educational ecosystem for national development in different contexts.

Readers of this book will have a wide spectrum of information on OER in the countries covered. However, I would like to draw their attention also to key findings of a major research project[9] on OER in the global south that highlighted some of the key concerns on OER adoption. It is important for all of us involved in OER to reflect on these questions to find answers in our own contexts to help mainstream the use of OER globally. These are as follows:

(1) what will enable localization of OER moving from just copying or "as is" use?
(2) what are the best practices in curation and rehosting of derivative works?
(3) how to improve utilization of existing OER repositories?
(4) what actions would help improve the quality assurance processes for OER creation, adoption, and sharing?
(5) how to provide feedback to the OER creators?

There are certainly no right or wrong answers to these questions. But, we as community of practitioners of OER need to focus on collective action. To a large extent, it is possible by addressing the issues related to policy, capacity building, and technological infrastructure.

The collection of case studies in this publication is a rich source of good practices, options, and solutions for both OER practitioners and policymakers. The valuable expertise and experiences of the editors to collate and synthesize the case studies help us to make better sense of the OER developments in some of the "Belt and Road" countries. I am sure this will be a valuable resource for anyone interested in mainstreaming of OER globally.

Sanjaya Mishra, Ph.D.
Education Specialist, eLearning
Commonwealth of Learning, Canada

---

[9]https://idl-bnc-idrc.dspacedirect.org/bitstream/handle/10625/56823/IDL-56823.pdf.

Preface

Open Educational Resources (OER) are becoming a widespread movement, supported, and adopted by several institutions, organizations, and governments. Paris Declaration 2012 and Incheon Declaration 2015 called upon realizing the potential of OER as a way of fulfilling the objectives of "2030 Agenda", Sustainable Development Goal (SDG) 4—ensure inclusive and equitable quality education and promote lifelong learning opportunities for all. Therefore, the Belt and Road (B&R) International Community for Open Educational Resources (OER) has been established in support of the OER movement and China's "B&R Initiative".

Therefore, this book presents the OER state-of-the-art with the focus on the countries covered by China's Belt and Road Initiative. Specifically, the book describes the OER current state in those countries from eight aspects, namely: infrastructure, policy, resources, open license, curriculum and teaching methodology, outcome, stakeholders, and impact. Additionally, the book offers valuable insights and recommendations for different stakeholders, including policymakers and educators to facilitate OER adoption as well as insights for inter-regional cooperation on OER.

The book is structured according to three parts, namely: (1) Introduction part: it contains the first chapter of this book which presents a general introduction to help readers understand the OER concept as well as the OER Belt & Road initiative; (2) Case studies: It contains eleven chapters, where each chapter discusses the current state of OER in a specific country. The covered countries are Austria, Estonia, Italy, Korea, Magnolia, Morocco, Palestine, Romania, Serbia, South Africa, and Turkey; and, (3) Conclusion part: It discusses the eleven case studies and presents a comparative study to identify the OER gaps in the Belt and Road countries. This can help several stakeholders, including policymakers and educators, provide more strategies and solutions to facilitate OER adoption in these countries.

Ronghuai Huang
Ahmed Tlili
Smart Learning Institute of Beijing
Normal University
Beijing, China

Acknowledgements

We would like to first thank all of the authors for their valuable contributions to this book by sharing the current state of Open Educational Resources (OER) in their countries. These studies and their reported findings definitely help readers learn about how OER is adopted and applied in each country within the OER Belt and Road (B&R) initiative.

We would also like to thank all of the reviewers who accept to review the submitted book chapters and give their constructive comments and suggestions for the authors to further enhance the quality of their book chapters, hence enhancing the overall quality of this book. We really appreciate them for giving their reviews in a timely manner that helps our book to meet the production timeline.

Special thanks also go to the series editors, namely, Prof. Ronghuai Huang, Prof. Kinshuk, Prof. Mohamed Jemni, Prof. Nian-Shing Chen, and Prof. Mike Spector for their comments and guidance to prepare this book, as well as all our colleagues in the Smart Learning Institute of Beijing Normal University, China for their support to finish this book project.

Beijing, China   Book Editors

Contents

Editors and Contributors

About the Editors

Ronghuai Huang is currently a Professor in Faculty of Education and Dean of Smart Learning Institute in Beijing Normal University, the Director of UNESCO International Rural Educational and Training Centre and the Director of National Engineering Lab for Cyberlearning and Intelligent Technology. He serves as Vice Chairman of China Association for Educational Technology; Vice Chairman of China Educational Equipment Industry Association; Deputy Director of Collaborative and Innovative Center for Educational Technology; Director of Digital Learning and Public Education Service Center; Director of Professional Teaching and Guiding Committee for Educational Technology; Director of Beijing Key Laboratory for Educational Technology.

Dejian Liu is the founder of NetDragon Websoft Holding Ltd., one of the most successful online gaming companies in China. In 2015, he was awarded the Special Allowance Expert in China's State Council. In 2010, he founded Huayu Education, a wholly-owned subsidary of NetDragon. Huayu integrates worldwide cutting-edge education resources with leading mobile internet technology. Huayu specializes in K-12 and life-long education for learners all over the world. Huayu Education recently earned a Smart Media Award from Academics' Choice for producing a top-quality product, 101 Education, which improves teachers' experience in preparing lessons. He is certified as a senior engineer by the China Association of Science and Technology, the highest level of proficiency awarded. He is co-dean and chair of the Council for the Smart Learning Institute, an academic department at Beijing Normal University. In this capacity, he teaches a course on Virtual Reality Applications in Education, and he co-teaches a doctoral-student seminar on virtual reality and Visualization in Education. Mr. Liu graduated with a B.S. from the University of Kansas in 1995.

Ahmed Tlili is a former Assistant professor of educational technology at the University of Kairouan, Tunisia, where he has (co)supervised over 30 students and taught different subjects, including Human Computer Interaction (HCI), game development, web development and software engineering. Dr. Tlili is now a postdoctoral fellow at the Smart Learning Institute of Beijing Normal University. He is currently leading teams in the fields of Open Educational Resources (OER) and Edutainment. Dr. Tlili is a member of IEEE, OER laboratory of Smart Learning Institute, China and the laboratory of Technologies of Information and Communication & Electrical Engineering (LaTICE), Tunisia. His current research interests include open learning, learning analytics, game-based learning, distance education, learner modeling, adaptive learning, artificial intelligence in education and educational psychology. Dr. Tlili has published several academic papers in international referred journals and conferences. He has served as a guest editor in the Smart Learning Environments journal, as a local organizing and program committee member in various international conferences, and as a reviewer in several refereed journals. Dr. Tlili is the co-chair of IEEE special interest group on Artificial Intelligence and Smart Learning Environments and APSCE's Special Interest Group on Educational Gamification and Game-based Learning (EGG). Dr. Tlili is also the editor of the Springer book entitled Data Analytics Approaches in Educational Games and Gamification Systems.

Yuan Gao is the former Director of Open Educational Resources Lab and Senior Researcher at Smart Learning Institute of Beijing Normal University. Her main research interests include development and implication of open educational resources, instructional design, teaching and learning in smart learning environment, educational technology, educational psychology, and foreign/second language learning and instruction. Based on her wide-ranging interests, she has several publications on the relevant disciplines, and some of them have been published in the world-leading journal including journal of educational psychology. Since 2016, she attended and led a series of academic/research activities under the framework of 'Belt and Road' initiatives proposed by Chinese government. She contributed to a number of publications related to open educational resources, and attended to establish an international community of OER, which includes more than 60 organizations from 43 countries.

Rob Koper is a distinguished (university) professor at the Open University of the Netherlands with a specific focus on the innovation of online education, including the use of learning analytics, learning designs, open education and big data. He studies the social and cognitive aspects of human learning, the effective use of ICTs for human learning and the improvement of educational institutions to facilitate teaching and learning. He has written more than four hundred scientific contributions in journals and books, and has developed many different ICT systems to support learning and teaching.

Contributors

A. Amarzaya Department of Mathematics, School of Arts and Sciences, National University of Mongolia, Ulaanbaatar, Mongolia

Diana Andone e-learning Center, Politehnica University of Timişoara, Timişoara, România

Rachid Bendaoud Trans ERIE - Faculty of Sciences Semlalia, Cadi Ayyad University, Marrakech, BP, Morocco

Khalid Berrada Trans ERIE - Faculty of Sciences Semlalia, Cadi Ayyad University, Marrakech, BP, Morocco

Marija Blagojević University of Kragujevac, Faculty of Technical Sciences Čačak, Čačak, Serbia

A. Bulgan Department of Mathematics, School of Arts and Sciences, National University of Mongolia, Ulaanbaatar, Mongolia

Daniel Burgos UNIR iTED, Universidad Internacional de La Rioja (UNIR), Logroño, Spain

B. Burmaa The ONE Foundation, Khan Uul District, Ulaanbaatar, Mongolia

Kursat Cagiltay Education Faculty, Middle East Technical University, Ankara, Turkey

Ting-Wen Chang International Cooperation Center, Smart Learning Institute, Beijing, China;
Smart Learning Institute of Beijing Normal University, Beijing, China

Gi Woong Choi Department of Computer Science, State University of New York at Oswego, Oswego, NY, USA;
396 Shineman, Oswego, NY, USA

Jaewoo Do Future Education Research Division, Korean Educational Development Institute, Jincheon-gun, Chungcheongbuk-do, Korea

Martin Ebner Graz University of Technology, Educational Technology, Graz, Austria;
Graz, Austria

Ilham Laaziz El Malti Ministère de l'Education Nationale et de la Formation Professionnelle, de l'Enseignement Supérieur et de la Recherche Scientifique, Rabat, Morocco

Gabriela Grosseck Department of Psychology, West University of Timişoara, Timişoara, România

Carmen Holotescu Faculty of Engineering, "Ioan Slavici" University of Timişoara, Timişoara, România

Ronghuai Huang Smart Learning Institute of Beijing Normal University, Beijing, China;
Faculty of Education and Dean, Smart Learning Institute, Beijing Normal University, Beijing, China

Jamil Itmazi Palestine Ahliya University, Bethlehem, West Bank, Palestine

Engin Kursun Kazim Karabekir Education Faculty, Ataturk University, Erzurum, Turkey

Mart Laanpere School of Digital Technologies, Tallinn University, Tallinn, Estonia

Daeyeoul Lee Purdue University, West Lafayette, IN, USA

Sofia Margoum Trans ERIE - Faculty of Sciences Semlalia, Cadi Ayyad University, Marrakech, BP, Morocco

Tony Mays Unit for Distance Education, Faculty of Education, University of Pretoria, Pretoria, Republic of South Africa;
University of Pretoria, Groenkloof, Pretoria, Republic of South Africa;
Unit for Distance Education, Faculty of Education, University of Pretoria, Hatfield, Republic of South Africa

Danijela Milošević University of Kragujevac, Faculty of Technical Sciences Čačak, Čačak, Serbia

Jewoong Moon Department of Educational Psychology and Learning Systems, Florida State University, Tallahassee, FL, USA;
Tallahassee, FL, USA

L. Munkhtuya Office of ICT and Distance Education, Mongolan National University of Education, Ulaanbaatar, Mongolia

Fabio Nascimbeni Universidad Interacional de La Rioja (UNIR), Madrid, Spain

T. Navchaa Department of Mathematics, School of Arts and Sciences, National University of Mongolia, Ulaanbaatar, Mongolia

Ivan Obradović University of Belgrade, Faculty of Mining and Geology, Belgrade, Serbia

Hans Põldoja School of Digital Technologies, Tallinn University, Tallinn, Estonia

David Porter Ontario Online Learning Consortium (eCampusOntario), Toronto, Ontario, Canada

Sandra Schön BIMS e.V., Reichenhall, Germany

Ranka Stanković University of Belgrade, Faculty of Mining and Geology, Belgrade, Serbia

Secil Tisoglu Education Faculty, Kastamonu University, Kastamonu, Turkey

Ahmed Tlili Smart Learning Institute of Beijing Normal University, Beijing, China;
University of Kairouan, Kairouan, Tunisia

D. Tumenbayar Department of Mathematics, School of Arts and Sciences, National University of Mongolia, Ulaanbaatar, Mongolia

Junfeng Yang Department of Educational Technology, Hangzhou Normal University, Hangzhou, China

Imane Zaatri Trans ERIE - Faculty of Sciences Semlalia, Cadi Ayyad University, Marrakech, BP, Morocco

Part I
Introduction

Chapter 1
Open Educational Resources and the Belt and Road Initiative

Ting-Wen Chang, Ahmed Tlili, Junfeng Yang and Ronghuai Huang

1 Open Educational Resources

Open Educational Resources (OERs) were first coined at UNESCO's 2002 Forum on Open Courseware and are defined as "teaching, learning, and research materials in any medium, digital or otherwise, that reside in the public domain or have been released under an open license that permits no-cost access, use, adaptation, and redistribution by others with no or limited restrictions." Typically, an OER could be any piece of educational material (e.g., content, video, presentation, and course) characterized by the metadata that describes it, such as author, subject, and language (de Oliveira et al., 2018). A variety of standards for OER metadata have been established, including the Dublin Core and the IEEE LOM ("Learning Objects Metadata"). Typically, a set of metadata is considered to tackle the issue of contextual dependence of educational resources, where same topics can occur in different educational or curricular contexts with a different meaning or content, hindering reuse of learning materials in different contexts (Koper, 2003).

The idea behind OERs is that those educational materials (such as applications and tools, documents, pictures, and videos) are commonly published in online repositories which in turn are defined as digital databases that include the learning resources (McGreal, 2011). In these repositories, learners can search for an OER, view, and

T.-W. Chang (✉)
Beijing Normal University, Smart Learning Institute, Beijing, China
e-mail: tingwenchang@bnu.edu.cn

A. Tlili
Beijing Normal University, Smart Learning Institute, Beijing, China

J. Yang
Hangzhou Normal University, School of Education, Hangzhou, China

R. Huang
Beijing Normal University, Smart Learning Institute, Beijing, China

© Springer Nature Singapore Pte Ltd. 2020
R. Huang et al. (eds.), *Current State of Open Educational Resources in the "Belt and Road" Countries*, Lecture Notes in Educational Technology,
https://doi.org/10.1007/978-981-15-3040-1_1

download it, as well as its metadata. Butcher et al. (2011) stated that OERs can enhance the quality of the provided learning content, as well as capacity building, and facilitate knowledge sharing.

The core characteristic of OERs is that they are published under specific licenses. Pomerantz and Peek (2016) mentioned that the meaning of "openness" has evolved in the late twentieth and early twenty-first centuries, thus its definition differs from one context to another. Specifically, in OER, "openness" means that a resource is freely available to use, but the way of using it is protected by intellectual property licenses. In other words, the OER movement introduced the idea of releasing educational resources (e.g., content, course designs) that anyone could freely access, retain (download, duplicate, store), reuse, revise (translate, adapt, modify), combine, and share *under specific licenses*, that in turn, offer no or limited restrictions, yet recognize authorship of work. Wiley (n.d.) mentioned five OER principles of using OERs, namely: (1) Retain—each person has the right to make and own copies of the published resource, such as downloading, storing or duplicating; (2) Reuse—each person has the right to use the content in different ways, such as in classrooms or on a website; (3) Revise—each person has the right to revise the content and enhance it; (4) Remix—each person has the right to create something new by combining the original content with other contents; and (5) Redistribute—each person has the right to share with others copies of the original, revised or remixed contents. Based on these five principles, openness is seen as a continuum rather than a simple binary (open, close). As the restrictiveness degree of the used license for a particular resource increases, the granted permissions provided to users for that resource decreases, and the less open the resource becomes. Based on the above descriptions, Fig. 1 summarizes the process of OER use in a given situation.

The Creative Commons (CC) (2016) open licensing has become the most used license for the OER community as it provides a comprehensive range of attributions, such as Share-alike (SA) and Non-commercial (NC), which define how to legally use an already published open resource in the public domain. Havemann (2016) agreed with Wiley's definition about openness, and mentioned that resources released under CC licenses that include the "no derivatives restriction" are not seen as truly open, as this restriction prohibits revising and remixing. On the other hand, educators or OER publishers who share their resources without a license are, arguably, already aligned with the OER movement, and yet are seen as operating outside of it. Amiel and Soares (2016) pointed out that open licenses provide a legal ground for the published open resources.

The OER paradigm was officially adopted during the 2012 World OER Congress (Paris declaration), demonstrating emphatically the increasing worldwide interest toward open education movements. The OER vision was to provide educational resources which, unlike in traditional learning in universities/schools, would be free and open for everyone. Since then, several institutions have started providing open courses to learners, mostly in the form of Massive Open Online Courses (MOOCs).

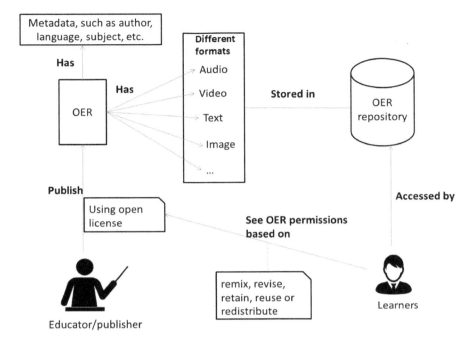

Fig. 1   OER use process

With the development of OER, more research and practice associated with OER emerged. In order to fully understand the research and practice of OER in a region or country, the following section will introduce the framework of OER evaluation.

2   The Framework for Evaluating OER State

To explore the current state of OER development in a country/region, eight factors are identified, namely infrastructure, policy, open license, stakeholders/users, resources, curriculum and teaching methodology, outcome, and impact. These factors are extracted from the literature based on a comprehensive literature review using several search keywords, including "open educational resources", "open education", "progress of open educational resources". The online search was in several online databases, including IEEE, Science Direct, and Springer. Only articles which are not written in English or discuss openness in other fields are excluded.

As shown in Fig. 2, the basis of this framework is built around the concept of a house. Infrastructure, policy, and open license are the foundations for OER development which make creating and publishing OER resources possible. It is followed by the strategies of integrating these resources into curriculum and the applied teaching methodologies to achieve successful educational outcomes. These processes are

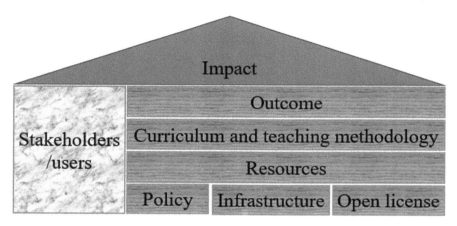

Fig. 2 Framework for evaluating OER state

inseparable from the engagement of stakeholders and users, and this is a two-way influence process. Each of these factors works together as a building block to facilitate education transformations, creating impact on educational equity and inclusiveness, and lifelong learning opportunities. Each of the eight factors is detailed below.

- *Infrastructure*: It is the basis to realize OER implementation, particularly ICT infrastructure. Although OER may not necessarily be digitized materials, however, with the support of technology, OER materials can be delivered cost effectively and more extensively. Infrastructure includes internet connectivity, software tools, repositories, and so on, which facilitate the creation, use, and sharing of OER. For instance, Wang and Zhao (2011) discussed that, in order to publish and adopt OER, technological infrastructure, including internet access, is a crucial factor. Nevertheless, in the circumstances where ICT infrastructure is limited, other innovative infrastructure can be adopted to support OER implementation.
- *Policy*: It is the main driver of OER movement in a country. OER policies can be a standalone policy framework, as well as an integral part of existing policies. Policies play a key role in supporting the integration of OER into educational processes, providing funding, establishing open licensing framework, building OER infrastructure, and so on. The development of OER policies involves governmental, institutional, and higher level organizational stakeholders. In this context, UNESCO released on 2019 an OER recommendation document which contains five objectives: one of these objectives is developing supportive OER policies (Tlili, Huang, Chang, Nascimbeni, & Burgos, 2019). Tlili et al. (2019) stated that universities should also update their policies to keep up with the OER paradigm, for instance, by including open access publications as one of the criteria to get promoted.
- *Open license*: It is the legal licensing framework that governs how OER is licensed for use. The open license protects a copyright holder's rights in environments where content (particularly when digitized) can so easily be copied and shared via the

internet without asking permission. In this context, Yawan and Ying (2013) found that educators avoid developing and publishing their open educational resources because they are afraid of copyright infringements. Particularly, they found that most people and institutions publish their OERs without an open license which defines how others should use these resources.

- *Resources*: They are educational materials appeared in various formats, such as open textbook, video, music, photographs, and so on that may be accessed, copied, used, reused, adapted, and/or distributed, depending on the open license (discussed above).
- *Curriculum and teaching methodology*: OERs are integrated into curriculum and teaching methodology to support teaching and learning. Curriculum refers to the contents of a series of subjects taught in a school or in a specific course or program, to achieve the pre-defined learning objectives or standards. Teaching methodology includes the teaching approaches or the strategies used to teach students the contents of a particular subject as set out in the curriculum. The use of OER for teaching in an innovative and collaborative environment is referred to as Open Educational Practices (OEP). Ehlers (2011) (p. 4) defined OEP as "practices which support the (re)use and production of Open Educational Resources through institutional policies, promote innovative pedagogical models, and respect and empower learners as co-producers on their lifelong learning paths."
- *Stakeholders/Users*: They are governments, organizations, and individuals involved in all OER development stages (e.g., educators, teacher trainers, librarians, learners, parents, educational policy makers, teacher and other professional associations, student associations, teacher, and student unions, as well as other members of civil society, and intergovernmental organizations and funding bodies).
- *Outcomes*: It refers to success and satisfaction of learners/educators using OER compared to the traditional learning method in classrooms or using online learning. For instance, several researchers (Hilton, 2016; Ozdemir & Bonk, 2017) investigated the perception of both educators and learners after using OER in learning.
- *Impact*: It refers to the impact of OER on educational transformation. In this context, Hilton, Bliss, Robinson, and Wiley (2013) developed a COUP framework that classifies OER impacts into four categories as follows: (1) Cost—investigates the financial impacts of OER adoption and reform; (2) Outcomes—investigates the learning impacts, such as academic performance, of OER adoption and reform; (3) Usage—investigates ways of using OER; and (4) Perceptions—investigates the opinions and feelings of learners as well as faculty members toward OER.

As noted above, OER is becoming a widespread movement, supported and adopted by institutions, organizations, and governments. Paris Declaration 2012 and Incheon Declaration 2015 called upon realizing the potential of OER as a means of meeting the objectives of "2030 Agenda", Sustainable Development Goal (SDG) 4—ensure inclusive and equitable quality education and promote lifelong learning opportunities for all. Therefore, the Belt & Road (B&R) International Community for Open Educational Resources (OERs) has been established in support of the OER movement and China's "B&R Initiative". This initiative is further detailed in the next section.

3   OER Belt & Road Initiative

China was one of the first Asian countries to adopt open education and its related strategies following the MIT OpenCourseWare Conference in Beijing in 2003. OER in China can be grouped into three categories (Tlili et al., 2019): OERs which are not protected by Chinese copyright laws or any other open licenses but are publicly available by Chinese institutions and libraries for use without any fee; OERs which are under an open license or protected by Chinese copyright laws that allow their free use and/or re-use; and OERs which are not under an open license and do not reside in the public domain yet are made available for free public use by government policies. Additionally, several initiatives have been launched in China to support the adoption and creation of OER, which are listed below.

(1) **Full coverage of digital educational resources for One-teacher school (2012)**
    https://jxd.eduyun.cn/cms/jxds/xmdt/
    The aim of this initiative is to provide high-quality digital education resources to 63,600 One-teacher schools across the country through IP satellites, internet, and other means, helping rural remote areas to access the national curriculum to meet the basic requirements of a good education. Basic hardware and resources are provided by Ministry of Finance, and the cost of project management, maintenance, and renewal is the responsibility of the local government's finance department.

(2) **National Quality Course**
    In 2003 the MoE initiated the National Quality Course (NQC) with the goal of reforming teaching content and enhancing courses. Approximately 750 universities participated in the development of NQCs and between 2003 and 2010, resulting in the development of 3,790 NQCs, of which 2,525 were general undergraduate courses, and 1,265 were vocational college and online education courses. While this initiative is noted as an OER, it is also noted that the NQCs adopted China's Copyright Law (all rights reserved).

(3) **Construction of National Quality Open Courses (NQOC) (2011)**—https://www.icourses.cn/home/
    This initiative focuses on sharing quality educational resources, showcasing best practices in teaching, encouraging independent learning, and supporting open learning using online platform. It also involves the building of 1,000 quality open video courses (QOVC) and 5,000 quality open resource course (QORC). The Ministry of Education provides subsidies for NQOCs, and local universities/colleges also provide funds for the development of quality open courses.

(4) *Five-Minute Course* (**2012**)—https://www.5minutes.com.cn
The five-minute course, initiated by Open University of China, aims to build 30,000 five-minute courses involving 100 subjects (academic and non-academic) in several fields including arts, history, language, economics, management, education, technology, science, philosophy, politics, and farming. Thus far, more than 30,000 five-minute courses have been developed, and the China's Copyright Law (all rights reserved) is used to protect the copyright.

(5) **XuetangX (2013)**—https://www.xuetangx.com
XuetangX is an initiative of Tsinghua and MOOC-CN Information Technology, which provides access to over 1,000 free courses from Tsinghua, Fudan, MITx, HarvardX, and other universities. The platform also includes some paid courses.

(6) **NetEase open courses (2010)**—https://open.163.com/cuvocw/**;NetEase cloud classroom (2012)**—https://study.163.com
NetEase, Inc. is a Chinese internet technology company providing online services centered on content, community, communications and commerce. Founded in 1997 by Lebunto, the company was a key pioneer in the development of internet services for China. Today, NetEase develops and operates some of China's online PC and mobile games, advertising services, email services, and e-commerce platforms. It is one of the largest internet and video game companies in the world. In November 2010, NetEase launched an "Open Course project", with the first batch of 1,200 courses placed online, including more than 200 video with Chinese subtitles. Users are able to freely access open courses from world-class and domestic universities such as Harvard University.

NetEase Cloud Classroom is an online platform for practical skills learning created by NetEase company, which is officially launched at the end of December 2012, which provides a large quantity of courses for learners, and the users can arrange their own study progress according to their own learning level.

(7) *One creative lecture per teacher, and one elite teacher per lecture* (**2014**)—https://1s1k.eduyun.cn/portal/html/1s1k/index/1.html
This initiative of the Ministry of Education and National Center for Educational Technology targets every teacher, particularly those in basic education. Starting in 2014, the initiative aims at fostering innovation in teaching and learning, promoting the integration of information technology and education teaching, and improving the quality of education through teachers' classroom use of OER. Currently, there are more than 16,975,318 lecturers from elite teachers in different discipline from different provinces in China. The subjects covered include language, math, English, science, music, arts, history, and physical education. The MoE allocates funds to each province according to the quality and quantity of courses uploaded the platform, and the education department in each province will use the money for teachers who provide the materials accordingly.

(8) *National Public Service Platform for Educational Resources* (**2012**)—https://www.eduyun.cn
The "National Public Service Platform for Educational Resources" is an innovation of the central government to provide basic public services for education. The platform, launched in December 2012, fully utilizes cloud computing and

other technologies to connect with regional educational resource platforms and enterprise resource service platforms. The platform brings together resources from famous schools and famous teachers. It also provides a personalized space for teachers and students throughout the country. By the end of December 2018, 12.52 million teacher spaces, 6.05 million student spaces, 5.56 million parents' spaces, and 400,000 school spaces were opened in the platform. Furthermore, 19 provincial platforms, 28 municipal platforms, and 26 district-level platforms were connected with this national platform. The national and provincial platforms are regarded as important OER platforms which are funded with public funds.

Paris Declaration 2012 and Incheon Declaration 2015 called upon realizing the potential of OER as a means of meeting the objectives of "2030 Agenda", *Sustainable Development Goal (SDG) 4—ensure inclusive and equitable quality education and promote lifelong learning opportunities for all.* Around the same time, China has proposed the "B&R initiative" which follows the historical symbol of the Silk Road Economic Belt and the twenty-first century Maritime Silk Road, aiming at establishing economic, political, and cultural partnerships with the countries along the Belt & Road. In response to the B&R initiative, the Ministry of Education initiated the "Proposed Actions on Jointly Building the Education of the Belt and Road" in 2016. This proposal highlights the importance of advancing educational collaborations among the Belt & Road countries, to strengthen cultural exchanges and facilitate capacity building.

Smart Learning Institute of Beijing Normal University has taken together the significance of OER and China's B&R initiative, using this opportunity to establish the B&R OER Community, with the aspirations of achieving quality education for all through knowledge sharing, combining expertise, and collaboration of its members.

The mission of the B&R OER Community is to leverage resources, knowledge, and expertise to catalyze quality education for all using OER, through joining forces of its members in Belt & Road countries. The Community aims to serve as a key enabler for meeting global educational challenges and generating long-lasting impact to contribute to a sustainable future. The Community emphasizes collaboration to extend outreach capacity, and to strengthen visibility and impact of its action on education in Belt & Road countries. The B&R OER Community aims to:

- Develop a policy framework for OER development in Belt & Road countries;
- Establish OER guidelines for developing and using OER in schools and educational institutions;
- Establish an OER platform for sharing knowledge and high-quality resources (i.e., Virtual Reality, STEAM Education, and Maker Education);
- Support the development and adaptation of OER in various languages and cultural contexts;
- Organize annual OER workshops and conferences;
- Conduct research and release publications associated with OER;

- Establish OER Research Centers in member countries, to further strengthen OER impact on education in Belt & Road countries;
- Invite partners, covering majority of the Belt & Road countries at the end of 2020.

4 Conclusion

This chapter started by explaining the term Open Educational Resource (OER) to readers and its impact on learning. It then presented a generic OER framework, which is composed of eight important factors, that researchers and practitioners should refer to when investigating the current state of OER in each country. Particularly, each factor of this framework is discussed to further present its importance within this framework. Finally, this chapter presents the Belt & Road initiative, and its main goal. The next part of this book will present the current state of OER according to the presented OER framework (Sect. 2) in several Belt & Road countries. Specifically, the findings of this investigation can help draw conclusions about the OER gaps and limitations that researchers and practitioners need to address in the B&R countries, hence provide the needed solutions accordingly. This may facilitate the OER adoption and progress in these countries.

References

Amiel, T., & Soares, T. C. (2016). Identifying tensions in the use of open licenses in OER repositories. *The International Review of Research in Open and Distributed Learning, 17*(3).

Butcher, N., Kanwar, A., Uvalic´-Trumbic´, S. (2011). *A basic guide to open educational resources (OER)*. Vancouver, Canada: Commonwealth of Learning, and Paris, France: UNESCO. Retrieved from https://www.col.org/oerBasicGuide.

de Oliveira, M. R., Sant'Anna, I. B., Ramos, G. S., de Bona, L. C. E., Castilho, M. A., Del Fabro, M. D., & Todt, E. (2018). Open educational resources platform based on collective intelligence. In *2018 IEEE 4th International Conference on Collaboration and Internet Computing (CIC)* (pp. 346–353).

Ehlers, U. D. (2011). Extending the territory: From open educational resources to open educational practices. *Journal of Open, Flexible, and Distance Learning, 15*(2), 1–10.

Havemann, L. (2016). Open educational resources. In M. A. Peters (Ed.) *Encyclopedia of educational philosophy and theory: Living edition*. Singapore: Springer Singapore. Retrieved from https://doi.org/10.1007/978-981-287-532-7_218-1.

Hilton, J. I. I. I. (2016). Open educational resources and college textbook choices: A review of research on efficacy and perceptions. *Educational Technology Research and Development, 64*(4), 573–590.

Hilton III, J., Bliss, T. J., Robinson, T. J., & Wiley, D. A. (2013). An OER COUP: College teacher and student perceptions of open educational resources. *Journal of Interactive Media in Education*.

Koper, R. (2003). Combining reusable learning resources and services with pedagogical purposeful units of learning. In *Reusing online resources* (pp. 64–77). Routledge.

McGreal, R. (2011). Open educational resource repositories: An analysis. In *The 3rd Annual Forum on e-Learning Excellence*, Dubai, UAE. Available at: https://elexforum.hbmeu.ac.ae/Proceeding/PDF/OpenEducationalResource.pdf.

Ozdemir, O., & Bonk, C. (2017). turkish teachers' awareness and perceptions of open educational resources. *Journal of Learning Development, 4*(3), 307–321.

Pomerantz, J., & Peek, R. (2016). Fifty shades of open. First Monday, 21(5).

Tlili, A., Huang, R., Chang, T. W., Nascimbeni, F., & Burgos, D. (2019). Open educational resources and practices in China: A systematic literature review. *Sustainability, 11*(18), 4867.

Wang, C., & Zhao, G. (2011). Open educational resources in the People's Republic of China: Achievements, challenges and prospects for development. Retrieved October 2, 2013.

Wiley. (n.d.). Accessed from: https://opencontent.org/definition/.

Yawan, L., & Ying, L. (2013). *A study on the use of open educational resources in China* (pp. 21–39). Open Education Resources: An Asian Perspective.

Dr. Ting-Wen Chang is the Associate Research Fellow and the Director of International Cooperation Center in Smart Learning Institute of Beijing Normal University (SLIBNU) for doing the research on smart learning as well as making many international cooperation projects since March 2014. As the Director of International Cooperation Center, he has made more than 50 international scholars/experts as well as several oversea institutions for SLIBNU in order to create lots of international cooperation about innovative and the cutting-edge technologies of smart learning. Dr. Chang was the workshop coordinator for some key workshops of SLIBNU, such as in 2017, the 1st Workshop on VR and Immersive Learning in Harvard University, The 4th Annual International Conference "Education & Global Cities: Smart Learning for World Universities" in St. Petersburg, Russia, and The 12th edition of the eLearning Africa Conference in Republic of Mauritius. On September 2017, Dr. Chang has also been responsible for the ME310 Global Project with School of Stanford University.

Dr. Ahmed Tlili is a former Assistant Professor of educational technology at the University of Kairouan, Tunisia, where he has supervised over 20 undergraduate students and taught different subjects, such as Human Computer Interaction (HCI), game development, web development, software engineering, and XML. Dr. Tlili is now working as a post-doctoral research fellow at the Smart Learning Institute of Beijing Normal University. He is currently leading projects in the fields of Open Educational Resources (OER) and Edutainment. Dr. Tlili is a member of IEEE, OER laboratory of Smart Learning Institute, China and the laboratory of Technologies of Information and Communication & Electrical Engineering (LaTICE), Tunisia. His current research interests include open education, learning analytics, game-based learning, distance education, learner modeling, adaptive learning, artificial intelligence in education and educational psychology. Dr. Tlili has published several academic papers in international referred journals and conferences. He has served as a guest editor in the Smart Learning Environments journal, as a local organizing and program committee member in various international conferences, and as a reviewer in several refereed journals. Dr. Tlili is also the co-chair of IEEE special interest group on Artificial Intelligence and Smart Learning Environments.

Dr. Junfeng Yang is a Professor and Dean of Department of Educational Technology in Hangzhou Normal University. He earned the title of "Zhejiang Young Zhijiang social science scholar", "Hangzhou new century 131 scholar". He has published more than 30 academic papers, including SSCI journal papers and outstanding Chinese journal papers. He serves as the associate editor of the journal of Smart Learning Environment published by Springer.

Dr. Ronghuai Huang is currently a Professor in Faculty of Education and Dean of Smart Learning Institute in Beijing Normal University, the Director of UNESCO International Rural Educational and Training Centre and the Director of National Engineering Lab for Cyberlearning and Intelligent Technology. He serves as Vice Chairman of China Association for Educational Technology; Vice Chairman of China Educational Equipment Industry Association; Deputy Director of Collaborative and Innovative Center for Educational Technology; Director of Digital Learning and Public Education Service Center; Director of Professional Teaching and Guiding Committee for Educational Technology; Director of Beijing Key Laboratory for Educational Technology.

Part II
Case Studies

Chapter 2
Open Educational Resources in Austria

Sandra Schön and Martin Ebner

1 Austria—Overview and Introduction

Austria ("Österreich" in German language) is a republic with about 8.8 million inhabitants in the middle of Europe and member of the European Union. Austria has German as its official language.

Austria is one of the well-developed parts of Europe, with a high living standard and an in general free educational system at school as well as university level. So education from primary to higher level can be consumed without any further costs. For some years a very small students' fee for universities was established (for EU citizens who take longer than the usual duration plus one tolerance semester each additional semester costs 360€ for the student union). Austria's general technical infrastructure is in general highly developed and reachable. This is especially illustratable with the fact that nearly all of the kids over 10 years have their own smartphone in Austria (Grimus & Ebner, 2016) with a high-speed Internet connection.

Nevertheless, the equipment in schools and teacher education concerning educational technologies still is lagging behind innovative countries such as others within the northern European Union (Baumgartner, Brandhofer, Ebner, Gradinger, & Korte, 2016). Usage of educational technologies in schools and universities is not bad, in general widespread, but on the other side still in development. An Austria-wide study for higher education (Bratengeyer et al. 2016) assessed the current status of

S. Schön
BIMS e.V., Reichenhall, Germany
e-mail: mail@sandra-schoen.de
URL: https://sandra-schoen.de

M. Ebner (✉)
Graz University of Technology, Educational Technology, Rechbauerstraße 12, 8010 Graz, Austria
e-mail: martin.ebner@tugraz.at
URL: https://elearningblog.tugraz.at

Münzgrabenstraße 36, 8010 Graz, Austria

© Springer Nature Singapore Pte Ltd. 2020
R. Huang et al. (eds.), *Current State of Open Educational Resources
in the "Belt and Road" Countries*, Lecture Notes in Educational Technology,
https://doi.org/10.1007/978-981-15-3040-1_2

e-learning. Therefore "all universities are already using e-learning today, although the intensity and the range of courses on offer vary greatly" (own translation ibid, p. 13).

Within Austria, Open Education Resource (OER) gained rising interest within the last 10 years. They are currently even part of the official strategies of the relevant ministry. Within the contribution an overview of the current state and last developments of OER activities in Austria will be given, also including the infrastructure, policy, existing resources, curriculum and teaching methodologies, outcome, stakeholders and impact. For this overview, we used an existing collection (Ebner, Freisleben-Teutscher et al., 2016), the National Education Report (Baumgartner et al., 2016) as well a broader overview of Austrian's OER activities (Schön, Ebner, & Hornung-Prähauser, 2017). Please note: Although "OER" includes software as well in the current OER definitions, the majority of activities that are coined as OER initiatives in Austria are related to educational content, such as textbooks, courses or similar materials—thus directly related to teaching and learning content.

2 Current Situation of OER

2.1 OER Infrastructure

Concerning OER, it is of interest, that the open-source learning management system Moodle is widely used in Austria (for higher education see Bratengeyer et al. 2016, for schools Baumgartner et al., 2016). With the start in 2016, according to the current IT strategy of the Austrian Federal Ministry of Education "Education 4.0" a new portal for "digital teaching and learning materials" will be created, called "Eduthek". According to the ministry, the materials should be available to teachers free of charge or openly licensed, but open licensing is not a prerequisite for admission (see Schön, Kreissl, Dobusch, & Ebner, 2017). The collection (BMP, 2017a) will include: "Teaching and learning materials, pedagogically recommended apps and games as well as innovative tools for modern teaching formats"; "Model application scenarios show teachers examples of how they can effectively integrate digital media into their teaching" (own translation). In the higher education sector, a so-called "e-infrastructure project" of an association of Austrian universities' libraries is developing a decentralized IT-architecture with the possibility to search in all available resources, as different systems are in use. Among other archived content, OER materials should also be made accessible through this infrastructure.

Austria contributes to the worldwide existing tools for the creation of OER especially with the following two very well-known projects: Geogebra and Catrobat.

At the turn of the millennium, the student Markus Hohenwarter from Salzburg developed the first version of Geogebra, a software on "dynamic geometry and algebra of the plane" (Hohenwarter, 2002) and continued his work as part of his doctoral thesis (Hohenwarter, 2006) and developed it further with colleagues. The software

GeoGebra is Open Source and its use and apps as well as contents are offered today by the "International GeoGebra Institute" for noncommercial purposes free of charge and therefore it enjoys high appreciation. Thus writes for example the CHIP editorship, where GeoGebra is led in the first place in the category "learning software" (CHIP, 2017). In addition to the software and apps there are numerous resources for GeoGebra, including several "books" on specific topics that include explanations and tasks. More than 140 "GeoGebra Institutes" are already established worldwide in 2017.

Wolfgang Slany, professor of computer science at Graz University of Technology, initiated the Catrobat project in 2010, which develops free software for children and young people with which they can "turn from passive users into creative developers": With the "Pocket Code" app and its visual programming language, children and young people can "create their own games, animations, stories or music videos directly on their mobile phones—anytime and anywhere" (Janisch, Ebner, & Slany, 2016). The project is successful worldwide and the headquarters of the "International Catrobat Association" is still Graz University of Technology. The project's successes include: According to OpenHub, Catrobat is among the 0.3% of the world's most active free open-source projects, was awarded the Austrian State Prize in 2013, the Lovie Award in 2015 (together with ESA, MSF and Red Bull), the EU Young Mind's Award in 2015, the Samsung Galaxy Game Jam in 2016 and many more. About 600 team members from more than 25 countries have been working on the nonprofit project for 7 years, with about 500,000 downloads of the Android version since 2014.

Smaller developments from Austria with international reach and role as OER infrastructures are, e.g. a template for a printed template for OER project development which was already translated at least into other 18 languages with the support of the international Open Education Group (see https://education.okfn.org/handbooks/oer-canvas/). Especially Graz University of Technology (TU Graz) already developed a set of apps that allows, e.g. to add the correct attributions to images from the Internet under open license or which helps when combining several different OER into a new one. Therefore Austria's OER developers also use software, websites as well as apps from outside Austria as well (Ebner, Scerbakov, & Schön, 2014).

2.2 Policy

OER movement in Austria began as a bottom-up movement at distributed initiatives of several educators but got eventually more drive through the establishment of the Creative Commons organization in Austria as well as through the research project OLCOS funded by the European Commission in the years 2005/2006. Later, the federal ministries funded numerous initiatives. However, the open licenses used were generally used due to the initiative of the participants and were not a prerequisite for the ministries or funding organizations (Schön, Ebner, et al., 2017). Nowadays OER can be seen as established part of Austria's current official educational strategies.

Already in the OECD study on OER, Austria is counted among the countries for which OER production or use is part of government policy (Orr, Rimini & van Damme, 2015, p. 129). Nevertheless, there is still no obligatory OER option for public funding; OER is still seen as an option among others. Although the ministries are interested to develop and implement new materials as OER and that an introduction of OER textbooks in schools was considered within a feasibility study (Schön, Kreissl, et al., 2017), there are currently no plans to change the whole system as such.

2.2.1 Governmental Policies

In Austria's National Report on Education 2016, OER is pointed out as a major topic for the first time; it is a focal point in the chapter "Promoting media competence—teaching and learning in the digital age" (Baumgartner et al., 2016). In 2016, the term "OER" was also mentioned for the first time in an Austrian government strategy paper, the "Digital Roadmap" (BKA and BMWFW, 2016). As a measure, it announces: "Gradual embedding of digital and interactive textbooks; making digital educational media and open and free educational content (Open Educational Resources, OERs for short) accessible; expanding offers for (self-organized) further education" (own translation). Since autumn 2016, the Federal Ministry of Education has been working intensively on the topic of open educational resources. On January 23, 2017, concrete projects were presented to the public (BMP, 2017a) (some of them are listed in Chap. 5.3); in addition, the press document on the digitization strategy of the Federal Ministry of Education (BMP, 2017b) presented the activities on digitization to date. In concrete terms, the press release in "Pillar 4: Digital Learning Tools" OER states: "To be able to convey digital content, teachers need simple and free access to teaching and learning materials. OER (Open Educational Resources) provides content and encourages the active use of digital media" (own translation). Under these activities, the ministry financed a feasibility study on OER schoolbooks in Austria (see Schön, Ebner, et al., 2017). The study addressed opportunities and challenges as well as presents possible scenarios and required changes for the introduction of OER schoolbooks in Austria. The main question here is whether and how the necessary changes for the development of OER schoolbooks (e.g. changed financing model) can be implemented by different stakeholders, especially as the current business model is well-established and appreciated by all stakeholders, besides the fact that no OER schoolbooks are available (ibid.). A newly established foundation with a special focus on digital learning (called "Innovationsstiftung Bildung") is currently asking for contributions for OER projects to modify existing OER (200.000 Euro for 2018/2019). Also for the ministry of research, science and economics, which was then responsible for higher education till 2017, OER was part of the strategy. The ministry developed, e.g. a strategy for OER certification (Ebner, Kopp, et al., 2017; Ebner, 2018) after the first white paper on "Open Educational Resources in Higher Education" was published in 2016 (Ebner, Freisleben-Teutscher, et al., 2016; Ebner, Kopp et al., 2016). Please note, that since 2018, there is (again) just one ministry responsible for schools as well as universities in Austria—ministry of education, science and research.

2.2.2 Institutional Policies

The University of Klagenfurt participated in the OpenCourseWare initiative from 2005 (last update 2009; see Ebner, Freisleben-Teutscher, et al., 2016); these activities were even part of an institutional strategy (see Kampl & Hofmann, 2007; Pfeffer, 2008). Graz University of Technology published—as far as we know–as the first university in German-speaking Europe an OER strategy in 2010 (Ebner & Stöckler-Penz, 2011). For the first time, OER was named and outlined on the level of higher education. Graz University Technology mentioned to put a focus on this topic and committed to further research projects.

Building upon this, the association of all universities in Graz organized an Austrian OER conference in 2011.[1] Currently, OER is part of several strategies for fostering educational technologies in education—for example the University of Vienna, the University of Graz or Graz University of Technology.

2.2.3 Higher Level Organizational Stakeholders Policies

The Internet Foundation Austria (IPA) has been systematically promoting the production of openly licensed Internet projects in Austria since 2006 with the "netidee" call for proposals. These are often open educational resources (usually software), especially in those years in which education topics have been the main focus of calls for proposals, e.g. 2011 "Education and the Internet". Approximately one million euros (as of 2016) are put out to tender annually, up to 50,000 euros per project. The tender is financed by the profits of the Internet directory services (Nic.at).

The association fnm-austria is the organization on teaching technologies of nearly all universities in Austria (in German called "Forum neue Medien in der Lehre Austria"). In 2016, fnm-austria published "Recommendations for the Integration of Open Educational Resources at Universities in Austria", outlining the advantages of OER and outlining a roadmap and necessary measures for the future of Higher Education (Ebner, Freisleben-Teutscher, et al., 2016). The working group OER of fnm-austria also presented a roadmap for recommendations for the integration of OER at universities in Austria. In cooperation with the responsible Federal Ministry of Science, Research and Economics as well as the OANA network, a concept for an OER certification of Austrian universities was developed in spring 2017 (Ebner, 2018). fnm-austria was also the organizer of the first Austrian OER Festival in May 2017.

Although the Austrian UNESCO commission is not funding or actively contributing to OER projects, it supports the OER movement in Austria through patronages of

---

[1] see http://iunig.at/o-e-r-2011/ (2016-01-03).

OER projects; for example for a project of the collaborative next edition of the open textbook on technologies for teaching and learning (L3T 2.0, see http://l3t.eu/2.0) and the OER MOOC platform iMooX.at.

2.3   Open License

Austria's policies and papers typically are referring to UNESCO's definition of OER (UNESCO, 2012). Due to copyright restrictions, free online materials or other resources may only be used in Austria to a very limited extent (e.g. for private use or under certain conditions as paper copies in school lessons, but not freely per se). In addition, copyrights cannot simply be abandoned or transferred (as is possible with the public domain regulation in the USA, for example). If one wants to use the materials of strangers, the regulations of the copyright law must be observed. In Austria, copyright holders, generally the authors of educational resources must be asked for permission before materials can be redistributed, modified and republished (Ebner, Lorenz et al., 2016). In Austria, as in all other countries of the European Union, individual agreements between the rights holders and potential users must therefore be drawn up in detail and, if necessary, negotiated individually (e.g. through contracts). In order to make them useable by third parties, i.e. teachers, students, parents, etc., legally safe and unambiguous, even without individual rights clarification, standardized open licenses are used in the case of OER. This is made possible by so-called open or free licenses (cf. Ebner, Vlaj, & Schön, 2013). Therefore, nowadays Austrian OER policies and projects are therefore typically using the following three Creative Commons licenses (Schaffert & Geser, 2008). Three license options of the Creative Commons licenses are most common and suggested: CC BY, CC BY-SA and CC 0 (see Table 1).

Please note, that OER also includes materials that are already in the public domain under Austrian law because the author has been dead for a very long time (this "happens" after 70 years since the death of the author).

There are of course several projects in Austria, especially projects, which were started in the early years of Creative Commons or from the field of open access, which also using more restricted Creative Commons variants such as CC BY-NC or CC BY-NC-ND.

2.4   Resources

Within the following paragraphs, an overview of OER originated in Austria or from projects co-organized from Austria's institutions is given.

Table 1 Open Licenses that are used typically in Austria (see OERdeckel, 2016; Creative Commons, 2016)

Name of the license	Requirements for the usage of the materials
CC BY	Use may be free of charge (including modification, commercial use), provided that the authors are named, details of the license are given, any changes made and any links are provided (e.g. link/URL to the license, original material)
CC BY-SA (SA stands for „Share Alike")	Use may be free of charge (including modification, commercial use), provided that the authors are named, details of the license are given, any changes made and any links are provided (e.g. link/URL to the license, original material). In addition, materials created using the resource must also be published under this license (CC BY-SA)
CC 0 ("Public Domain")	The use may take place without any copyright restriction

2.4.1 Early Developments of OER in Austria

In Austria there have been initiatives on OER in the narrower sense for more than 10 years, i.e. learning and teaching resources that may not only be used free of charge but may also be modified and republished, i.e. licensed openly. However, the now widespread Creative Commons licenses CC BY and CC BY-SA were only just emerging. Of special importance and relevance till today is the "Austria Forum" initiative (formerly AEIOU), which was launched as an online encyclopedia for Austria (Neuhold, Ebner, & Maurer, 2018). Since 1995 Hermann Maurer (today em. Prof. of TU Graz) and his team have been collecting a wide variety of materials, texts and pictures, which are freely available (due to legal issues not always under open license, e.g. because it is just to complicate to identify all relevant copyright owner of objects collected in early 1980). Werner Stangl, then assistant professor at the University of Linz, began publishing "Werner Stangl's Worksheets" in 1997. He was also one the early OER developers and his extensive online collection is now under the (restrictive) license CC BY-NC-ND. Both initiatives can be outlined as individual ones, driven by Hermann Maurer respective Werner Stangl.

2.4.2 Open Access Materials as (Potential) OER

With the increasing dissemination of the Open Access movement, Austrian journals have not only started to publish their articles online free of charge, but also to make use of the Creative Commons licenses. The journal "Zeitschrift für Hochschulentwick-lung" (formerly "Zeitschrift für Hochschuldidaktik") is financed by the Ministry of Science, Research and Economics (BMWFW). Since 2006 its contributions have been under the (comparatively restrictive) CC BY-NC-ND license. The articles of the journal "Medienimpulse. Beiträge zur Medienpädagogik" are published since 2009 under the license CC BY-NC-ND 3.0 AT. The articles of the "erwachsenenbildung.at" magazine financed by the Federal Ministry of Education have been freely accessible since the first issue in 2007 and published under an open license since 2016 (CC BY).

2.4.3 OER for School Sector

There are also several initiatives on OER in the area of schools in Austria. The Ministry of Education also supported some of these, but there is no final list of the projects or the production of OER that was often not part of the tender or required part of the tenders, but the participants decided in favor of OER. Since 2013 "OER activities are increasingly actively supported by Austrian ministries" (Ebner, Freisleben-Teutscher, et al., 2016, p. 11). These projects include (see Schön, Ebner, et al., 2017):

- In the DigiComp and DigiCheck project, a working group of the ministry of education, arts and culture (BMUKK) defined reference frameworks for digital competences at different school levels and collected a series of openly licensed (CC BY) teaching examples (Bundeskanzleramt 2013).
- "E-Learning 1 × 1" is an openly licensed handbook with teaching recommendations for teachers of the Virtual PH online campus with the eLSA and NMS e-learning networks and was produced on behalf of the Federal Ministry of Education and Women (CC BY-SA; Dobidia, Nárosy & Waba, 2014).
- Since about 2014/2015, small "e-learning appetizers" have been called "eTapas" within the framework of the "eLC2.0—eLearning Cluster Project" (elC2.0) network supported by the Austrian Federal Ministry of Education and Women (BMBF) and are openly licensed teaching proposals and materials relating to the use of digital technologies (see Neumann & Muuß-Merholz, 2016, p. 56).
- The EU project IDERBLOG ("Individually DifferEnziert Richtig schreiben", funded by Eramus) started in 2015 and provides comprehensive learning and teaching materials to improve writing skills, including software for text capture and analysis of children's contributions. In Austria, PH Vienna, KPH Krems, PH Styria and TU Graz are involved in the project (Steinhauer et al., 2017).

As mentioned, many of these OER were also (co-) financed with public funds. These materials are located on different platforms and educational servers of Austria's states. Additional materials, even if they "call" themselves OER or are definitely OER, are only accessible with registration; many of them are not marked with open licenses as OER as well.

By mid-2016 the ministry of education (BMB) had not yet set any guidelines regarding accessibility or licensing of the materials. Teachers with experience in the OER field and individual representatives of textbook publishers complain about the lack of or hidden licensing and thus unclear terms of use of the materials (Schön, Kreissl, et al., 2017), as this prevents the continued use of copies in other directories, for example, even though the initiatives were financed with public funding. With the year 2016 (see Sect. 3.1), increased support was given to OER. For example, from September to December 2016 an accompanying study was conducted on behalf of the ministry of education (BMB), in which digital materials were developed as OER in addition to the digital versions of the textbooks and the use was tested ("EBOOK IN ACTION") and in 2017 the first chapters of an openly licensed computer science textbook were published by the Graz University of Technology and further activities for basic computer science education were made available, including an openly licensed Moodle course on Pocket Code (Grandl, Höllerbauer, Ebner, & Slany, 2017). In 2018 the first OER schoolbook about the use of "BBC micro:bits in classrooms" had been developed by a group of educators and published online as well as a textbook by the ministry of education.

Examples of these projects which do not use open licenses, but which are often allowed to use the materials at least in public schools themselves, e.g. the photo collection for teachers Bilderpool.at or http://bilder.tibs.at/ is based on an initiative of the Tiroler Bildungsservices (TiBS) in cooperation with the Education Group (CC BY-NC-SA), the platform LMS.at (for students from Austria) or the materials of saferinternet.at (CC BY-NC).

2.4.4   OER in Higher Education

The textbook project "L3T" with more than 50 chapters about learning and teaching with technologies was published under CC BY-NC-ND in 2011. The new edition, published in 2013 is under CC BY-SA (Ebner & Schön, 2013). The textbook project is widely seen as "OER flagship project" and also got in 2016 an award by the German UNESCO commission for its impact on the German-speaking community. Besides its textbooks chapter itself, it got a lot of attention for its approach of an intense use of collaborative activities and a broad community: Version 2 of the textbook was edited within 7 working days with the support of 280 people (Ebner & Schön, 2012). Besides that, several Austrian universities worked within OER projects, which are already named within the last paragraphs as projects for school or do OER within international projects. One of the current bigger initiatives is "Open Education Austria", a so-called "university space structural funds project" approved for 2016–2018 by the Austrian Federal Ministry of Science and Research. It is a project of Austrian universities for the joint development of a national infrastructure for Open Educational Resources (OERs). For the first time, attempts are being made to link the services of e-learning centers, IT Services and libraries of partner universities in order to support teachers in the production of OER materials for self-study and teaching. Among other things, the project offers an open online OER course (COER17, see 5.6); an OER festival dealing with questions and challenges on the topic of Open Educational Resources has served about 100 participants. In addition, further education offers for universities are being developed.

Especially the Austrian MOOC platform iMooX.at has to be mentioned as a university project with a wide impact on teaching and learning beyond the university sector (Khalil & Ebner, 2016). The iMooX.at platform offered the first free and openly licensed online courses in 2014 and is based on a cooperation between University of Graz and Graz University of Technology. Under the auspices of the Austrian UNESCO Commission, it has specialized in openly licensed courses for a large number of participants (massive open online courses, in short MOOCs).

Last, but not least, OER as a research topic is regularly addressed within a special book-series of scientific contributions on OER called O3R.eu.

2.4.5   Other OER for Other Target Groups

Besides materials for schools and universities, Austria has additional OER projects as well, examples are:

- The project "WerdeDigital.at", launched in 2014 and cofinanced by the Federal Chancellery under the direction of Meral Akin-Hecke, bundles all materials on the subject of media competence and publishes e-books, materials and webinars under open license as well as a map with offers in the subject area (CC BY-SA).
- Digi4family is an initiative of former Federal Minister Sophie Karmasin (then Federal Ministry for Families and Youth) for media education of parents that started in autumn 2015. All webinars and materials are made available as OER (Röthler, 2016).

2.5   *Curriculum and Teaching Methodology*

As it was already mentioned and shown, OERs are already implemented in teacher education, teacher further education as special open online courses about OER or as topics within modules about technology-enhanced teaching. As sketched in the paragraph on higher education, the platform iMooX.at plays an important and significant role here; not only for providing OER-MOOCs itself but also with MOOCs about OER.

- In 2014, one of the first online courses of the newly founded MOOC platform iMooX.at is aimed at teachers, namely the online course "Learning on the Net": It provided an overview of current trends in online including OER.
- The Austrian State Prize for Adult Education was awarded to the openly licensed online course on the iMooX platform and the cooperation project "Free Online Learning" with more than 1,000 participants in the "Digital Literacy" category—it also introduced to OER (Ebner et al., 2015)
- Graz University of Technology also initiated the specialized open online course on OER (COER15) on the iMooX.at platform; it was repeated in 2016 (COER16) and modified in 2017 (COER17) and 2018 (COER18).
- In 2017, the openly licensed online course for digitization in adult education (EBmooc) under the direction of CONEDU at iMooX.at was the largest German-language adult education initiative to date. More than 3,000 registered participants

were counted, more than 1,000 have successfully completed the course where OER itself was a topic as well. This initiative was financed with funds from the Federal Ministry of Education and will be repeated in 2018 (Ebner, Khalil et al., 2017).

Besides this open online course, OER as a topic is already implemented in teacher further education, e.g. the Austrian wide offer of "T3C" for professors at educational universities. Finally, also the "Virtuelle Pädagogische Hochschule", responsible for the online education of all teachers in Austria, offers online course, e-lectures and content mostly based on the usage of OER. Furthermore, they also established online counseling for copyright questions where OER also plays an important role.

2.6   Outcome

Besides the potential direct usage of Austrian OER, the development of OER within several projects initiated concrete outcomes besides the pure materials themselves. We therefore want to emphasize the easy (re-) usage of materials that also makes new collaborations possible (Schön, Ebner, et al., 2017). Good examples for this from Austria are organizations that organized learning activities along the online courses "Gratis Online Lernen" as well as "EBmooc" because it is allowed, also with commercial intend (e.g. fees or marketing for new participants). These new cooperations spread the reach of the online courses and, e.g. the number of people who got already certificates for their course participation at the platform iMooX.at— in sum 4 thousands (June 2018). Furthermore, also new didactical concepts, called Inverse Blended Learning, can be seen as a result of this extensive OER usage (Ebner, Khalil et al., 2017).

2.7   Stakeholders/Users

Stakeholders for educational resources in Austria are teachers, pupils/students/learners, schools and universities, the ministries for (higher) education as well as content provider. Two developments could be seen as important and can eventually explain why Austria adapted OER several years before Germany: One year earlier than in Germany, since 2003, there are official Creative Commons contact persons in Austria. In 2004, they presented the first Austrian licenses at the Ars Electronica Festival. Today, the Austrian Computer Society (OCG), among others, coordinates the Austrian CC activities. Additionally, the first project on OER, called olcos.org, cofinanced by the European Commission was coordinated by an Austrian organization, Salzburg Research. In 2007, the "OLCOS Roadmap" appeared as a frequently quoted contribution on how open educational resources and open educational practices can gain importance in the future (Geser, 2007). The project was concluded at the international EduMedia conference in Salzburg entitled "Open Education enhanced by Web 2.0—Open Educational Practices and Resources for Lifelong Learning", which was the first conference on the topic of open educational resources in German-speaking countries (cf. Mruck, Mey, Schön, Idensen, & Purgathofer, 2013). These early developments are accompanied with a series of initiatives and projects from educators and researchers—several were already mentioned within this chapter. They can be typically seen as bottom-up or grass-root initiatives, although they eventually got public money, as the open licenses were not obligatory (and are not till today). For comparison: The first conference on OER in Germany was not held until 2013 under the leadership of the Wikimedia Foundation in Berlin (Ebner, Köpf et al., 2015, p. 21).

From the perspective of universities the role of their association on teaching with technologies (fnma-austria) was already described above. Additionally, as also described, the libraries from Austrian universities are already working on establishing OER measures as well.

Other civilian organizations in Austria which address issues of OER were, e.g.

- The Vienna Chamber of Labor published an article on the topic "Textbook Campaign Digital—Perspectives for Open Education in Austria" (Dobusch, 2015).
- The students' union established and organizes a "month of free education" since several years. It is associated with the idea of free access to education in general, but includes OER as well.

Textbook and schoolbook publisher from Austria are currently not actively supporting the development of OER, as this challenges their traditional business model although there is no direct need (e.g. action from ministry) to develop OER (see feasibility study on OER schoolbooks in Austria by Schön, Kreissl, et al., 2017).

The relevant ministry (currently the Austrian Federal Ministry of Education, Science and Research) is actively supporting the implementation and development of OER within their policies. Nevertheless, the development of OER is still not obligatory for public funds.

2.8 Impact

The impact of OER on educational transformation in Austria, although it is only the beginning, is manifold. Even, as experienced researchers on the topic we underestimated the different outcomes and developments, because OER is not only about the content itself it changes the whole educational system in the long run as well as innovates the educational field as such. One of the reasons why this is different in relation to other technological induced innovations is simple: OER costs nothing and if it is once published, it will not get lost as a resource, as it is possible to update, reuse, etc., also years later.

Mail impacts are simple that OER can be used as the Austrian copyrights rules limit the usage of schoolbooks and other materials rigidly (in comparison, e.g. with the US and the fair use principle). Today OER is seen as a solution, especially in

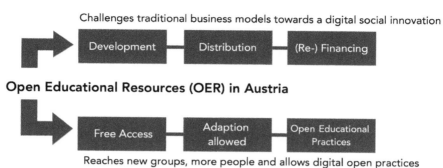

Fig. 1 OER influences business models and educational practices

the Higher Education sector. Based on the fact that a lot of teaching materials are produced by lecturers themselves for their lectures, open licensing is not only simple possibly it will also help to deal with things easily in the long run. So if for example, lecture handouts were OER the institution would know how to deal with the content when lecturers leave—same for the lecturers themselves. Also students can and will know how to work with the material. Shortly, OER will innovate the use of content and especially help in countries with a very strict copyright law. As shown, the usage and reach of OER developed in Austria is worldwide (e.g. Geogebra, Catrobat) or influencing the German-speaking world (e.g. L3T, iMooX.at).

How OER influences the development and usage of educational resources in OER can be seen as a complex change (see Fig. 1). OER influence not only the traditional business models (see Schön, Kreissl, et al., 2017) but also the educational practices including, e.g. the collaborations of organizations (Schön, Ebner, et al., 2017).

OER influences didactical concepts. In the case of MOOCs for example a new didactical approach, called Inverse Blended Learning has been developed in Austria. This concept describes the opposite of Blended Learning. Blended Learning means that a typical face-to-face lecture is extended and alternated by online components, whereas Inverse Blended Learning describes the enhancement of a MOOC with regular-presence meetings of learners and instructors (Ebner, Khalil, et al., 2017). Those presence meetings can be offered anywhere by anyone, even in a commercial setting, because the MOOC is offered as a central OER resource.

2.9 Conclusion and Discussion

It can be concluded that Austria plays an important role in terms of OER for central Europe. In comparison, especially to the other German-speaking countries, it seems that the current developments are exemplary.

2.9.1 Reflections and Issues

OER plays an important role in terms of dealing with the copyright issue and is extremely helpful to avoid problems or even punishments. On the other side, as described beforehand, it allows new didactical approaches or new possibilities in learning and teaching. Furthermore, the whitepaper on OER (Ebner, Kopp et al., 2016) points out 7 crucial advantages of OER:

1. OER increases access to free education.
2. OER provides substantial support to open learning scenarios.
3. OER produced by academics is generally of high quality.
4. OER expands the didactic opportunities for lecturers as well as students.
5. OERs are not automatically barrier-free, they make a valuable contribution to inclusion.
6. OER may also strengthen the collaboration between Higher Education institutions and corporations, especially start-ups in the fields of innovation and research.
7. OER improves the publicity of Higher Education institutions.

2.9.2 Challenges and Strategies

Despite the great initiatives and work about OER there are many barriers we have to overcome in the next years. Mostly, we need a better understanding from the public sector. Shortly, public funding should only fund open licensed content, so we need a mandatory commitment to OER. Furthermore, we have to encourage stakeholders to invest more in nationwide information systems who store OER and foster cooperation and exchange. Higher education institutions need a strong commitment to OER and have to offer educational programs to their lecturers. Finally, we need clear strategies on how we would like to deal with OER in the future.

2.9.3 Future Pathways

The future of OER in Austria should be a success in the long run. Nevertheless it is a hard way, because it needs a change in the educational system and the way that we deal with educational content today. Our main focus must be that the grass-root movement has to become mainstream. From our personal perspective, Austria is on a good path, on the right direction and should continue to do so.

One of our next steps is to work on the OER certification for Higher Education and to establish an educational program about "How to use OER in my daily teaching practice" for all educational sectors. Finally, the IT infrastructure should be elaborated more so that we can exchange learning objects in a fast and meaningful way.

References

Baumgartner, P., Brandhofer, G., Ebner, M., Gradinger, P., & Korte, M. (2016). Medienkompetenz fördern – Lehren und Lernen im digitalen Zeitalter. In M. Bruneforth, F. Eder, K. Krainer, C. Schreiner, A. Seel & C. Spiel (Hrsg.), *Nationaler Bildungsbericht Österreich 2015, Band 2: Fokussierte Analysen bildungspolitischer Schwerpunktthemen* (pp. 95–132). Graz: Leykam. January 3, 2017, https://www.bifie.at/public/downloads/NBB2015/NBB_2015_Band2_Kapitel_3.pdf.

Bratengeyer, E., Steinbacher, P., Martina, F., Neuböck, K., Kopp, M., Gröblinger, O., & Ebner, M. (2016). Die österreichische Hochschul-E-Learning-Landschaft. Book on Demand.

Bundeskanzleramt (2013). Bundesrecht konsolidiert: Gesamte Rechtsvorschrift für Familienlastenausgleichsgesetz 1967.

Bundeskanzleramt und Bundesministerium für Wissenschaft, Forschung und Wirtschaft (2016). Digital Roadmap. Die digitale Strategie der österreichischen Bundesregierung. December 3, 1999, https://www.digitalroadmap.gv.at/.

Bundesministerium für Bildung (2017a). Schule 4.0 – jetzt wird's digital. Presseunterlage, 23.1.2017. March 5, 2017 https://www.bmb.gv.at/schulen/schule40/index.html.

Bundesministerium für Bildung (2017b). Schule 4.0 – bisherige digitale Initiativen. Presseunterlage, 23.1.2017 (online nicht verfügbar).

CHIP (2017). GeoGebra. Beitrag der CHIP Software-Redaktion zur Version vom 8.3.2017. March 14, 2017, http://www.chip.de/downloads/GeoGebra_20747798.html.

Creative Commons (2016). Website Creative Commons. December 23, 2016, http://de.creativecommons.org.

Dobidia, A., Narosy, T., Waba, S. (2014). E-Learning 1x1. February, 2020, https://tablets.schule/wp-content/uploads/2012/09/1x1_E_Learning_1108_mit_Umschlag.pdf

Dobusch, L. (2015). Schulbuchaktion Digital: Perspektiven für Open Education in Österreich. AK Infos, Wien. February 14, 2017, http://www.dobusch.net/pub/pol/AK-Info-Folder_Schulbuch_digital.pdf.

Ebner, M. (2018). OER-certification in higher education. In *Proceedings of EdMedia: World Conference on Educational Media and Technology* (pp. 1–6). Amsterdam, Netherlands: Association for the Advancement of Computing in Education (AACE).

Ebner, M., Khalil, M., Schön, S., Gütl, C., Aschemann, B., Frei, W., & Röthler, D. (2017) How inverse blended learning can turn up learning with MOOCs? In *Proceedings of the International Conference MOOC-MAKER 2017* (pp. 21–30). Antigua Guatemala, Guatemala, November 16–17, 2017.

Ebner, M., Kopp, M., Hafner, R., Budroni, P., Buschbeck, V., Enkhbayar, A., Ferus, A., Freisleben-Teutscher, C. F., Gröblinger, O., Matt, I., Ofner, S., Schmitt, F., Schön, S., Seissl, M., Seitz, P., Skokan, E., Vogt, E., Waller, D. & Zwiauer, C., (2017). Konzept OER-Zertifizierung an österreichischen Hochschulen. Forum Neue Medien in der Lehre Austria.

Ebner, M., Freisleben-Teutscher, C., Gröblinger, O., Kopp, M., Rieck, K., Schön, S., Seitz, P., Seissl, M., Ofner, S., & Zwiauer, C. (2016). Empfehlungen für die Integration von Open Educational Resources an Hochschulen in Österreich. Forum Neue Medien in der Lehre Austria, 22 S. http://www.fnm-austria.at/fileadmin/user_upload/documents/Buecher/2016_fnma-OER-Empfehlungen_final.pdf.

Ebner, M., Kopp, M., Freisleben-Deutscher, C., Gröblinger, O., Rieck, K., Schön, S., et al. (2016b). Recommandations for OER integration in Austrian higher education. *Conference Proceedings: The Online, Open and Flexible Higher Education Conference, EADTU, 2016*, 34–44.

Ebner, M., Lorenz, A., Lackner, E., Kopp, M., Kumar, S., Schön, S., & Wittke, A. (2016) How OER enhance MOOCs —A perspective from German-speaking Europe. In M. Jemni, Kinshuk, & M.K. Khribi (Eds.), *Open Education: from OERs to MOOCs*. Lecture Notes in Educational Technology (pp. 205–220). Springer.

Ebner, M., Köpf, E., Muuß-Mehrholz, J., Schön, M., Schön, S., & Weichert, N. (2015). Ist-Analyse zu freien Bildungsmaterialien (OER). Die Situation von freien Bildungsmaterialien

(OER) in Deutschland in den Bildungsbereichen Schule, Hochschule, berufliche Bildung und Weiterbildung im Juni 2015. December 24, 2016, http://l3t.eu/oer/images/band10.pdf.

Ebner, M., Schön, S., & Käfmüller, K. (2015). Inverse Blended Learning bei "Gratis Online Lernen" – über den Versuch, einen Online-Kurs für viele in die Lebenswelt von EinsteigerInnen zu integrieren. In N. Nistor, & S. Schirlitz (Hrsg), *Digitale Medien und Interdisziplinarität* (pp. 197–206). Waxmann, Medien in der Wissenschaft Bd 68.

Ebner, M., Scerbakov, N., & Schön, S. (2014). How open content servers can be made beneficial for learning and teaching. *Transactions on Internet Research, 10*(2), 26–30.

Ebner, M. & Schön, S. (2013). Lehrbuch für Lernen und Lehren mit Technologien (L3T). December 3, 2016, http://l3t.eu.

Ebner, M., & Schön, S. (2012). *L3T – ein innovatives Lehrbuchprojekt im Detail: Gestaltung*. Apps und Finanzierung, Book on Demand, Norderstedt: Prozesse. ISBN 978-3-8448-1013-4.

Ebner, M., & Stöckler-Penz, C. (2011). Open educational resources als lifelong-learning strategie am Beispiel der TU Graz. In N. Tomaschek, E. Gornik, (Hrsg.), *The Lifelong Learning University* (pp. 53–60). Waxmann, Oldenburg, S. http://o3r.eu/.

Ebner, M., Vlaj, G., & Schön, S. (2013). Lehrunterlagen als E-Books – Überblick über weltweite Initiativen. In P. Micheuz, A. Reiter, G. Brandhofer, M. Ebner, B. Sabitzer, (Hrsg.), *Digitale Schule Österreich* (pp. 336–344). Eine analoge Standortbestimmung anlässlich der eEducation Sommertagung 2013.

Geser, G. (2007). Open educational practices and resources—OLCOS Roadmap 2012, Salzburg 2007. abrufbar unter November 12, 2013, http://www.olcos.org/english/roadmap/.

Grandl, M., Höllerbauer, B., Ebner, M., Slany, W. (2017) Ein offenes Unterrichtskonzept für den Einstieg in die Programmierung mit Hilfe von "Pocket Code". Coding als Baustein der digitalen Grundbildung (pp. 32–37). Schule Aktiv (Sonderheft des BMB).

Grimus, M. & Ebner, M. (2016). Mobile phones and learning—perceptions of austrian students aged from 11 to 14 years. In *Proceedings of EdMedia: World Conference on Educational Media and Technology 2016* (pp. 106–115). Association for the Advancement of Computing in Education (AACE).

Hohenwarter, M. (2002). GeoGebra—ein Softwaresystem für dynamische Geometrie und Algebra der Ebene. Diplomarbeit, Universität Salzburg. January 2, 2017, http://www.geogebra.org/publications/diplomarbeit_geogebra.pdf.

Hohenwarter, M. (2006). GeoGebra—didaktische Materialien und Anwendungen für den Mathematikunterricht. Dissertation zur Erlangung des Doktorgrades der Naturwissenschaften, vorgelegt am Fachbereich Fachdidaktik und LehrerInnenbildung der Paris-Lodron-Universität Salzburg.

Janisch, S., Ebner, M., & Slany, W. (2016) Pocket code—freier online-Kurs für kinder. In: Schule Aktiv, *Sonderheft Oktober 2016* (pp. 43–46). CDA-Verlag.

Kampl, R. & Hofmann, B. (2007). Offene Lehre ist freie Lehre ist gute Lehre. In Freie Netze. Freies Wissen. Echomedia, Linz. December 8, 2016, http://www.freienetze.at/pdfs/fnfw-kapitel3.pdf.

Khalil, M., & Ebner, M. (2016). When learning analytics meets MOOCs: A review on iMooX case studies. In G. Fahrnberger, G. Eichler, & C. Erfurth (Eds.) *Innovations for Community Services: 16th International Conference, I4CS 2016*, Vienna, Austria, June 27–29, 2016 (pp. 3–19). Cham, Springer International Publishing.

Mruck, K., Mey, G., Schön, S., Idensen, H., & Purgathofer, P. (2013). Offene Lehr- und Forschungsressourcen. Open Access und Open Educational Resources. In: M. Ebner, & S. Schön (Hrsg.), Lehrbuch für Lernen und Lehren mit Technologien (L3T). November 12, 2016, http://l3t.eu/homepage/das-buch/ebook-2013/kapitel/o/id/112/name/offene-lehr-und-forschungsressourcen.

Neuhold, P., Ebner, M., & Maurer, H. (2018). Mobile applications for encyclopedias. In S. Yu, M. Ally, & A. Tsinakos (Eds.), *Mobile and Ubiquitous Learning, Perspectives on Rethinking and Reforming Education* (pp. 229–247). Singapore: Springer.

Neumann, J., & Muuß-Merholz, J. (2016). OER Atlas 2016. Open Educational Resources: Akteure und Aktivitäten in Deutschland, Österreich und der Schweiz. Berlin: OER World Map.

OERdeckel (2016). Website OERdeckel. December 23, 2016, http://oerdeckel.wordpress.com.

Orr, D., Rimini, M., & van Damme, D. (2015). Open educational resources: a catalyst for innovation. *Educational Research and Innovation, OECD Publishing, Paris*. https://doi.org/10.1787/9789264247543-en.

Pfeffer, T. (2008). OpenCourseWare Klagenfurt: Ziele, Erfahrungen, Ausblicke. In V. Hornung-Prähauser, M. Luckmann & M. Kalz (Hrsg.), *Selbstorganisiertes Lernen im Internet. Einblicke in die Landschaft der webbasierten Bildungsinnovation* (pp. 209–213). Innsbruck: Studienverlag. January 21, 2017, http://www.uni-klu.ac.at/ocw/downloads/2008_pfeffer_ocw_klagenfurt.pdf.

Röthler, D. (2016). Medienbildung für Eltern – digi4family. Vortrag im Rahmen der edudays 2016, Krems.

Schaffert, S., & Geser, G. (2008). Open educational resources and practices. In *eLearning Papers*, 7, February 2008.

Schön, S., Ebner, M., & Hornung-Prähauser, V. (2017). Digital social innovation within education: Five insights on the role of digital tools in the field of Open Educational Resources (OER) projects. In R.V. Nata (Ed.), *Progress in Education*, vol. 49 (pp. 167–188). Nova publisher.

Schön, S., Kreissl, K., Dobusch, L., & Ebner, M. (2017). Mögliche Wege zum Schulbuch als Open Educational Resources (OER). Eine Machbarkeitsstudie zu OE Jakob Haringer Strasse 5/III|5020 Salzburg, AustriaR-Schulbüchern in Österreich. Band 15 der Reihe "Beiträge zu offenen Bildungsressourcen" (http://o3r.eu). http://l3t.eu/oer/images/band15.pdf.

Steinhauer, N., Gros, M., Ebner, M., Ebner, M., Huppertz, A., Cormann, M., et al. (2017). Learning analytics to improve writing skills for young children: An holistic approach. *Journal of Research in Innovative Teaching & Learning, 10*(2), 143–159.

UNESCO. (2012). *Paris OER Declaration*. Paris: Juni.

Sandra Schön is researcher and project manager in the field of digital social innovation and open educational resources. Her research focus lies on innovative forms of learning and working with technologies, e.g. Open Educational Resources and Maker Education.

Martin Ebner is currently head of the Department Educational Technology at Graz University of Technology and therefore responsible for all university-wide e-learning activities. He holds an Adjunct Prof. on media informatics (research area: educational technology) and works also at the Institute for Interactive Systems and Data Science as a senior researcher. His research focuses strongly on seamless learning, learning analytics, open educational resources, maker education and computer science for children. Martin has given a number of lectures in this area as well as workshops and keynotes at international conferences. For publications as well as further research activities, please visit his website: http://martinebner.at

Chapter 3
Open Educational Resources in Estonia

Hans Põldoja and Mart Laanpere

1 Case Overview

Estonia is a small country situated in Northern Europe. With a population of 1.3 million people, it is one of the smallest countries in the European Union. Despite having a turbulent history with various rulers, Estonia has maintained its cultural traditions and language. The Estonian educational system consists of general education, vocational education and higher education. General education is divided into pre-school, basic and upper-secondary education. Various studies have recognized the quality of Estonian education, for example the most recent PISA study showed that the Estonian basic education is among the best in Europe and in the world (OECD, 2016). Most important developments in the area of education are guided by the Lifelong Learning Strategy for 2014–2020 (MER, 2014), which lists five strategic goals: (1) a change in the approach to learning; (2) competent and motivated teachers and school leadership; (3) the concordance of lifelong learning opportunities with the needs of the labor market; (4) a digital turn in education; and (5) equal opportunities and increased participation in lifelong learning.

H. Põldoja (✉) · M. Laanpere
School of Digital Technologies, Tallinn University, Narva mnt 25, 10120 Tallinn, Estonia
e-mail: hans.poldoja@tlu.ee
URL: http://www.hanspoldoja.net

M. Laanpere
e-mail: mart.laanpere@tlu.ee
URL: http://www.mart.laanpere.eu

© Springer Nature Singapore Pte Ltd. 2020
R. Huang et al. (eds.), *Current State of Open Educational Resources in the "Belt and Road" Countries*, Lecture Notes in Educational Technology,
https://doi.org/10.1007/978-981-15-3040-1_3

2   Current Situation of OER

2.1   Infrastructure

The OER infrastructure in Estonia consists of learning object repositories (LOR), learning resource authoring tools, assessment platforms, virtual learning environments (VLE) and supporting systems such as metadata application profile and single sign-on (SSO). There is a large number of educational information systems that are managed directly by the Ministry of Education and Research (MER) or by other organizations working under the ministry. An analysis conducted in 2014 mapped more than 300 educational information systems. Currently the ministry is in the process of consolidating these information systems under the central concept of Hariduspilv (Education Cloud) (2014). Education Cloud covers also information systems for authoring, publishing and using digital learning resources. While not all of these systems support open educational resources, it is important to examine them as part of the wider educational infrastructure.

The main learning object repository for general education is e-Koolikott (e-Schoolbag), which was launched in 2016 by MER. Currently the repository contains more than 18,700 learning resources. These include open educational resources, resources without an open license and also some commercial content from the textbook publishers. Teachers are able to create collections of content which contain existing resources in the repository and their own content. The collections can be shared with students and other users of e-Koolikott. The possibility to create collections leads teachers to upload their own resources to the repository. While the Creative Commons licenses are prominently presented in the publishing interface, the search interface does not yet allow users to search content by open licenses.

Together with the development of e-Koolikott, a learning resource metadata application profile EstCORE was compiled based on IEEE Standard for Learning Object Metadata and The Learning Resource Exchange metadata application profile by the European Schoolnet. This work was inspired by other localized metadata application profiles such as NORLOM in Norway. A detailed four-level classification taxonomy allows connecting each resource to a subject domain, school subject, topic and subtopic. This taxonomy is based on the most recent (2014) versions of national curricula for primary, secondary and high schools. The EstCORE metadata application profile is implemented in several repositories that are linked to e-Koolikott portal that is automatically harvesting the metadata of recently added or edited learning objects from all these repositories. The metadata harvesting takes place once a day, using the OAI-PMH protocol. The future plans envisage switching to the next version of EstCORE that is based on LRMI (instead of LOM), in connection to the upcoming curriculum reform in 2021.

There are two other large repositories that are not developed further after launching e-Koolikott. Both of these repositories are managed by the Information Technology Foundation for Education (HITSA). Koolielu was used as the main repository for general education between 2001 and 2016. During these years teachers published more than 5,700 learning resources, more than 3,300 of these under Creative Commons licenses. The metadata of most of the high-quality resources from Koolielu has been transferred to e-Koolikott. The second repository managed by HITSA was focused on higher education and vocational education. It was taken into use in 2009 and contains more than 4,600 learning resources, all under Creative Commons licenses. The main aim of this repository was to store resources that were developed in various content development projects which were funded by European Social Fund.

Some projects and communities have set up their own OER repositories. LeMill was a collaborative authoring platform and repository for OER, which was used widely by the Estonian teachers between 2006 and 2014 (Leinonen, Purma, Põldoja, & Toikkanen, 2010). During these years, Estonian teachers published more than 3,400 OERs on LeMill platform, all under CC BY-SA license. Another noteworthy initiative is KAE Kool, which was inspired by Khan Academy and contains more than 150 educational videos under CC BY-NC-SA license.

Foundation Innove is managing the Examination Information System (EIS) which is used for preparing test tasks and conducting online tests. EIS provides 30 different question types that can be used in tests. The system is integrated with the Estonian ID-card infrastructure which provides a safe solution for authenticating students who take the tests. EIS is currently mostly used for conducting standard-determining tests in schools. Currently it is not possible to publish test items under open licenses, but EIS is an important part of the national digital learning resources infrastructure.

The main VLE used in vocational and higher education is Moodle, which is provided on a central hosting platform by the HITSA foundation. Tallinn University has developed their own VLE named eDidaktikum, which is used mostly in teacher training programs. Primary and secondary schools use study information systems eKool and Stuudium. These systems have started out as a digital gradebook and tool for communicating with parents. However, both of the systems now also provide simple tools for managing assignments and learning content. Tallinn University has developed several tools for managing open learning environments where learners use blogs such as LePress (Tomberg, Laanpere, Ley, & Normak, 2013), Dippler (Laanpere, Pata, Normak, & Põldoja, 2014) and EduFeedr (Põldoja, Duval, & Leinonen, 2016). The latter one of these is still in use for organizing master level courses in a MOOC-like open format. EduFeedr enables any interested learner to enroll to the course with their personal blog, aggregates all posts and comments from participants' blogs and displays some simple learning analytics visualizations.

There is currently no OER authoring tool that is offered as a free online service for a wider community of interested educators. School teachers are mostly using standard office software and Web 2.0 tools for authoring open educational resources. The common strategy is to use Weebly, Blogger, WordPress or Google Sites as a simple content management system and to combine this with embedded resources from external services such as YouTube, SlideShare, LearningApps.org and others. The lack of central authoring platform means that often teachers do not take additional steps to submit their learning resources to the repository. Also these generic content management tools do not provide any support for learning resource metadata. Tallinn University has developed a special authoring platform DigiÕppeVaramu based on

Drupal and H5P. Several new interactive content types were developed for DigiÕppe-Varamu in addition to the existing content types provided in H5P. It has been used in a large OER development project, but it is not yet offered as a service for wider audience.

In higher education there are currently no state-level initiatives to support authoring and adoption of OER. University of Tartu has set up their own learning content authoring platform based on OpenScholar. Some of the websites developed on this platform are published as OERs. In Tallinn University, there have been some experiments with Xerte Online Toolkits, but it has not been taken into wider use. Some lecturers use WordPress or other simple content management systems to build websites that are published under open licenses.

In order to provide single sign-on between different educational information services, TAAT infrastructure (The Estonian Academic Authentication and Authorization Infrastructure) has been developed, using SimpleSAML technology. Instead of having a separate user account for each service the users can use their existing account and authentication system in their home institution. TAAT has been used mainly by larger universities and HITSA. A new identity management system HarID is currently being piloted, and it is based on OpenID/OAuth technology. The aim of HarID is to provide a possibility to use the same user account for authentication in all online systems related to education, be it on the school, municipality or national level. Such SSO service will work across all education levels and forms, allowing development of next-generation learning analytics services. Until now, only a few small-scale learning analytics initiatives have been piloted within research projects.

The use of open educational resources and digital technologies puts learner into a more active role which requires teachers to plan their lessons in a new way. To support teachers in planning their lessons and sharing the lesson plans, Tallinn University has developed an online platform named LePlanner (Pata, Beliaev, Rõbtšenkov, & Laanpere, 2017). This platform enables teachers to create visual lesson plans in which teacher's and learners' activities are connected to the resources used in these activities. Learning scenarios may combine both OER and other content, making it also easy to share a collection of related resources to the learners. All learning scenarios created in LePlanner are published under CC BY license.

A simplified architecture of the digital learning resources infrastructure used in Estonia is presented in Fig. 1. We have selected four steps from the typical usage scenario of OER suggested by Camilleri, Ehlers, and Pawlowski (2014) as a basis for describing the architecture: authoring, publishing, integrating and using. Other steps suggested by Camilleri et al. (2014) are not that clearly supported by specific software applications or can be seen as sub-processes of authoring, publishing and using.

As can be seen from the figure, there are two alternative workflows for OER. The aim of DigiÕppeVaramu authoring tool and e-Koolikott repository is to provide a simple workflow that allows teachers develop OER, publish them in the repository and create collections which combine their own OER with resources from other teachers and from external websites such as YouTube or Kahoot! However, a lot of teachers still prefer to use their own tools such as Weebly or other simple website

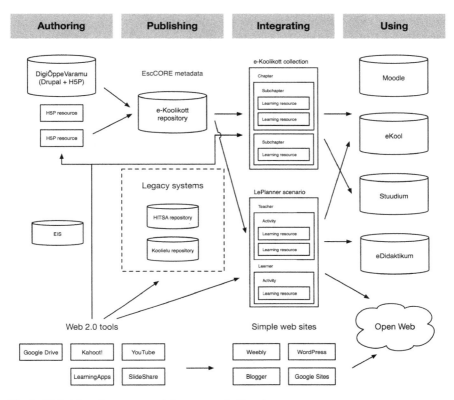

Fig. 1 Digital learning resources infrastructure in Estonia

building tools for integrating their resources and making them available for the learners. e-Koolikott repository and main VLE's (Moodle, eKool) are integrated with SSO solutions. However, the possibilities of learning analytics are largely not used. Also, a lot of learning activities that take place in the open web are loosely integrated with the rest of the digital learning resources infrastructure.

2.2 Policy

The Estonian Lifelong Learning Strategy 2020 defines availability of Bring-Your-Own-Device compliant open educational resources as one of the policy indicators related to the digital turn program in primary and secondary education. In order to implement the Lifelong Learning Strategy and to apply modern digital technologies (mainly learners' own devices, BYOD) in all levels of education in a more efficient way, MER has launched the first phase of the Digital Turn program on 2015–2018. This program requires that learning resources developed with public funding should be distributed under Creative Commons Attribution (CC BY and CC BY-SA) license. The use of Creative Commons licenses (both CC BY and CC BY-SA) has been a requirement also in several funding instruments that support the development of learning resources by the school teachers and university lecturers. However, there exists no specific open education strategy in Estonia. Until 2014, the professional accreditation policy for primary and secondary school teachers provided a powerful incentive to develop and publish OER in Koolielu repository, as the authors of validated learning resources received a certificate that helped them to move to the next category (a senior teacher, with 20% salary increase). Unfortunately, the current professional qualification system for teachers does not provide any incentives like this and teachers' motivation to publish OER without pay has decreased significantly.

2.3 Open License

The Copyright Act entered into force in 1992 and has been updated numerous times, because of new technical possibilities and a need to comply with European Union directives. Copyright applies from the moment that the work is created and lasts during author's lifetime and 70 years after their death. The copyright act specifies author's moral and economic rights, as well as principles of free use of works. Section 19 of the Copyright Act regulates the free use of works for scientific, educational, informational and judicial purposes. Under certain conditions, it is permitted to make summaries and quotations from a work, use the work as an illustration, reproduce copies for teaching and scientific research, and process a work for text and data mining.

The Creative Commons 3.0 licenses were localized by the HITSA foundation in 2010. All localized CC licenses were listed in the required metadata field in the main local learning object repositories and introduced in various teacher training programs. However, the localizations have not been actively maintained in recent years, and CC version 4.0 has not been localized yet.

There have been various in-service teacher training programs which also cover copyright issues and open licenses for digital learning resources. Therefore, there is some level of awareness about open licenses among teachers and educators. Regarding the license choice, two tendencies come out from the repositories' statistics. At first, university lecturers and vocational school teachers are more restrictive and prefer licenses with Non-Commercial restriction. In fact, the most used license in HITSA repository was CC BY-NC-ND, which does not allow users to create derivative works from the resources. School teachers have always been more open with the license choice, while CC BY-NC-SA was still the most used license in Koolielu repository; it was followed by CC BY-SA (35%). The fact that in e-Koolikott the majority of content is under CC BY license does not mean that there has been an important shift in teachers' use of CC licenses. This is related to recent large content development projects in which MER required authors to use CC BY license.

2.4 Resources

Main repositories used in Estonia were introduced in Sect. 2.1. Most of them combine both open educational resources and other content that is not published under open licenses. Only HITSA's repository is limited to CC-licensed content.

The largest and most recent repository e-Koolikott contains more than 18,700 learning resources, more than 11,700 of these are under Creative Commons licenses. Most of these resources are for basic and upper-secondary education. The most commonly used license in e-Koolikott is CC BY (61% of OERs), followed by CC BY-NC-SA (28% of OERs). Koolielu, which was previously the main repository for general education, contains more than 3,300 open educational resources. The majority of OERs in Koolielu are under CC BY-NC-SA (57%) or CC BY-SA (35%) licenses. In general education, teacher trainings, competitions and other non-financial measures have been used to encourage teachers to share their learning resources as OER. Both Koolielu and e-Koolikott have a network of subject experts for assuring the quality of published resources. In Koolielu, all the resources were moderated by the subject experts before they were made public in the repository. Experts suggested changes to the resources, when it was required. e-Koolikott allows teachers to publish their resources immediately, but subject experts are still following the updates in their subject area.

The second largest repository of open educational resources is HITSA's repository, which contains more than 4,600 OERs for vocational and higher education. As mentioned earlier, the main aim of HITSA's repository was to host content that was developed the financial support from The European Social Fund. Only less than 5% of resources are not related to any funded content development project. In these projects, many of the authors used Creative Commons license only because it was required. This reflects also on the preferred licenses: 46% of resources are under the most restrictive CC BY-NC-ND license, followed by 41% of resources under CC BY-NC-SA license. After the financial support for content development ended, the growth of the repository dropped significantly.

Within the Digital Turn program, MER has focused on more coordinated, systemic and large-scale development of digital learning resources. For instance, recently MER has funded the largest ever national OER development project DigiÕppeVaramu, where Tallinn University coordinated the development of more than 10,000 interactive learning objects that covered all of the compulsory and elective courses in the national curriculum for upper-secondary schools (grades 10–12) in four subject domains out of six: mathematics, science, social studies and arts. For example, in science the resources consist of 6 courses in physics, 4 courses in chemistry, 3 courses in geography, 5 courses in biology, teacher's book and additional resources for vocational schools. One course in a school equals to 35 lessons. More than 120 experienced subject teachers from upper-secondary schools were hired as authors to create these learning objects on Drupal platform, using interactive templates of H5P. All the resources are described with appropriate metadata and classified using a four-level taxonomy (subject domain, school subject, topic and subtopic) according to EstCORE metadata application profile. All produced learning resources passed through a rigorous quality assurance procedure and 20% of the resources were piloted by teachers in 30 schools in spring term of 2018. These resources are published in Estonian language under Creative Commons Attribution license, available for using and editing by all teachers and students in the e-Koolikott platform.

MER has recently funded also some specific digital OER development projects, targeting learners with special needs or development of highly prioritized competences (e.g. swimming or computing skills). For the main subjects in primary and lower-secondary education, MER preferred to procure licenses of commercially published digital textbooks collected to the online platform called Opiq.

Several Estonian universities have provided their courses as MOOCs. In Tallinn University, some lecturers have experimented with cMOOC format in which all learners use their personal blogs and Wikiversity (Kikkas, Laanpere, & Põldoja, 2011). University of Tartu is developing open online courses in highly successful series of MOOCs in which video lectures and course readings are combined with quizzes and discussion (Leito, Helm, & Jalukse, 2015; Lepp et al., 2017).

In addition to OER and MOOCs, research groups in Tallinn University and University of Tartu have been involved in the development of a number of open source learning tools for open education. These include OER authoring tools (Leinonen et al., 2010) and various learning platforms (Pedaste et al., 2015; Põldoja, Duval, & Leinonen, 2016).

In non-formal and informal education, OERs are rarely used in Estonia. Although driving schools use actively online learning resources (e.g. teooria.ee), these are usually copyrighted and not open.

2.5   Curriculum and Teaching Methodology

The current national curricula for basic schools and for upper-secondary schools entered into force in 2014. The national curricula does not refer to open educational resources, but it acknowledges that study material shall include resources based on contemporary information and communication technologies. Furthermore, the national curricula states that studies may be organized also in virtual study environments.

Studies show that Estonian teachers actively participating in professional development activities (OECD, 2014). Several ICT-related teacher training programs cover OER. However, the percentage of teachers using innovative teaching practices (group work, ICT, projects-based learning) frequently is below average in TALIS 2013 study (OECD, 2014).

Regarding teaching methodology, we can point out some interesting open educational practices from the higher education level. In Tallinn University, several lecturers run their courses in a blended learning format in which the online activities take place not in a closed learning management system, but in an open and distributed learning environment based on learners' personal blogs and other social media tools.

This open course format allows any interested person to take part in online learning activities. The pedagogical design of these courses follows the principles of self-directed learning by giving more control and responsibility to the learner. In addition to designing and controlling their personal learning environment, learners plan their learning goals and strategy using personal learning contracts (Väljataga & Laanpere, 2010). Learning contracts are also used for self-assessment in the end of the course. In some courses there have been experiments with using Open Badges for assessment (Põldoja, Jürgens, & Laanpere, 2016). In the educational technology Master program, about half of the courses are based on this kind of open course format.

It is not clear, how many universities and schools are adopting OER in their teaching programs. However, based on the resources published in HITSA repository we can conclude that lecturers from five public universities out of six have shared their resources as OERs. Regarding schools, it can be estimated that the majority of upper-secondary schools are going to use some resources from DigiÕppeVaramu project, which covers mathematics, science, social studies and arts in upper-secondary level.

2.6 Outcome

There are no studies on the outcomes of using OER in Estonia. In DigiÕppeVaramu project there has been an initial piloting of the developed resources in 30 schools. However, this initial pilot study focused on the quality and interactivity aspects of the developed resources. Learners' success and satisfaction of using OER is a topic for future studies. It must be also studied how the openness of resources changes teachers' practices.

2.7 Stakeholders

Implementation of the Estonian Lifelong Learning Strategy is led by the Ministry of Education and Research. Several activities related to the ICT infrastructure and content development are delegated to two foundations that work under the ministry: The Information Technology Foundation for Education (HITSA) and Foundation Innove. There are six public universities in Estonia. Tallinn University and University of Tartu, the main providers of initial teacher education, are more active than others in developing open educational resources and practices. There is no formally established open education community in Estonia, but some internet communities work on open content (Wikimedia Estonia, KAE Kool, various subject teacher communities). The main national OER initiatives have been recently coordinated and funded by MER, HITSA and Innove.

2.8   Impact

There are no in-depth studies on the impact of OER on educational transformation in Estonia. In 2016, six Estonian teachers were interviewed about their perception and application of copyright for a study that was carried out in five European countries (Kasprzak, Jurkowska, & Tarkowski, 2017). However, on a practical level it can be said that OERs have a certain impact, as the majority of resources in the national learning object repositories are under Creative Commons licenses.

3   Discussion and Conclusion

When discussing the situation with the open educational resources in Estonia, we have to take into account that implementing OER in a small country which use their own language is a different challenge than implementing OER in a large English-speaking country (Krelja Kurelovic, 2015). To summarize our current situation, we have outlined some aspects that can be considered successful and areas in which we need improvement.

At first, it must be pointed out that digital learning resources in schools are a priority area in our educational policy because of the Lifelong Learning Strategy and the Digital Turn program. However, we must acknowledge that the openness is not the main reason behind the focus on digital learning resources. In media the parents have often expressed their concerns about the fact that thick textbooks make school bags too heavy. The ministry has also used this as an argument for moving toward digital textbooks. This reflects also in the name of the new digital learning resources repository, which can be translated as e-Schoolbag.

There is a relatively good cooperation between MER, universities, textbook publishers and foundations that deal with developing the educational system and use of ICT in education. In a small country there are less experts working in the field and more personal contacts between the people. These contacts are strengthened by regular informal networking events such as seminars organized by the HITSA foundation and the universities. Also there has been a strong network of about 50 active teachers who do in-service teacher training courses on using digital technologies. We can rely on this network when promoting the idea of OER among the wider community of school teachers.

Having good direct contacts to important decision makers in MER has helped us to promote the understanding that publicly funded resources should be published under open licenses. In the beginning it was a challenge to gain wider understanding about the differences and compatibility issues between Creative Commons licenses. The decision makers tended to prefer more restrictive CC BY-NC-SA licenses. However, in several recent projects it has been a requirement to make the developed resources available under CC BY license, which gives more possibilities for reuse and building upon the content.

Finally, we must point out that in a recent project four subject fields of upper secondary education (mathematics, natural science, social studies and art subjects) were covered with more than 10,000 interactive OERs made available under CC BY license. This enables to introduce the idea of OER to a wider teacher community, encourage different kind of reuse of digital resources and provide possibilities to study how the use of OER changes the educational practices in schools.

However, there are still a number of areas in which the situation needs improvement. At first, there is a lack of specific OER policy in state and institutional level. A lot of recent developments, such as the move toward a more liberal CC BY license, are based on good personal contacts to the decision makers. Having a state-level OER policy would guarantee that these decisions are systematically followed also in the future. There is a lack of coordinated OER initiatives in higher education. Some universities have set up their MOOC initiatives, but this is seen more as a marketing tool than a way to open up learning. University lecturers are also not sharing their resources in the repositories, although there are lecturers who use open licenses and have set up web pages for their OERs. This is related to general awareness about OER and open licenses. While school teachers are more willing to share their resources openly, lecturers in higher education have a more skeptical attitude toward sharing their resources. As a small country, we do not have a functional open education community, although uncoordinated OER development is relatively active and increasing. However, we have several other open communities such as open source community, open data community and Wikipedia community, which sometimes turn attention to education. Related to community building, there is also little participation in international networks. For example, Estonia is not anymore actively involved in some networks where we participated earlier (such as EdReNe network of educational repositories). Some of the previous good practices have been discontinued with the move from Koolielu repository to e-Koolikott and reorganization of tasks between the foundations working in the field. As a result, we have less systematic approach on quality assurance and OER topics are not anymore in focus in in-service teacher training system. Also there is inconsistent approach to developing digital learning resources for basic schools and upper-secondary schools. While there was a large initiative to cover upper-secondary curriculum with OER, digital learning content projects in basic education have been targeted to textbook publishers who only make their content available with restricted access.

Finally, there is a lack of research to assess the actual outcome and impact of OER. Most of related research in Estonia has focused on design and development of software tools for open education and on pedagogical practices related to open education. The possibilities of learning analytics have been little used. It is our challenge to use the existing digital learning resources infrastructure and good cooperation with MER and other stakeholders to develop a deeper research on the topic.

References

Camilleri, A. F., Ehlers, U.-D., & Pawlowski, J. (2014). *State of the art review of quality issues related to Open Educational Resources (OER)*. Report No. EUR 26624 EN. Retrieved from Institute for Prospective Technological Studies website. https://is.jrc.ec.europa.eu/pages/EAP/documents/201405JRC88304.pdf

Hariduspilv (Education Cloud). (2014). Retrieved from https://www.hm.ee/en/activities/digital-focus/hariduspilv-education-cloud

Kasprzak, T., Jurkowska, O., & Tarkowski, A. (2017). *Creator, rebel, guardian, unsuspecting user: Teachers and modern educational practices* (pp. 1–34). Warsaw: Communia. Retrieved from https://rightcopyright.eu/wp-content/uploads/2017/04/Teachers-and-modern-educational-practices.pdf

Kikkas, K., Laanpere, M., & Põldoja, H. (2011). Open Courses: The next big thing in eLearning. In A. Rospigliosi (Ed.), *Proceedings of the 10th European Conference on e-Learning* (pp. 370–376). Reading: Academic Publishing Limited.

Krelja Kurelovic, E. (2015). Advantages and limitations of usage of open educational resources in small countries. *International Journal of Research in Education and Science, 2*(1), 136–142.

Laanpere, M., Pata, K., Normak, P., & Põldoja, H. (2014). Pedagogy-driven design of digital learning ecosystems. *Computer Science and Information Systems, 11*(1), 419–442. https://doi.org/10.2298/CSIS121204015L

Leinonen, T., Purma, J., Põldoja, H., & Toikkanen, T. (2010). Information architecture and design solutions scaffolding authoring of open educational resources. *IEEE Transactions on Learning Technologies, 3*(2), 116–128. https://doi.org/10.1109/TLT.2010.2

Leito, I., Helm, I., & Jalukse, L. (2015). Using MOOCs for teaching analytical chemistry: Experience at University of Tartu. *Analytical and Bioanalytical Chemistry, 407*(5), 1277–1281. https://doi.org/10.1007/s00216-014-8399-y

Lepp, M., Luik, P., Palts, T., Papli, K., Suviste, R., Säde, M., & Tõnisson, E. (2017). MOOC in programming: A success story. In L. Campbell & R. Hartshorne (Eds.), *12th international conference on e-Learning (ICEL 2017)* (pp. 138–147). Sonning Common: Academic Conferences and Publishing International.

MER. (2014). *The Estonian lifelong learning strategy 2020*. Retrieved from https://www.hm.ee/sites/default/files/estonian_lifelong_strategy.pdf

OECD. (2014). *Talis 2013 results: An international perspective on teaching and learning*. OECD Publishing. https://doi.org/10.1787/9789264196261-en

OECD. (2016). *PISA 2015 Results (Volume I): Excellence and equity in education*. Paris: OECD Publishing. https://doi.org/10.1787/9789264266490-en

Pata, K., Beliaev, A., Rõbtšenkov, R., & Laanpere, M. (2017). Affordances of the LePlanner for sharing digitally enhanced learning scenarios. In M. Chang, N.-S. Chen, R. Huang, Kinshuk, D. G. Sampson, & R. Vasiu (Eds.), *IEEE 17th international conference on advanced learning technologies* (pp. 8–12). Los Alamitos, CA: IEEE Computer Society. https://doi.org/10.1109/ICALT.2017.77

Pedaste, M., De Vries, B., Burget, M., Bardone, E., Brikker, M., Jaakkola, T., et al. (2015). Ark of inquiry: Responsible research and innovation through computer-based inquiry learning. In H. Ogata, W. Chen, S. C. Kong, & F. Qiu (Eds.), *Workshop proceedings of the rd international conference on computers in education ICCE 2015* (pp. 187–192). Asia-Pacific Society for Computers in Education.

Põldoja, H., Duval, E., & Leinonen, T. (2016). Design and evaluation of an online tool for open learning with blogs. *Australasian Journal of Educational Technology, 32*(2), 64–81. https://dx.doi.org/10.14742/ajet.2450

Põldoja, H., Jürgens, P., & Laanpere, M. (2016). Design patterns for badge systems in higher education. In M. Spaniol, M. Temperini, D.K.W. Chiu, I. Marenzi, & U. Nanni (Eds.), *Advances in web-based learning—ICWL 2016* (Vol. 10013, pp. 40–49). Cham: Springer. https://dx.doi.org/10.1007/978-3-319-47440-3_5

Tomberg, V., Laanpere, M., Ley, T., & Normak, P. (2013). Sustaining teacher control in a blog-based personal learning environment. *The International Review of Research in Open and Distance Learning, 14*(3), 109–133. https://dx.doi.org/10.19173/irrodl.v14i3.1397

Väljataga, T., & Laanpere, M. (2010). Learner control and personal learning environment: A challenge for instructional design. *Interactive Learning Environments, 18*(3), 277–291. https://doi.org/10.1080/10494820.2010.500546

Hans Põldoja works as head of studies and associate professor of educational technology in the School of Digital Technologies at the Tallinn University. He is teaching a number of courses in the Educational Technology and Human–Computer Interaction Master's Programs in Tallinn University. His research belongs to the field of technology enhanced learning and human–computer interaction. More specific areas of interest and expertise include open education, learning environments, digital learning resources and interaction design. Hans Põldoja has more than 15 years of experience in designing learning environments and learning resource authoring tools. He has been responsible for the interaction design for several internationally recognized projects (LeMill, EduFeedr) and a number of learning environments that are widely used in Estonia. In 2016 he defended his doctoral dissertation "The Structure and Components for the Open Education Ecosystem: Constructive Design Research of Online Learning Tools" in the Media Lab at the Aalto University School of Arts, Design and Architecture.

Mart Laanpere received Ph.D. in educational science from Tallinn University. He works as a senior research fellow at the Centre for Educational Technology in the School of Digital Technologies, Tallinn University. His research interests include pedagogy-driven design of online learning environments, next-generation digital textbooks, technology-enhanced assessment and digital competences. He is teaching the masters' courses on basics of instructional design, development of digital learning resources and managing the digital innovations. He has been coordinating several projects in OER domain, such as development of Estonian teachers' portal and LOR Koolielu.ee, technical specification for current Estonian OER catalogue e-Koolikott.ee, national LOM application profile EstCORE and a large-scale OER production initiative for Estonian high schools DigiÕppeVaramu.

Chapter 4
Open Educational Resources in Italy

Connecting the Macro, Meso and Micro Levels, Towards a National OER Ecosystem

Fabio Nascimbeni

1 Case Overview: Education and ICT in Italy

The Italian population is around 60,391,000 (ISTAT 2019) with a per-capita GDP of 32.110 USD per year (World Bank 2019). Compared to other European countries, Italy is lagging behind both in terms of internet home diffusion and broadband access (European Commission 2019). Also, although internet access has been steadily increasing over the years, disparities between the north and the south of the country remain, reflecting the longstanding socio-economic gap which exists between the two regions. These disparities exist also in education, that is characterized by wide and persisting regional gaps in terms of learning outcomes (European Commission 2018).

The Italian education systems have been under reform for the last couple of decades, as a critical field where governmental changes have been reflected in a series of somehow discontinuous reforms. Education is compulsory from 6 to 16 years of age and is divided into five stages: kindergarten (*scuola dell'infanzia*), primary school (*scuola primaria*), lower secondary school (*scuola media inferiore*), upper secondary school (*scuola media superiore*) and university (*università*). Italian universities, the great majority of which are state-supported, are among the oldest in the world; in particular the University of Bologna (founded in 1088), is said to be the first university in the western world.

Since 2003 the Ministry of Education, University and Research (MIUR) has been supporting schools in the use of ICT for teaching and learning. In line with the priority assigned to digital competence by the European Commission, in 2007 ICT has been included as a key competence to be acquired during the first and second cycle of education. During this period and until the present days, some important public initiatives were launched with the aim of reforming the school administration and

F. Nascimbeni (✉)
Universidad Interacional de La Rioja (UNIR), Calle Almansa 106, Madrid, Spain
e-mail: fabio.nascimbeni@unir.net

© Springer Nature Singapore Pte Ltd. 2020   49
R. Huang et al. (eds.), *Current State of Open Educational Resources
in the "Belt and Road" Countries*, Lecture Notes in Educational Technology,
https://doi.org/10.1007/978-981-15-3040-1_4

innovating teaching and learning methodologies in line with the emerging knowledge society paradigms. The major initiatives have concerned supplying schools with multimedia equipment, connecting schools to the Internet, setting up networks and services and training teachers on the pedagogical use of ICT.

2   Current Situation of OER

The Italian education and training system is lagging behind with respect to most OECD countries in terms of equipment and use of ICT in education, both as far as schools (Avvisati et al. 2013) and universities are concerned (Ghislandi and Raffaghelli 2016). Also, the capacity of teachers of using ICT remains a challenge in Italy, as demonstrated by the OCSE TALIS report (2013) that places Italy in the first place as far as the need for teacher training and educational needs in ICT are concerned. In this report, 36% of interviewed teachers declared to be insufficiently prepared for ICT-enhanced teaching against an average rate in Europe of 17%.

Nevertheless, probably following the innovation push received by the European Union, connected to the availability of European funds for innovation, the attention of Italian educational stakeholders towards the innovative use of technology, including the adoption of open licenses for education and Open Educational Resources (OER), is on the rise (Ghislandi and Raffaghelli 2016). This is demonstrated by the constant presence of OER and Open Education as key issues in the programmes of EMEM,[1] the main Italian Conference on e-learning, and of other academic events in the field.

In order to understand the state of the art of OER use and adoption in Italy and to extract some critical points, it is useful to distinguish among three levels: the macro level, connected to the national and regional policies in the field, the meso level, that deals with representative stakeholders networks and communities, and the micro level, that considers the single institutions and projects dealing with OER.

2.1   Macro Level: OER Policy

At the policy level, OER are included as a component of the national policy for digitalization in schools and are encompassed in some regional initiatives. On the other hand, in the higher education sector neither a specific policy on OER nor a mention to OER in existing public policy initiatives exist (Tammaro et al. 2016).

---

[1] See https://www.ememitalia.org/.

2.1.1 School Education

In the school sector, OER is present in public policy since 2013, with a mention to open content in the national policy on digital textbooks. Two years later, also following the priority assigned to OER by the European Commission with its *Opening Up Education* Communication (European Commission 2013), OER were put at the core of one of the 27 actions of the National Digital School Plan (*Piano Nazionale Scuola Digitale—PNSD*), an initiative launched by the Ministry of Education, University and Research with the aim to increase digital-supported innovation across Italy's school system. The OER-related action, which aims at building a system of rights and licenses that is sensible and functional for OER, was not equipped with a dedicated budget and should have started in 2016 mainly through local projects to be developed within schools. Unfortunately, to date, just a limited number of these projects have started and therefore it is difficult to document any impact. Apart from this specific action, the National Digital School Plan is inspired by a rather holistic vision on open education, understood both in terms of teaching practices and of learning resources (Inamorato dos Santos et al. 2017). Openness is indeed transversally permeating the policy, as a way to promote critical citizenship and an active approach towards ICT and online knowledge. Apart from current funding from the MIUR for school education, funds from other Ministerial services as well as regional funds from the European Social Fund have been activated, and synergy happened with other Ministries, for example to ensure the provision of broadband connectivity for schools. In terms of impact, the policy has been able to activate 8300 *digital animators*,[2] one per school, this being probably the biggest change that schools have embraced rather enthusiastically.

Apart from this national policy, in the school sector some government-supported OER initiatives exist, such as *A scuola di Open Coesione*,[3] a project working with secondary schools on open data monitoring and data journalism that pays attention to release all its resources as OER. The project, which was launched in 2013 within the open government strategy on cohesion policy carried out by the National Government, has recently launched a Massive Open Online Course (MOOC) on open data journalism and is reaching good visibility in the national high school community.

2.1.2 Higher Education

In the Higher Education sector, a comprehensive public policy for the promotion of OER does not exist. The only initiative in the field by the Ministry of Education and Research is the initiative *Talent Italy*,[4] a competition for the development of MOOCs by and for national universities and schools launched in 2014 with an overall award of 160,000 Euros, whose winners were announced in 2016. Also, the Ministry has

---

[2]http://www.istruzione.it/scuola_digitale/prog-animatori-digitali.shtml.
[3]http://www.ascuoladiopencoesione.it.
[4]https://talentitaly.it/.

been financially supporting the setup of the EduOpen initiative, a multi-university MOOC platform that will be described later in the chapter.

The low attention devoted to OER and openness in Higher Education by the Italian government is rather discouraging, especially if compared for example with the one of the French government, that has launched in 2013 the initiative *Universite Numerique* with an overall funding of 29 Million Euros, resulting in a rather successful national MOOC platform called *FUN—French Université Numerique*,[5] that is having an important impact on the overall innovation capacity of the French university system (Ministère de l'Enseignement supérieur, de la Recherche et de l'Innovation 2019).

2.2 Meso Level: Advocacy for OER

Looking at the developments at the meso level, the level between public policy and grassroots initiatives, is useful to understand the national debate as well as to try to anticipate policies, that can possibly originate from the work of representative associations that work at this level. In Italy, a number of activities at this level must be reported especially in the higher education field, where the Italian Conference of Rectors (CRUI) has been advocating for an increased use of OER through a number of activities.

In 2010, CRUI started to devote attention to OER by running a survey in collaboration with the Italian publishers association and copyright association, aiming to understand the state of the art of the management of intellectual property rights for e-learning in the country. The survey showed a rather immature OER ecosystem, with only 14% of the responding universities using Creative Commons licenses, 5% having an OpenCourseWare policy, and 28% authorizing the reuse of their resources outside the university. On the positive side, 90% of respondents declared willingness to use OER in their courses (Tammaro 2015). These results were somehow confirmed by another survey run in 2011 by a newly established CRUI working group dedicated to OER, with the mission to prepare a set of guidelines to encourage universities to innovate their educational practices through the adoption of open content. This second survey confirmed the slow adoption of OER and the practical absence of OER-related strategies in Italian universities: 50% of responding institutions reported a basic knowledge of OER, but no experience of producing open content. On the other hand, 65% of respondents stated their involvement in some kind of pilot projects on OER, mainly targeting regular students and not society at large (Tammaro et al. 2016).

In 2016, CRUI started focusing on MOOCs, by launching a set of guidelines for the preparation of quality MOOC by Italian universities, together with an institutional framework for the mutual recognition of credits by universities and a system of benchmarking for the evaluation of MOOCs quality (Fondazione CRUI 2015). This initiative, which was again turning the attention of the Italian academic community on

---

[5]https://www.fun-mooc.fr/.

Open Education, was alleged to possibly take an overly regulatory approach given the start-up phase of the Italian MOOCs community, that would require a certain degree of freedom to experiment (Tammaro et al. 2017).

More recently, in the conclusions of a Digital University meeting organized in 2018 gathering all major players of the Italian higher education system, CRUI stated that OER shall be considered as a priority, advocating for action on this at the ministerial level. "The university system is asking the institutional system for support to develop didactic innovation in priority areas such as the development of a culture and practice of OER in all forms including MOOCs through stimulus to institutional and interinstitutional projects for the reuse, sharing and production of OER by Italian universities" (CRUI 2018, p. 3).

These activities of CRUI, apart from having raised data that can help understanding the state of the art of OER adoption among Italian universities, are showing genuine interest within the national higher education community on Open Education. The expectation is that this advocacy work might inspire action at the governmental level in the future.

Another interesting development at the meso level is represented by the grassroots network *Open Education Italia*.[6] Created in 2016 with the objective of connecting different individuals and stakeholders active on OER and Open Education, the network has been organizing events and developing small research and advocacy actions, mostly on a voluntary basis and by building on the activities of its members. Apart from its impact on knowledge sharing and capacity building in the area of Open Education, the network, which gathers academics, school stakeholders, companies and civil society actors, would represent a bottom-up counterpart for a balanced policy development in the field, as it is happening with *OER Coalitions* in other EU countries such as Germany, Poland or Romania.

2.3 Micro Level: Platforms and Resources

2.3.1 Higher Education

Thanks to the advocacy work of CRUI as well as to the generalized interest for the MOOCs phenomenon, the Italian higher education community is rather active in terms of OER use, especially with regard to MOOCs. This is witnessed by the fact that two of the major global conferences in the field of Open Education in 2019 are taking place in Italy: the eMOOC19 Conference hosted by the University Federico II di Napoli and the OEGlobal Conference by the Politecnico di Milano.

The international debate on whether—and under which conditions—MOOCs can be considered OER (Chiappe-Laverde et al. 2015) is quite lively in Italy (CRUI 2018). In an international context where the major MOOCs providers are not releasing their content with open licenses and where access to these content is increasingly being

---

[6]www.educazioneaperta.eu.

limited to defined time windows, Italy seems to be a positive exception. Most Italian MOOCs providers are in fact releasing their course content with open licenses. This is probably due to the fact that differently from more privately oriented higher education contexts such as the ones in the US or in the UK, the Italian university system is still mostly based on state subsidy and therefore universities do not assign a clear market value to their open courses.

The first example of this *OER MOOCs* approach is *EduOpen,*[7] a multi-university MOOCs platform launched in 2013 that gathers today 17 middle-size universities and offers more than 100 courses, either as individual learning experiences or organized in learning pathways, that include a group of courses connected to each other. At the end of the course, participants can get a free participation certificate and an open badge, and can additionally take a face to face examination and get a paid certificate with credits. The second example is the *Federica*[8] online learning platform, launched by the University Federico II in Naples already in 2007, that counts today with more than 300 courses whose content is released through open licenses (De Rosa and Zuccarini 2011). Also, Politecnico di Milano is releasing all the content of the courses hosted by *POLIMI OpenKnowledge*[9] through open licenses (and through a dedicated YouTube channel). This platform is particularly interesting since it focuses on the transition moments from school to university, from bachelor to master and from higher education to employment, and has inspired a similar recent development in the University of Bologna, called *BOOK—Bologna Open Knowledge.*[10] The *Sapienza*[11] University in Rome offers six courses through Coursera, allowing users to download the videos of these courses.

Interesting developments can be found within European projects with Italian participation. The *EMMA* project has resulted in a rather rich platform[12] that offers around 40 MOOCs in different languages. In the case of EMMA, each course provider is deciding which license to use, so on the platform we can find both OER and restricted content. Other projects that have produced OER in Italian are the *ECO* project,[13] which has developed a social portal fostering inclusive MOOC-based learning, and the *OERUp!* project,[14] that has produced an open course on OER targeting adult learners.

If we move beyond the MOOCs scene, we notice that at the level of the single universities many educators are releasing their teaching content as OER, even if this is mostly connected to their decision is not corresponding to institutional policies (Tammaro 2013). Some examples of OER-related initiatives are hereby provided.

---

[7]http://eduopen.org.

[8]https://federica.eu.

[9]https://www.pok.polimi.it.

[10]https://book.unibo.it/.

[11]https://www.coursera.org/sapienza.

[12]http://platform.europeanmoocs.eu/.

[13]https://www.facebook.com/ecolearning.eu/.

[14]www.oerup.eu.

The *FARE* website[15] is a collection of openly licensed learning materials created by a professor of the Politecnico di Torino that includes a set of open content and guidelines for its use. The *WikitoLearn* platform[16] is a rather unique development: created by a group of students to facilitate the sharing and documentation of university courseware, it is a powerful online tool to produce open textbooks that counts with more than 1000 chapters produced by users and that is being used internationally in Europe and beyond. Finally, BESTR is the Italian national open badges platform.[17]

2.3.2   School Education

In the school sector, a number of publicly funded platforms containing OER exist. Indire, the national agency for school innovation and research, is planning to launch *DI share*, a platform that will put a number of quality digital resources at the disposal of school teachers. This platform should collect the heritage of a number of rather successful previous projects that were collecting OER for school teachers, such as PuntoEdu. Also managed by Indire, *Scuola valore*[18] is an online repository of learning paths, activities and resources for school teachers, providing access to more than 800 resources in several subjects, adapted to the different levels of the Italian school system and downloadable without the need to register. In copyright terms, the platform is allowing teachers to use the content for non-commercial educational and scientific purposes, but at the same time all the content of the platform is copyright protected, therefore not allowing remixing of resources. This portal is rather paradigmatic of the OER scene in the school sector in Italy, where good intentions are in many cases not mirrored by the most suitable approaches.

At the regional level, a rather well-known project is *Trio*[19] by the Tuscany region, which collects around 1.800 courses mainly targeting vocational training and professional development. Also in this case, all content is usable under the educational exception and remains property of the funding entity. If we move to the digital libraries ecosystem, the portal *Internet Culturale* has been developed in 2010 as a search engine providing integrated access to digital catalogues and content. Internet Culturale is working across the various collections of Italian libraries, linking digital assets on many disciplines, and adopts the licenses used by the different libraries, guaranteeing nevertheless free access to its content. Finally, the *Rai Scuola*[20] portal, managed by the national public television, must be mentioned: its videos, which are subject to copyright but can be used and shared under the educational exception rule, are organized according to the possible curricular positioning in different

---

[15] https://fare.polito.it/.

[16] www.wikitolearn.org.

[17] https://bestr.it.

[18] http://www.scuolavalore.indire.it/.

[19] http://www.progettotrio.it/trio/.

[20] http://www.raiscuola.rai.it/.

school grades and a service for the creation of lessons based on the existing videos is available.

Two OER private initiatives are worth mentioning. *WeSchool*[21] defines itself as an "online school" created by a group of students offering a great amount of videos, texts and exercises—produced and uploaded by teachers and experts as well as by students—on many subjects, with a feature of social rating. All the content of this platform is released with Creative Common licenses. *Alexandria*[22] is an open repository for school resources based on a full OER philosophy, where teachers are invited to upload their content and to produce online resources through a dedicated editing system. This portal offers the possibility to choose whether to adopt Creative Commons or closed licenses, and in this last case gives the option to sell, through a specific marketplace section, the resources produced.

OER can be also found in the large ecosystem of sites, blogs and social networks pages managed directly by individual teachers. In most cases, these OER individual repositories are difficult to be found and are not collected in an overall repository (Fini 2012a, b). Examples are *Il Filo di Arianna,*[23] a collection of CC-released courses for secondary schools curated by a team of teachers, Matematicamente,[24] a collaboratively built collection of resources on mathematics released with an open license, and *Bookinprogress,*[25] a portal with open textbooks on various subjects curated by a network of secondary schools. Finally, the Bricks open access journal[26] must be mentioned, which has been collecting articles on a number of OER-related good practices, often written by teachers.

2.4   *Copyright and Open Licenses*

The Italian copyright law is strongly based on authors' rights, with limited exceptions to authors' exclusive rights and with no provision for fair use or fair dealing. In legal terms, in Italy, resources created by teachers and commercial publications are not distinguished: in both cases, compensation or remuneration must be in place, potentially acting as a deterrent to teachers to create OER. Also, Italian legislation does not allow translation or adaptation of copyrighted resources for educational purposes (Nobre 2017). However, displays provided in the context of educational activities are not considered as public performances, and are therefore excluded from copyright protection. What remains to be seen is how Italy will adopt the recent Copyright Reform of the European Union, that can be interpreted in more or less restrictive terms. The main challenge for OER production and use in terms

---

[21] https://library.weschool.com/.

[22] http://www.alexandrianet.it.

[23] http://www.ariannascuola.eu.

[24] https://www.matematicamente.it.

[25] https://www.bookinprogress.org/.

[26] http://www.rivistabricks.it.

of copyright is a *weak opening* of Italian copyright legislation that, while it allows the use of low-quality images and videos from the web, it gives the possibility to publishers and publishers associations of allowing that use or not (De Rosa and Zuccarini 2011). Across all Italian educational sectors, the challenge of who owns the intellectual property rights of the resources produced by teachers, and therefore who can decide which (possibly open) license to apply, is still a key problem. Reaching a clear understanding whether the owner is the person who produced the resource or of the institution would indeed be necessary to build transparent OER initiatives addressing at the same time accessibility and sustainable viability.

2.5 Curriculum and Teaching Methodology

Italy is not an exception in the Open Education movement, that is witnessing a focus shift from OER, licenses and technological interoperability towards a more holistic vision focused on Open Educational Practices (OEP) as well as other dimensions such as recognition, collaboration and research (Inamorato dos Santos et al. 2016). This is confirmed by the results of the CRUI surveys mentioned earlier, that report a generalized positive expectation by Italian universities on the impact of OER on students' achievements (Tammaro 2013). The potential impact of OER on pedagogical innovation was recognized by the Italian Ministry of Education already in 2013, by mentioning the use of digital textbooks and OER as ways to promote pedagogic and technologic innovation within school settings (MIUR 2013). In line with this approach, a number of the projects presented in paragraph 2.3, such as for example Trio and Scuola Valore, do indeed pay attention to the teaching innovation that the use of OER can bring, giving importance to OEP and moving the focus from the content to the processes.

A general challenge for teaching innovation in university settings is connected to the fact that in Italy, similarly to what happens in other countries, teachers are recruited on the basis of their scientific production and not on their teaching capacity. Because of this, and despite the increasing cases of universities providing incentives for innovative pedagogical practices, in many cases educators are devoting marginal effort to teaching activities, to the detriment of teaching innovation, especially given the effort required to produce and use quality OER and more in general to put in place innovative ICT-based teaching strategies (Comba 2008).

2.6 Perceived Benefits and Challenges of OER

The main benefits and challenges of using OER have been investigated, limitedly to the higher education sector, by the two surveys by CRUI presented in paragraph 2.2, whose results have been jointly analysed by Tammaro (2015). In terms of perceived benefits, 50% of responding universities have connected those to teaching internationalization, this being related to the fact that most OER used within higher education are in English, 39% to cost reduction, 32% to the visibility of both the educator and the institution. Importantly, a set of perceived benefits are connected to improved didactics: 71% of respondents appreciated the possibility of using OER with flipped classroom methodologies and 54% noted an increased students' motivation connected to the use of OER. Also, 37% reported an increased collaboration among universities as a perceived benefit. The results of the 2015 survey on MOOCs are similar in terms of perceived benefits: the majority of respondents appreciated the potential impact on teaching innovation (85%) and flexibility (67%), the increased visibility of the university (69%) and the increased contact with professional communities and companies (52%) (Tammaro et al. 2013).

Also in terms of challenges, a certain convergence between the results of the CRUI surveys on OER and MOOCs exist. The main reported obstacle is the absence of OER promotion institutional policies, that is connected with the low support, capacity building and incentive mechanisms for teachers, and with the lack of working business models for OER.

Filtering these findings through the work of Parrish and Kuna Parrish (2018), four main categories of barriers to the use of OER in Italy that are common across educational sectors can be identified: quality perception, searchability and language, lack of teachers capacity and lack of institutional strategies. The first barrier is connected to the common perception that free resources are most likely of inferior quality. Despite the demonstrated quality of the work of the producers of open resources, especially in the higher education sector, suspicion about free resources remain. The problem with searchability is connected with resources granularity in terms for example of level of difficulty, fit and scope, context needs of students. Also, the language of the resource can limit searchability. Language barriers are not just due to unavailable translation in Italian, but also in appropriate style and cultural expressions. Also, the perception of potential negative impacts of OER repositories from English-speaking countries are a barrier. Lack of teachers capacity in a key problem in the country: teachers feel that reuse of OERs inhibits their self-expression and are reluctant to adapt or reuse resources because they "belong" to others. Institutional barriers connected to the lack of an OER strategy are also multidimensional: these refer to the proprietary nature of educational content in some institutions, to the institutional regulations that prevent sharing internal resources, even when developed under public funding, and to the lack of incentives, including recognition and compensation, for creating OER material.

3 Discussion and Conclusions

The content of the previous paragraphs is mainly based on few attempts that were made in the last years to analyse the state of the art of OER in Italy (see Comba 2008; Fini 2012a, b; Uggeri 2014, 2015) and on the surveys on OER and MOOCs run by the Italian Rectors Conference between 2011 and 2013, which have been later analysed and discussed by the OER community (Tammaro et al. 2015, 2016; Lepore and Vellani 2017). Regrettably, it was not possible to find more recent attempts to describe the developments of the OER ecosystem in Italy.

As far as higher education is concerned, the actual OER panorama (including the majority of the national MOOCs platforms that as we have seen can be considered OER) is rather lively, both at the community and at the institutional level. The majority of the existing analysis agree that the main barrier that prevents the Italian universities OER ecosystem to fully develop its potential is the absence of a national Open Education or OER policy for higher education. Such a policy, which exists with different declinations in other European countries such as France and Germany (Inamorato do Santos et al. 2017), would be fundamental to provide a push for university to formalize into institutional strategies the many activities connected with the use of open content that they are actually running, often in a scattered and uncoordinated way and without appropriate technical and pedagogical support (Tammaro 2013). The absence of institutional OER or Open Education policies was identified already in 2013 as one of the main weaknesses of the OER Italian ecosystem, impacting negatively on the motivation of individual teachers to use OER (61% of respondents), on the support mechanisms for teachers in the use of OER (68%), on the sustainability of OER projects (61%) and on the national and international cooperation dynamics (57%).

Such a national policy could be implemented through a number of activities, building on and articulating the existing achievements and efforts of universities and of universities networks in the field of OER. First, the OER and MOOCs guidelines developed by CRUI should be updated, also considering some important recent European developments such as the work of the JRC of the European Commission (Inamorato do Santos et al. 2017) and could constitute the normative—but flexible—core of the Italian approach to OER implementation. Second, the existing capacities of university educators in the use of OER and OEP should be valorised and strengthened, both in terms of initial and continual teachers professional development, and accompanied by a system of incentives for those teachers who are producing and sharing OER (Banzato 2014). Third, official inter-universities recognition mechanisms for the competences acquired through open courses should be promoted, strengthening existing national experiences such as the EduOpen MOOCs platform, moving towards OER-based university ecosystems such as the one of the OER University in New Zealand (McGreal et al. 2014).

In the school sector, whereas we have seen OER are present in the current national school innovation policy, the main problem seems to be the fragmentation of initiatives. Many OER projects exist at the local, institutional and often at the individual teachers' level, but they are rarely connected in a system view, and especially they are not linked to other sectors and to the labour market. Further, around these innovative OER-based projects, a generalized lack of knowledge and scepticism exist among school stakeholders, including teachers, leaders and parents. Putting in place a systemic Open Education policy entails a significant cultural, pedagogical and ethical change, that passes through a general acceptation of sharing practices to eventually transform teaching practices around learners and learners–teachers knowledge co-creation open practices. In the school sector as well as in higher education, the relation between openness and collaboration is in fact the keystone for sustainable pedagogic innovation, beyond the use of open license and the production of freely accessible online courses (Nascimbeni and Burgos 2016).

A number of actions could be put in place in order to *defragment* the Italian school OER ecosystem. According to a OECD review of the Italian Strategy for Digital Schools (Avvisati et al. 2013), a useful development would be a central platform for teachers to publish and search existing OER, building on the several past projects (most of which have unfortunately been discontinued) and especially connecting the existing communities that work around the production and use of open teaching content, from the individual teacher to the *Rai Scuola* selection of videos, functioning as a *broker* of communities of practice. Such a meta-platform would be possible today thanks to some Artificial Intelligence search systems that could actually connect existing repositories without having to centralize all their content. To be useful, this system should be organized according to the Italian school curriculum and should provide ideas for teachers on how to meaningfully use OER in their classroom. Such a resource bank in itself could act as an incentive and support mechanism to develop further resources. Also, an effort should be made to build teachers capacity, not only in a technical way but also with the objective of transforming teachers as gate-openers of their communities of practice (Tosato and Raffaghelli 2011) and of instilling a culture of openness in the Italian school system (Fulantelli et al. 2011).

Building an integrated OER-based school ecosystem would need a more structured—and possibly dedicated—policy. This would help tackling the underlying problem of OER use within Italian schools, that is the low awareness of the opportunities offered by open content not only in terms of technical and pedagogical innovation, but also as a driver for social development through more equal education. Also, this would contribute to the long due transformation of the Italian education system in a real lifelong learning perspective, as advocated for the last couple of decades by the European Union.

Open lifelong learning should be the objective of both a new higher education policy and of a renewed and more systemic school policy in the field of OER, or better in the field of Open Education, intended as an area that includes OER but also open course design, open teaching practices and open assessment, and that is connected with areas such as Open Data or Open Access. Being able to rely on these policies in a context such as the one of Italy, that as we have seen is rather rich in terms of bottom-up initiatives and networks and where openly licensed content seems to be the norm also in the field of MOOCs, would contribute to the needed transition from a vision of Open Education as a way to reduce costs and increase access without losing quality towards a more holistic understanding, advocated by the European Commission (2013) and UNESCO (2017) among others, of how Open Education can represent one of the keys for a deep modernization of the national education system.

Acknowledgements Gratitude goes to Eleonora Pantò and Matteo Uggeri for the precious review of the chapter and for the ideas and experiences provided.

References

Avvisati, F., et al. (2013). Review of the Italian Strategy for Digital Schools. *OECD Education Working Papers*, No. 90. Paris: OECD Publishing.

Banzato, M. (2014). Open Educational Resources: una prospettiva allo sviluppo sostenibile in ambito formativo ed educativo. Formazione & Insegnamento. *Rivista internazionale di Scienze dell'educazione e della formazione, 9*(3), 59–74.

Chiappe-Laverde, A., Hine, N., & Martínez-Silva, J. A. (2015). Literature and practice: A critical review of MOOCs. *Comunicar, 22*(44), 9–1.

Comba, V. (2008). Risorse didattiche aperte: aspetti sociali ed economici.

CRUI. (2015). MOOCS Massive Open Online Courses. Prospettive e opportunità per l'Università italiana.

CRUI. (2018). ATTI I Magnifici Incontri CRUI 2018 - Piano Nazionale Università Digitale.

De Rosa, R., & Zuccarini, M. (2011). Federica: la via italiana alle risorse educative aperte. *TD. Tecnologie Didattiche, 19*(2), 96–101.

European Commission. (2013). Communication "Opening up education: Innovative teaching and learning for all through new technologies and open educational resources", COM/2013/0654 final.

European Commission. (2018). *E&T monitoring report*. Luxembourg: Publication Office of the European Union.

European Commission. (2019). The digital economy and society index. Retrieved June 20, 2019, from https://ec.europa.eu/digital-single-market/en/desi.

Fini, A. (2012a). Ieri Learning object, oggi "risorse": dove reperirli e come (ri)usarli? *Rivista Bricks, 1*(2012).

Fini, A. (2012b). Risorse educative aperte. Principali orientamenti e prospettive di sviluppo. In M. Ranieri (a cura di), *Risorse educative aperte e sperimentazione didattica: le proposte del progetto Innovascuola - AMELIS per la condivisione di risorse e lo sviluppo professionale dei docenti* (pp. 19–42). Firenze: Firenze University Press.

Fulantelli, G., Gentile, M., Taibi, D., & Allegra, M. (2011). La centralità dei docenti per il successo delle risorse educative aperte. *TD Tecnologie Didattiche, 19*(2), 80–87.

Ghislandi, P., & Raffaghelli, G. (2016). Opening-up higher education. Analisi di strategie attraverso un caso di studio. In *Proceedings of the 2013 SIeL Conference*.

Inamorato dos Santos, A., Punie, Y., & Castaño-Muñoz, J. (2016). *Opening up education: A support framework for higher education institutions*. JRC Science for Policy Report, EUR 27938 EN. Retrieved from https://doi.org/10.2791/293408.

Inamorato dos Santos, A., Nascimbeni, F., Bacsich, P., Atenas, J., Aceto, S., Burgos, D., et al. (2017). *Policy approaches to open education—case studies from 28 EU Member States (OpenEdu Policies)*. EUR 28776 EN, Publications Office of the European Union, Luxembourg.

ISTAT. (2019). Indicatori Demografici. Retrieved June 20, 2019, from https://www.istat.it/it/archivio/226919.

Lepore, V., & Vellani, S. (2017). Open education in Italia: stato e prospettive. *Bibelot, 23*(1), 30–38.

McGreal, R., Conrad, D., Murphy, A., Witthaus, G., & Mackintosh, W. (2014). Formalising informal learning: Assessment and accreditation challenges within disaggregated systems. *Open Praxis, 6*(2), 125–133.

Ministère de l'Enseignement supérieur, de la Recherche et de l'Innovation. (2019). Stratégie numérique pour l'enseignement supérieur. Retrieved June 20, 2019, from http://www.enseignementsup-recherche.gouv.fr/cid74147/france-universite-numerique-enjeux-et-definitions.html.

Ministero dell'istruzione, dell'università e della ricerca. (2013). Decreto Libri digitali, 27 settembre 2013, Allegato 1 – estratto.

Nascimbeni, F., & Burgos, D. (2016). In search for the open educator: Proposal of a definition and a framework to increase openness adoption among university educators. *International Review of Research in Open and Distributed Learning, 17*(6). https://doi.org/10.19173/irrodl.v17i6.2736.

Nobre, T. (2017). *Copyright and education in Europe: 15 everyday cases in 15 countries.* COMMUNIA International Association of the Digital Public Domain.

Parrish, P., & Kuna-Parrish, M. (2018). Barriers and benefits of open educational resources. In *Proceedongs of the Open Education Global Conference,* Krakow, Poland.

Tammaro, A. M. (2015). Oer nelle Università italiane: risultati di un'indagine conoscitiva. In M. Cinque (a cura di), *MOOC Risorse educative aperte* (Vol. 4, pp. 53–65). Universitas Quaderni.

Tammaro, A. M., et al. (2013). OER nelle Università italiane: primi risultati di un'indagine conoscitiva del Gruppo CRUI OA-OER. In *Proceedings del convegno SIeL 2013*, SIeL Editore.

Tammaro, A. M., Ciancio, L., De Rosa, R., Pantò, E., & Nascimbeni, F. (2017). Digital libraries in open education: The Italy case. In C. Grana & L. Baraldi (Eds.), *Digital Libraries and Archives: 13th Italian Research Conference on Digital Libraries, IRCDL 2017*, Modena, Italy, January 26–27, 2017.

Tammaro, A. M., De Rosa, R., Pantò, E., & Nascimbeni, F. (2016). Open education in Italia: stato dell'arte e proposte per una politica di sistema. In *Proceedings oft he GARR Conference,* Rome 2016.

Tosato, P., & Raffaghelli, J. (2011). Risorse Educative Aperte e professione docente nell'era dell'accesso. *TD-Tecnologie Didattiche, 53,* 20–27.

Uggeri, M. (2014). OER: policies e iniziative nella scuola. Il racconto di una (tentata) mappatura della situazione italiana ad oggi. *Bricks, 3*(4).

Uggeri, M. (2015). Oer: policies e inizitive. Una mappatura della situazione italiana. In M. Cinque (Ed.), *MOOC Risorse Educative Aperte* (Vol. 30). Universitas Quaderni.

UNESCO. (2017). *Ljubljana OER action plan.* Paris: UNESCO.

World Bank. (2019). GDP per capita. Retrieved June 20, 2019, from https://data.worldbank.org/indicator/.

Fabio Nascimbeni works as Assistant Professor at the Universidad Internacional de la Rioja (UNIR), where holds the Telefonica Chair on Digital Society and Education. He is a Senior Fellow of the European Distance and eLearning Network (EDEN), a member of the Advisory Board of the Open Education Working of the Open Knowledge Foundation, a fellow at the Centro de Estudos sobre Tecnologia e Sociedade of the University of Sao Paulo (USP) in Brazil and at the Nexa Centre of the Politecnico di Torino. He has been active in the field of learning innovation and ICT for learning since 1998, by designing and coordinating more than 40 research and innovation projects and promoting European and international collaboration in different areas, from school education to higher education, to lifelong learning, to ICT research. He has been working across Europe as well as in Latin America, the Caribbean, the South Mediterranean and South-East Asia. His main research interests are open education, learning innovation, digital literacy, social and digital inclusion. Fabio is among the founders of the Italian Open Education community Educazioneaperta.eu.

Chapter 5
Open Educational Resources in Korea

Gi Woong Choi, Jewoong Moon, Jaewoo Do and Daeyeoul Lee

1 Introduction

In recent years, Open Educational Resources (OERs) have emerged as a hot topic of interest within the educational realm. Open Courseware and Massive Open Online Courses (MOOCs) are good examples of OERs' success (Conole & Weller, 2008; Miyazoe & Anderson, 2013; Nikoi & Armellini, 2012). Due to OER's cost-free and accessible nature, many forecast that OER could be one of the key solutions that can lessen the digital divide, balancing educational levels between developed and developing countries, and challenging restrictions given by content providers (Olcott, 2012).

The term OER was first used at UNESCO's Forum on the Impact of Open Courseware for Higher Education in Developing Countries in 2002 (UNESCO, 2002). In the

G. W. Choi
Department of Computer Science, State University of New York at Oswego, Oswego, NY, USA
e-mail: giwoong.choi@oswego.edu

396 Shineman, 30 Centennial Drive, Oswego, NY 13126, USA

J. Moon (✉)
Department of Educational Psychology and Learning Systems, Florida State University, 600 W College Ave, Tallahassee, FL 32306, USA
e-mail: jewoong.moon@gmail.com

Stone Building, Hull Drive, Tallahassee, FL 32303, USA

J. Do
Future Education Research Division, Korean Educational Development Institute, 7, Gyohak-ro, Deoksan-eup, Jincheon-gun, Chungcheongbuk-do 27873, Korea
e-mail: jaewoo.do@gmail.com

D. Lee
Purdue University, 100 N. University Street, West Lafayette, IN 47907, USA
e-mail: lee1895@purdue.edu

© Springer Nature Singapore Pte Ltd. 2020
R. Huang et al. (eds.), *Current State of Open Educational Resources in the "Belt and Road" Countries*, Lecture Notes in Educational Technology,
https://doi.org/10.1007/978-981-15-3040-1_5

forum, OER was defined as "the open provision of educational resources, enabled by information and communication technologies, for consultation, use and adaptation by a community of users for non-commercial purposes." (UNESCO, 2002, p. 24). Since then, UNESCO and The William and Flora Hewlett Foundation commonly defined OER as follows:

> Teaching, learning and research materials in any medium – digital or otherwise – that reside in the public domain or have been released under an open license that permits no-cost access, use, adaptation and redistribution by others with no or limited restrictions (Open Educational Resources, n.d., paragraph 7).

The popularity of OER is a worldwide phenomenon, and the resources are publicly open to people from all over the world. However, there may be contextual differences between countries due to their differences in policy, language, culture, etc. In this chapter, we focus on the case of Korea, which is considered to be one of the technologically innovative countries. Throughout the chapter, we discuss OER in Korea in a number of ways. First, we discuss the history of OER, then we continue on to list and describe two contextual factors that are in play for Korean OERs: technological development and policy-driven implementations. We also introduce resources that are currently in use and address copyright issues as well as relevant pedagogies for Korean OERs. Lastly, limitations and future directions are discussed.

2   Current State of OER in Korea

Figure 1 represents the overview of current state of OER in Korea.

2.1   History of OER in Korea

According to Shin et al. (2018), the EDUnet Bulletin Board System (BBS), which was used in the late 1980s, is regarded as the first OER in Korea. It provided information about educational institutions, educational policy, educational software programs, and online education. It also offered a place for consultations and discussions about the topics in education. People could access information and resources for free. The next iniative involved a governmental intervention. With explosive development of the Internet in the 1990s (Chon, Park, Kang, & Lee, 2005), the Korean Ministry of Education established a plan to provide computers in schools. According to the plan, every school in Korea would have had at least 31 computers by the end of 1996, and 90 educational software programs would have been developed and offered to schools by the end of the 1990s.

As the needs to utilize multimedia in computers for education have increased, the Korean Ministry of Education and the Korea Education and Research Information Service (KERIS) launched a web portal called EDUNET on September 11, 1996.

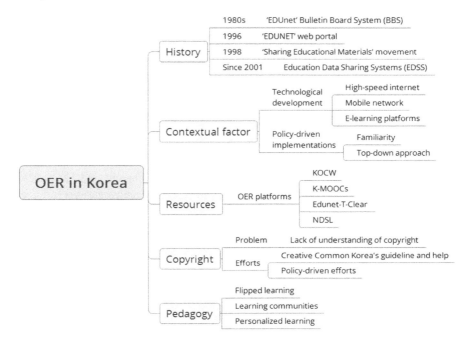

Fig. 1 Overview of OER in Korea

The web portal was initially launced with the address https://edunet.nmc.nm.kr, but it has changed to https://www.edunet.net since 1999. By providing organized resources and services for learning and teaching as well as web-based learning materials, the EDUNET web portal has become a web-based platform where learners can interact with learning contents, which was beyond the scope of what EDUnet BBS initially planned to offer (Shin et al., 2018). In accordance with the efforts of the government, *JoongAng Ilbo*, which is one of the premier newspaper companies in Korea, started *Sharing Educational Materials* movement in 1998. This movement was about collecting educational materials developed by individuals or groups with the goal of utilizing them in schools. The educational materials consisted of learning and teaching materials as well as materials of career education for students, research materials, and multimedia, which do not require permission from the copyright owners (Hong, 1998).

Since 2001, all elementary, middle, and high schools in Korea (Total of 10,064 schools) were provided with the Internet and the school management information system. In addition, personal computers were given to 340,000 teachers (Chon et al., 2005). With the growing use of the Internet and computers in schools, the number of educational materials and multimedia that were developed by several educational institutions including schools and the Regional Office of Education operated in each city or province grew exponentially. Education Data Sharing Systems (EDSS) was developed to make searching more convenient. EDSS is a system that collects educational materials through Korea Education Metadata (KEM) and provides metadata (Shin et al., 2018). Raw data are stored in the Office of Education or educational institutions.

2.2   Contextual Factors

In Korea, there are two contextual factors that played an important role in fostering the development of OER movement: (1) technological development and (2) policy-driven implementations. Technological development explains how various forms of Korea's technological infrastructures supported OER, and the policy-driven implementations depict how the Korean government facilitated the rapid and nationwide development of its OER environment.

2.2.1   Technological Development

The technological advancement of Korea has significantly contributed in fostering a rapid growth of OER platforms and their adoptions. Evidence supports that several key characteristics explicate the technological development in Korea: (1) high-speed internet, (2) mobile network, and (3) e-learning platforms. First, to date, Korea has been ranked as one of the top countries that largely support high-speed internet network systems (Kim et al., 2007). Due to its highly-equipped network system, the Korean Ministry of Education was able to rapidly release its plan to develop and facilitate information and communications technology (ICT)-enriched learning environments.

Second, mobile technologies in Korea also encouraged OER-related systems to be naturally adopted in the fields of higher education. According to the Organization for Economic Cooperation and Development (OECD), Korea is equipped with the highest-quality wireless connection services among 38 The Organisation for Economic Co-operation and Development (OECD) countries. Since the emerging of mobile learning (Baek & Cheong, 2005), the OER movement in Korea increasingly expanded itself with the help of its extensive Wi-Fi network system. To date, many Korean institutions in higher education have adopted mobile-learning-supportive systems that allow learners to easily access variant information resources beyond traditional web-based networks (Kim, Lee, & Kim, 2014). Subsequently, the wireless Internet connection in Korea has facilitated students' high interactions in technology-enhanced environments, including online and offline environments.

Third, multiple forms of e-learning platforms that were propelled by Korean government influenced the OER movement. Since KERIS was established in the 1990s, various online education platforms have also emerged. First, the Korean government launched Educational Broadcasting System (EBS), which develops and disseminates multiple forms of educational resources through television and radio systems

(Heo & Choi, 2014; Kwak, 2017). EBS aims to distribute a variety of OERs to a broad spectrum of target learners. EBS played a critical role in lowering students' budgets, as well as providing massive supplementary learning materials tailored to fulfill diverse students' needs. In addition, in the field of higher education, KERIS also initiated the Korean OpenCourseWare (KOCW) platform to share high-quality college lectures publicly. KOCW was designed to archive and distribute a wide array of video-recorded lectures for anonymous learners. This movement also influenced several universities' open courseware initiatives (e.g., SNOU, SNOW, and HOWL) as well as facilitated the development and distribution of video-based lecture materials from open universities.

2.2.2 Policy-Driven Implementations

Policy-driven implementations led by governmental supports have also contributed to the development of OER systems in Korea. There are two key characteristics that describe the policy-driven implementations of OER systems: (1) prior experience and (2) top-down approach.

First, most Korean students were already familiar with the concept of using OERs because of their experience of using learning materials provided by EBS. EBS is a public broadcasting organization that develops and publishes various educational resources for teachers and students for free. EBS started its service in 1974 as a radio school service and launched two satellite TV channels in 1997 to broadcast video classes that had supplementary materials published as print materials. In 2000, EBS launched its first Internet service (EBS, 2019). EBS now plays a crucial role in ensuring accessibility and openness in education for all students through the implementation of advanced information and communication technologies. EBS remains as one of the best-known and widely accessed OER platforms in Korea. According to EBS, their goals are (1) enhancing public education, (2) reducing private education cost, and (3) improving equality in education (EBS, 2019). These goals align with the purpose of OER, which aims to provide high-quality teaching, learning, and research materials that are free for people everywhere to use and repurpose (Smith & Casserly, 2006). Most primary/secondary teachers and students have utilized EBS since it was mandated by the Korean Ministry of Education for all schools to integrate EBS-produced materials as supplementary learning resources. For example, the ministry established its policy to require the assessment items of the College Scholastic Ability Test (CSAT) to be based on existing EBS resources (KICE, 2019). As a result, learning resources produced by EBS have been considered to be essential materials for students if they want to achieve better academic performance. Because EBS had been already providing public resources to students, emerging of OER in 2002 was not considered to be an educational paradigm shift for Korean teachers and students. In fact, they were already used to finding, accessing, and using free educational resources.

Second, most Korean OER platforms have been developed by government-related agencies with a top-down approach (Korean Ministry of Education, 2015b). In other words, most of the platforms have been implemented and funded in the form of government projects (Joo & Kim, 2017; Lim & Kim, 2014). For instance, the analysis of 10 representative OER platforms in Korea showed that six platforms were under direct government control. Three platforms were managed by universities, and two were public universities. Only one OER platform on the list has been developed by a private organization.

The propulsion of the nationwide education agenda called SMART also demonstrates how governmental support had led the OER movements in the field of elementary and secondary education (Kim, Cho, & Lee, 2012). This national plan sought to build key learning environment conditions (i.e., self-directed, motivated, adaptive, resource-enriched, technology-embedded) that can promote students' twenty-first-century skills. Aligning with this strategic plan, the KERIS implemented a digital-textbook-development project to build a learner-centered OER environment that enables learners to access highly qualified learning materials for free (Jang, Yi, & Shin, 2016). Those efforts showed that governmental investments considerably contributed to the OER infrastructures and support systems in Korea.

Such top-down approach in the development of OER platforms has brought both strengths and limitations to OER in Korea. First, securing educational resources was easier for OER platforms that were developed with governmental support and guidance. Various educational institutions, such as research institutes, universities, and companies, that received government funding have actively contributed to the production and distribution of OER contents (Lim & Kim, 2014). The Korean government requires universities to provide information about its number of open courseware in the KOCW and make that information available to the public (Korean Ministry of Education, 2015a). In addition, *JoongAngIlbo*, a renown Korean university evaluation agency, reflects the number of open courseware in its university evaluation (JoongAngIlbo, 2013). These requirements led institutions to register their educational resources in OER platforms. As a result, Korea's OER platforms now have abundant amount of resources despite their relatively short history. For instance, K-MOOC only had ten courses when it first launched in 2015 but exceeded 500 courses in number by 2018 (K-MOOC, 2019).

As illustrated by examples, governmental support and intervention have enabled smooth and stable operation of OER platforms in Korea. When OER platforms are initialized as government projects, they can be managed by specialized entities within governmental institutions that are under the umbrella of the Ministry of Education. This means that government-related OER experts can help administer the platform. Moreover, more stable operation is possible with the funding provided by the government.

However, there are limitations in this approach. The biggest limitation would be the low utilization rate of the OERs (Jang, 2013). Because the contents of these OERs are mostly developed based on government policy and funding needs rather than user needs and requests, the OERs are not likely to fully reflect users' motivation and needs. Therefore, user engagement in OER platforms may be lacking. Similarly, content providers' motivation for participation remains low. In the case of OCW, professors develop courses to meet governmental or university requirements rather than fulfilling the purposes of OCW (Lee & Kim, 2015). The studies show that the development of government-sponsored OER platforms has resulted in a low utilization rate for users and a low level of motivation for content providers.

2.3 Resources

Based on existing reviews of OER platforms (Shin, Jeon, & Kim, 2016; Shin et al., 2018), there are several major OER platforms in Korea. To illustrate the current state of Korean OER platforms and compare them, we set five criteria: educational purpose, resource type, openness, administration, and history.

- Educational purpose: This category is about target users' educational levels/purpose for usage.
- Resource type: This category provides information on what types of resources are being provided.
- Openness: This category is about the openness and accessibility of these platforms, including registration requirements as well as the cost of use and support for multiple languages.
- Administration: This category provides information about who operates each platform. It also includes information about whether the system is operated by the government or not.
- History: This category provides information about the history of each platform, including when the platform was created as well as its development history.

Based on these criteria, we selected twelve major OER platforms that have been implemented in Korea. Table 1 shows the selected OER platforms in Korea. Among these platforms, four platforms are discussed in detail.

- KOCW (https://www.kocw.net): KOCW is the most famous and the biggest OER platform in Korea. KOCW is a free service that provides recorded lectures and learning materials in higher education to college students, professors, and anyone (KOCW, 2019). KERIS, which is a public research institution under the Korean Ministry of Education, manages this platform. KOCW is the biggest OER platform in higher education and has 33,232 courses and 406,844 course materials as of May 2019. In 2017, KOCW launched the English page for overseas users.
- K-MOOC (https://www.kmooc.kr): K-MOOC was established in 2015 as an open online service to provide free courses to anyone, anywhere (K-MOOC, 2019). National Institute for Lifelong Education is in charge of managing the platform. This service is operated through the close collaboration between a total of 87 institutions, including universities, colleges, companies, and government institutes. Even though it has a short history, K-MOOC shows continued growth. The cumulative number of applicants for K-MOOC stood at 55,559 in 2015, but the cumulative number of applicants for classes grew sharply to 696,185 in 2018.

Table 1 Major OER platforms in Korea

	Educational purpose	Resource type	Openness (registration/cost to use/language)	Administration	History
KOCW	Higher education	Online courses	No/free/Korean	Korea Education and Research Information Service (Government)	2007
K-MOOC	Higher education	Online courses	No/free/Korean, English	National Institute for Lifelong Education (Government)	2015
U-KNOU	Higher education	Online courses	Required/partly free/Korean	Korea National Open University (University)	2018
SNU Open Courseware	Higher education	Course materials (lecture notes, study materials)	No/free/English	Seoul National University (University)	2006
Sookmyung Network for Open World	Higher education	Online courses	No/free/Korean, English	Sookmyung Women's University (University)	2009
Edunet-T-Clear	Primary and secondary education	Education materials (videos, textbooks, learning materials)	No/free/Korean	Korea Education and Research Information Service (Government)	1996
COOLSCHOOL	Primary and secondary education	In-service teachers' narratives as to teaching and classroom management	No/free/Korean	Jiranjigyo Comms	2016
Classting	Primary and secondary education	Interactive learning management under a social media platform	No/free for users (paid by subscribed institutions)/Korean, English	Classting	2012

(continued)

Table 1 (continued)

	Educational purpose	Resource type	Openness (registration/cost to use/language)	Administration	History
EBS Clipbank	Primary and secondary education	5 min of educational videos	No/free/Korean, English subtitle	Korea Educational Broadcasting System (Government)	2009
Indischool	Primary education	Education materials	Required (only teacher)/free/Korean	Non-profit Organization (Private)	2000
RISS	Research	Academic content (papers, books, courses, reports)	Required/partly free/Korean	Korea Education and Research Information Service (Government)	1998
NDSL	Research	Academic content in science and technology	Required/partly free/Korean	Korea Institute of Science and Technology Information (Government)	2008

- Edunet-T-Clear (https://www.edunet.net): Edunet-T-Clear is an OER platform that provides teaching and learning materials to primary and secondary teachers and students (Edunet-T-Clear, 2019). Edunet-T-Clear is the first comprehensive educational information service platform in Korea. KERIS launched Edunet in 1996, and Edunet subscribers turned 5 million in 2002. In 2017, KERIS changed its name from Edunet to Edunet-T-Clear. Edunet-T-Clear provides various contents related to primary and secondary education including teaching and learning materials for all subjects, research results, best class videos, educational policy information, digital textbook, teacher training programs, and teacher and student community.
- NDSL (https://www.ndsl.kr): NDSL, which stands for the National Digital Science Library, is an OER platform that provides science and technology materials, such as journal articles, patents, technical reports, standards, and trends for researchers, educators, and industries (NDSL, 2019). NDSL is operated by Korea Institute of Science and Technology Information (KISTI) since 2008. As of May 2019, NDSL has 130 million contents related to science and technology by cooperating with more than 400 domestic and international institutions. In 2010, KISTI launched NDSL Open Service (NOS) that allows the public to easily connect and integrate content and services using OpenAPI (Hyun, Lee, & Kim, 2014).

2.4 Policy

Even though a variety of platforms have been developed and each of those platforms has provided a large number of OER contents in Korea, the practices in terms of the establishment and execution of policies for using OER are still limited. South Korea's current OER policy focuses on the correct use of Creative Commons (CC). More specifically, OER platforms operated by government institutions, such as KOCW and Edunet-T-Clear, provide a general description on CC and include an option to report on copyright issues.

At its current state, the only policy-level execution of Korea's OER platforms is related to the Creative Commons License. In fact, among the 12 platforms reviewed for this chapter (see Table 1), none of them had posted their institutional policy on the OER contents usage. Most platforms only listed general terms and conditions which can be seen in general websites. Terms and conditions on each platform contained policies about the protection of personal information, user agreements, and general rules for using the platform's services, but they did not specify concrete policies on the OER usage. This indicates that the existing OER platforms in Korea do not have clear institutional OER policies that reflect the characteristics of OER and their institutions. Instead of providing a detailed description on the policies for the use of these platforms, each OER institution provides a separate section or file with guidelines for accessing the OER contents that can aid the actual use of their services. These guidelines include step-by-step instructions on OER usage and use-cases that demonstrate the best use of the OER.

Another policy initiative worth mentioning relates to credits and certifications. In 2019, the Korean government announced its Basic Plan for Korean Massive Open Online Course (K-MOOC). According to the plan, if any adult learner (i.e., those who are not college students) takes a course from K-MOOC, his/her participation can be recognized in the form of credits, which can count toward obtaining a bachelor's degree in the future. Such effort by the government is to transform the informal learning experience of MOOCs into a formal learning outcome.

2.5 Copyright

Ever since the first introduction of OER in Korea, a lack of understanding about copyright issues has been a concern in using OER in Korea. For example, in a survey presented by Kim (2013), the fear of copyright infringement was one of the biggest barriers faced by respondents. When asked about Creative Commons (CC), 59 percent of the respondents indicated that they had heard of CC, and 34.4 percent replied that they would be confident to explain it (Belliston, 2009; Butcher, 2015).

In order to address copyright issues, the CC Korea hosted events—introducing various copyright infringement cases as to OER distributions. This organization offered basic guidelines for correct CC implementations. The CC Korea helped general users to identify fundamental features of license laws and apply CC concepts when using OERs.

Moreover, there have been policy-driven efforts from the government in dealing with OER license issues. One of the examples is the Elementary and Secondary Education Act which dictates that certified professionals in formal educational institutions have more access than others in terms of editing and distributing OERs. The purpose of the act is to guarantee instructor/trainers' flexible uses of learning materials, which are aligned with the goal of OERs.

2.6 Pedagogy

2.6.1 Flipped Learning

The early movements of OER focused on providing learners with opportunities in terms of accessing quality-assured materials. Later, scholars have further addressed how to promote learners' engagement through OERs. Although widespread uses of blended learning have emerged since the 2000s (Keller, 2008; Welsh, Wanberg, Brown, & Simmering, 2003), the question remains regarding which ways can better promote students' meaningful learning in distance education contexts. Scholars have focused on developing specific instructional design models and coming up with strategies to support teachers' seamless implementations of blended learning.

Some of the studies in Korea have proposed the adoption of flipped learning in implementing OERs in both formal and informal education. Flipped learning is a modified version of blended learning that facilitates interactive face-to-face learning activities combined with asynchronous online lectures (Lee, Lim, & Kim, 2017). Under the notion of mastery learning (Bergmann & Sams, 2014), flipped learning focuses on highly interactive group discussions that encourage students to perform in-depth reflections when compared to traditional blended learning environments. A series of current studies in Korea attempted to apply flipped learning to various educational contexts. A design and development research by Lee et al. (2017) introduced the entire development steps of the instructional design model, especially for Han, Lim, Han, and Park (2015) also proposed specific instructional strategies and example practices for promoting flipped learning in a college course. These study findings illustrated that there were empirical practices in designing models for flipped learning in various education contexts in Korea.

2.6.2 Learning Communities

The notion of learning communities (Palincsar & Brown, 1986; Vescio, Ross, & Adams, 2008) is another topic that are relevant to OERs in Korea. The learning communities are defined as a purposeful group that aims to share expertise in a specific field (Hou, 2015). Several web platforms allow educational professionals to construct their learning communities to exchange teaching and learning resources. For instance, the service WEDORANG in EDUNET—a web-based environment launched by KERIS in Korea—is a good example that shows the role of administrative support in developing professional learning communities. WEDORANG was intended to support teachers' instruction design competencies in preparing lesson plans and to increase learners' accessibility of various OER resources via open learning communities. This cloud-based platform is also connected to an existing digital-textbook system that encourages students to access various learning resources.

Building learning communities is not necessarily restricted within the boundaries of government-initiated OER infrastructures. In fact, there are example cases of social-media-initiated communities (Shin & Lee, 2017). There are communities that function as interdisciplinary agora where sharing of various educational resources happen. For example, COOLSCHOOL is an online community that allows education professionals to share their narratives regarding how they had utilized various educational technologies in classroom contexts (COOLSCHOOL, 2019). This microblogging webpage allows teachers to better provide case examples, as well as instructional strategies in chronological order. Also, small group communities in social media platforms in Korea contributed to distributing OERs. The interactions from these small groups in social media enhance individual users' easy and quick access to various web-based links to learning resources. Also, the emergence of a Korean corporation called CLASSTING inspired another wave of the learning communities. This adaptive web platform focuses on serving users that are interested in aligning existing formal school curriculum (CLASSTING, 2012). Since CLASSTING was introduced in 2012, a total of four million users—including parents, teachers, students—have enrolled. The platform has implemented interaction patterns that are similar to existing social media platforms (e.g., *Facebook* and *Naver Band*). The system provides a service called Open Class that allows students to freely share their learning resources in their class projects.

Several studies have proposed various instructional support models for OER frameworks (e.g., Kwon, Han, Lee, & Bang, 2012; Lee & Yoon, 2014). The results of these studies suggest that facilitating teachers to engage in social media usage is beneficial in increasing the number of OER being used, as well as maintaining quality-assured materials that are verified by fellow professionals within the community.

2.6.3 Personalized Learning

Many of the previous studies have highlighted instructional design for maintaining high-quality assurance of OERs. While they were useful studies, it had some limitations. For instance, early OER studies focused on learners' use of open learning resources in a limited way. Many current OER studies go further by discussing how learners' diverse needs can be captured based on their profiles. In fact, recent OER studies have featured uses of OERs especially tailored to students' personalized learning. Personalized learning generally stresses adaptive learning support that is tailored to students' background and interests (Bernacki & Walkington, 2018; Walkington, 2013). This approach suggests that customizing diverse OERs for individual students is essential in drawing students' attention. Since OER platforms target the general public, there is an increasing need for providing personalized instruction for individual online learners.

In Korea, ever since several universities began creating K-MOOCs, interests toward designing personalized learning environments in distance education have increased (Joo, So, & Kim, 2018; Kim, 2015). As a result, recent studies explored the potential of learning analytics to understand students' different learning profiles and propose an adaptive support design for them. With real-time data collection of students' learning resource uses, the learning-analytic technique portrayed diverse learning curves that necessitate individuals' personalization.

A few studies introduced how variant learning analytics can be used to collect learners' preferences in online environments. Park and Lim (2015) collected students' log from social media to extract and analyze both learners–teachers social interests during learning activities. Park, Yu, and Jo (2016) implemented cluster analysis to examine study participants' learning profiles and suggested suitable learning strategies for specified learner groups. Moreover, Kim, Jo, and Park (2016) investigated the effect of the learning analytics dashboard that was designed to facilitate students' self-regulation in MOOCs. These study findings coherently informed that practical implementations of learning analytics in using OERS have evolved.

3 Current Limitations and Future Directions

3.1 Policy-Related Suggestions

At its current state, OER initiatives are heavily driven by the Korean government and its agencies. There are pros and cons of government-driven implementations. First, government-led implementations guarantee reliable operations, rapid growth, and sourcing of professional staffs. Also, there is an abundance of available resources. However, there are issues of lower utilization rate and quality control. The future directions regarding OER initiatives need to consider motivating both content providers and users to develop and use OER as a way to promote effective utilization of OERs beyond quantitative growth. In order to accomplish this goal, more partnerships between government-led initiatives and user-driven OERs need to be established.

Another implication would be on international collaboration. Currently, OER created in Korea is consumed only within domestic boundaries. There needs to be more efforts to develop OERs at the international level as well. Korea has pursued OER partnership with large non-government organizations (NGOs) including the World Bank's Open Learning Campus (Keskin et al., 2017) which was developed in partnership with the Republic of Korea's Ministry of Economy and Finance. However, international collaboration is still in its infancy. Facilitating international network of OERs as well as understanding of how OERs are being developed through partnership need to be explored.

Lastly, the implication would be reducing the redundancy of platforms. Korea government currently holds two major platforms for OER: KOCW and K-MOOC. While these two platforms are different in nature, with one being a MOOC platform, there are overlapping characteristics since both platforms are managed under the Ministry of Education. In order to avoid duplication of contents and functionalities, the role of these platforms needs to be differentiated.

3.2 Research Directions

While there are many studies that explore OER in Korean contexts, there are still some areas that could be explored more. In fact, more research on effective use of OERs needs to be conducted in addition to previous research on how to develop OER platform and contents. One of the areas that could be addressed would be studies on copyright issues. Although OER adoptions in Korea have been prolific, only a few empirical studies were conducted to investigate how copyright issues of OER are effectively managed. There need to be more explanatory and investigative case studies that aim to examine how educational professionals can manage copyright issues.

Another area that could be explored more is quality assurance of OER environments. While there are emerging studies that propose various instructional design models and case studies that explore OER-supporting environments, not many studies deal with how quality assurances of those environments were implemented. Quality assurance is essential in understanding how various OERs are qualified and standardized for distribution. Although research has increasingly emphasized quality assurances in the context of OER (Camilleri, Ehlers, & Pawlowski, 2014; Kawachi, 2014), only a few studies examined how quality assurances were designed and implemented with Korean contexts. In terms of flipped learning, either instructional strategies or instructional design models for flipped learning have been proposed by researchers. Future research needs to examine the effectiveness of them within the context of OERs to better understand effective practices for instructional design or strategies in adopting OER in education. In addition, although learning communities have been one of the essential components of OERs in Korea, little has been known about how teachers or students interact with each other in learning communities. Future research needs to examine such interactions by using social network analysis or content analysis.

4 Conclusion

OERs in Korea have grown over the last few years. We argue that policy has played an important role in establishing groundworks for OER in Korea. Driven by government-led initiatives, several OER platforms have emerged, and they are still managed under the umbrella of the Korean government. Moreover, technologies played an important role during the development process of OER in Korea. Korea has been one of the leading countries in terms of technological infrastructure. Among different technologies, high-speed Internet, mobile network, and e-learning platforms were crucial in fostering OER in Korea. First, high-speed Internet enriched ICT-specialized learning environments. High-speed Internet enabled different modes of learning resources to be transferred via the Internet. This is crucial because different forms of media cannot be afforded with low-speed or poor Internet connections. Second, mobile network affords learners to access learning materials seamlessly. As a result, educational professionals have been implementing ubiquitous learning in classrooms via mobile supportive systems. Third, multiple innovative e-learning platforms initiated by multiple parties have contributed in providing a stable marketplace for comprehensive OER access.

In terms of pedagogy, several notions of learning have impacted OER usage in Korea. First, the notion of flipped learning expanded the role of online learning when using OERs. OERs are being used to support and foster highly interactive discussions in classrooms. In these cases, students are instructed to access class materials that are provided with OER and focus on deep reflections while in classrooms. In fact, there are emerging studies that build on instructional design models and present case examples especially for flipped learning contexts. The second notion is on learning communities. Online learning communities of educational professionals also fostered the active uses of OER materials. The web-/cloud-based platforms of the learning communities enabled users/learners to share their knowledge and learning resources. This chapter reviewed a couple of learning community cases in Korea.

- **Governmental-led**: The service WEDORANG hosted by KERIS
- **Bottom-up**: COOLSCHOOL (microblogging website)/CLASSTING (learning management system).

Third, the notion of personalized learning also impacted OER in Korea. Recent studies on online learning have emphasized how OERs can be provided through personalization (Joo et al., 2018; Kim, 2015). Studies aimed to answer how OER provisions can be tailored to learners' diverse needs. K-MOOC is an example. Several studies in MOOCs introduced how the adoption of learning analytics in predicting students' online learning behaviors under their learning profiles (Kim et al., 2016; Park & Lim, 2015; Park et al., 2016). The findings of these studies indicated that emerging uses of learning analytics helped to identify students' needs for personalized learning in distance education.

We have also discussed research and practical implications. We discussed future directions of government-led OER initiatives in terms of quality improvement,

improvement in utilization rate, both international and domestic collaboration, and redundancy of platforms. We also discussed the need for studies that focus on copyright issues and quality assurance studies.

Analyzing OER in Korean contexts is meaningful due to Korea's advanced technological infrastructure and its centralized initiatives led by government. Also, people's familiarity with using OERs and taking online courses could provide insights for not only Korean researchers and educators but also those who are from other cultures.

References

Baek, Y. K., & Cheong, D. U. (2005). *Present and future prospects for mobile learning in Korea.* Paper presented at the IEEE International Workshop on Wireless and Mobile Technologies in Education (WMTE'05).

Belliston, C. J. (2009). Open educational resources: Creating the instruction commons. *College & Research Libraries News, 70*(5), 284–303.

Bergmann, J., & Sams, A. (2014). *Flipped learning: Gateway to student engagement.* International Society for Technology in Education.

Bernacki, M. L., & Walkington, C. (2018). The role of situational interest in personalized learning. *Journal of Educational Psychology, 110*(6), 864–881.

Butcher, N. (2015). *A basic guide to open educational resources (OER).* Commonwealth of Learning (COL).

Camilleri, A. F., Ehlers, U. D., & Pawlowski, J. (2014). *State of the art review of quality issues related to open educational resources (OER).* Luxembourg: Publications Office of the European Union.

Chon, K., Park, H., Kang, K., & Lee, Y. (2005). A brief history of the Internet in Korea. *Korea Internet History Project.* Retrieved from https://net.its.hawaii.edu/history/Korean_Internet_History.pdf.

CLASSTING. (2012). Retrieved from https://en.classting.com.

Conole, G., & Weller, M. (2008). Using learning design as a framework for supporting the design and reuse of OER. *Journal of Interactive Media in Education, 5.*

COOLSCHOOL. (2019). Retrieved from https://www.coolschool.co.kr/

EBS. (2019). Korean Educational Broadcasting System. Retrieved from https://about.ebs.co.kr/kor/main/index; https://en.wikipedia.org/wiki/Educational_Broadcasting_System

Edunet-T-Clear. (2019). Retrieved from https://www.edunet.net

Han, H., Lim, C., Han, S., & Park, J. (2015). Instructional strategies for integrating online and offline modes of flipped learning in higher education. *Korean Journal of Educational Technology, 31*(1), 1–38.

Heo, H. J., & Choi, M. R. (2014). Flipped learning in the middle school math class. *Advanced Science and Technology Letters, 71*, 94–97.

Hong, S. (1998). The initiation of 'Sharing Educational Materials' movement. Retrieved from https://news.joins.com/article/3602365

Hou, H. (2015). What makes an online community of practice work? A situated study of Chinese student teachers' perceptions of online professional learning. *Teaching and Teacher Education, 46*, 6–16.

Hyun, M. H., Lee, H. J., & Kim, H. S. (2014). *Effect of NDSL Open Service (NOS) on sharing S&T information.* Paper presented at the Proceeding of ICCC.

Jang, D. H., Yi, P., & Shin, I. S. (2016). Examining the effectiveness of digital textbook use on students' learning outcomes in South Korea: A meta-analysis. *The Asia-Pacific Education Researcher, 25*(1), 57–68.

Jang, S. (2013). The analysis of learner's needs based on the current usages of e-learning open educational resources in higher education. *The Korean Journal of Educational Methodology Studies, 25*, 289–315.

Joo, Y. J., & Kim, D. (2017). A study of satisfaction and intention to use MOOC based on UTAUT2 in Korea. *Journal of Lifelong Learning Society, 13*(1), 185–207.

Joo, Y. J., So, H., & Kim, N. (2018). Examination of relationships among students' self-determination, technology acceptance, satisfaction, and continuance intention to use K-MOOCs. *Computers & Education, 122*, 260–272.

JoongAngIlbo. (2013). 2013 University Evaluation Indicator. Retrieved from https://univ.joongang. co.kr/new/university/index_view.asp?pg=1&ps=10&pb=10&sf=0&sw=&tf=&sm=&cf=0&sc= &ix=13&ht=

K-MOOC. (2019). Retrieved from https://www.kmooc.kr

Kawachi, P. (2014). Quality assurance guidelines for open educational resources. *TIPS Framework.* Commonwealth Educational Media Centre for Asia (CEMCA).

Keller, J. M. (2008). First principles of motivation to learn and e3-learning. *Distance Education, 29*(2), 175–185.

Keskin, N. Ö., Koutropoulos, A., De Waard, I., Metcalf, D., Gallagher, M., Anzai, Y., et al. (2017). National Strategies for OER and MOOCs From 2010 to 2020: Canada, Japan, South Korea, Turkey, UK, and USA. In K. Buyuk, S. Kocdar, & A. Bozkurt (Eds.), *Administrative leadership in open and distance learning programs* (pp. 188–212). USA: IGI Global.

Kim, H., Lee, M., & Kim, M. (2014). Effects of mobile instant messaging on collaborative learning processes and outcomes: The case of South Korea. *Journal of Educational Technology & Society, 17*(2), 31–42.

Kim, J. I. (2015). A study on the K-MOOC platform standardization measures. *International Journal of Software Engineering and Its Applications, 9*(1), 221–236.

Kim, J., Jo, I. H., & Park, Y. (2016). Effects of learning analytics dashboard: Analyzing the relations among dashboard utilization, satisfaction, and learning achievement. *Asia Pacific Education Review, 17*(1), 13–24.

Kim, K. J., Jeong, I. J., Park, J. C., Park, Y. J., Kim, C. G., & Kim, T. H. (2007). The impact of network service performance on customer satisfaction and loyalty: High-speed internet service case in Korea. *Expert Systems with Applications, 32*(3), 822–831.

Kim, T., Cho, J. Y., & Lee, B. G. (2012). *Evolution to smart learning in public education: A case study of Korean public education.* Paper presented at the IFIP WG 3.4 International Conference on Open and Social Technologies for Networked Learning.

Kim, Y. (2013). Open educational resources in Korea. *Open Education Resources: An Asian Perspective*, 107–118

KOCW. (2019). Korean OpenCourseWare (KOCW). Retrieved from https://www.kocw.net.

Korea Institute for Curriculum and Evaluation (KICE). (2019). Action Plan for the 2020 College Scholastic Ability Test.

Korean Ministry of Education. (2015a). A Proposal for Implementation of Korean Massive Open Online Courses (K-MOOC).

Korean Ministry of Education. (2015b). University and Graduate School Information Disclosure Guidelines.

Kwak, S. (2017). How Korean language arts teachers adopt and adapt Open Educational Resources: A study of teachers' and students' perspectives. *The International Review of Research in Open and Distributed Learning, 18*(4), 193–211.

Kwon, S., Han, S., Lee, J., Bang, S. (2012). Development of a smart e-learning model for liberal arts education. *Journal of Lifelong Learning Society. 8*(3), 115–152.

Lee, E., & Kim, K. (2015). A study of Korean professors' experiences in the adoption and use of Open Course Ware. *The Journal of Curriculum Studies, 33*(1), 65–91.

Lee, J., Lim, C., & Kim, H. (2017). Development of an instructional design model for flipped learning in higher education. *Educational Technology Research and Development, 65*(2), 427–453.

Lee, S., & Yoon, O. (2014). An exploration on instructional support model for convergence education with the form of class-specific courses in general education. *Korean Journal of General Education, 8*(2), 129–160.

Lim, K., & Kim, M. H. (2014). A SWOT analysis of design elements of Korean MOOCs. *Journal of Digital Convergence, 12*(6), 615–624.

Miyazoe, T., & Anderson, T. (2013). Interaction equivalency in an OER, MOOCS and informal learning era. *Journal of Interactive Media in Education, 2013*(2), 1–15.

NDSL. (2019). National Digital Science Library Retrieved from https://www.ndsl.kr

Nikoi, S., & Armellini, A. (2012). The OER mix in higher education: Purpose, process, product, and policy. *Distance Education, 33*(2), 165–184.

Olcott, D., Jr. (2012). OER perspectives: Emerging issues for universities. *Distance Education, 33*(2), 283–290.

Open Educational Resources. (n.d.) Retrieved from https://hewlett.org/strategy/open-educational-resources/

Palincsar, A. S., & Brown, A. L. (1986). Interactive teaching to promote independent learning from text. *The Reading Teacher, 39*(8), 771–777.

Park, J., & Lim, H. (2015). Analysis of social learning activities learners with educational data mining techniques. *The Journal of Korean Association of Computer Education, 19*(1), 31–35.

Park, Y., Yu, J. H., & Jo, I.-H. (2016). Clustering blended learning courses by online behavior data: A case study in a Korean higher education institute. *The Internet and Higher Education, 29*, 1–11.

Shin, H., & Lee, E. (2017). Searchin the potential of OER for overcoming the educational inequality in the digital era. *Asia-pacific Journal of Multimedia Services Convergent with Art, Humanities, and Sociology, 7*(5), 273–283. https://dx.doi.org/10.14257/ajmahs.2017.05.57

Shin, N., Jeon, M., & Kim, S. (2016). A review of selected OER platforms through the developed analysis indicators. *The Journal of Educational Informatio and Media, 22*(3), 561–582. https://dx.doi.org/10.15833/KAFEIAM.22.3.561

Shin, N., Shin, H., Jang, S., Meruyert, A., Park, J., Kim, S., … Jeon, M. (Eds.). (2018). *Open education resource for open education innovation*. Seoul: PYMate

Smith, M. S., & Casserly, C. M. (2006). The promise of open educational resources. *Change: The Magazine of higher learning, 38*(5), 8–17.

UNESCO. (2002). *Forum on the impact of open courseware for higher education in developing countries: Final report*. Retrieved from Paris https://unesdoc.unesco.org/images/0012/001285/128515e.pdf.

Vescio, V., Ross, D., & Adams, A. (2008). A review of research on the impact of professional learning communities on teaching practice and student learning. *Teaching and Teacher Education, 24*(1), 80–91.

Walkington, C. A. (2013). Using adaptive learning technologies to personalize instruction to student interests: The impact of relevant contexts on performance and learning outcomes. *Journal of Educational Psychology, 105*(4), 932–945.

Welsh, E. T., Wanberg, C. R., Brown, K. G., & Simmering, M. J. (2003). E-learning: emerging uses, empirical results and future directions. *International Journal of Training and Development, 7*(4), 245–258.

Gi Woong Choi is an assistant professor of human–computer interaction at State University of New York at Oswego. He earned his Ph.D. in Learning, Design, and Technology from Penn State University and has a background in human–computer interaction and user experience. His current research interests include HCI in education, mobile learning, informal learning, problem-solving, makerspaces, educational affordances of emerging technologies, AI in Education, etc.

Jewoong Moon is a Ph.D. candidate at the Department of Educational Psychology and Learning Systems at Florida State University. His research interests include learning analytics, educational data mining, game-based learning, and inclusive e-learning design. Specifically, he is interested in designing and developing a real-time adaptive system in technology-enhanced environments for learners with disabilities.

Jaewoo Do is a Ph.D. in Educational Technology. Currently, he works at Korean Educational Development Institute as an associate research fellow. He is in charge of managing open secondary schools of Korea and discovering research topics related to public online learning in Korea. His research interests include synchronous online course design, design thinking, equity in education and qualitative research.

Daeyeoul Lee is a Ph.D. candidate at the Department of Curriculum and Instruction at Purdue University. His main research interest is self-regulated learning. He is especially interested in self-regulated learning in Massive Open Online Courses (MOOCs) and online learning environments.

Chapter 6
Open Educational Resources in Mongolia

A. Amarzaya, D. Tumenbayar, T. Navchaa, A. Bulgan, B. Burmaa, David Porter and L. Munkhtuya

1 Case Overview

Mongolia is a country located in Central and East Asia bordering Russia and China. Its population is over 3.1 million with the least population density in the world of 1.92 people per square kilometer. According to World Bank data the country's Gross National Income (GNI) per capita in 2017 was 3,590 US dollars.

A. Amarzaya (✉) · D. Tumenbayar · T. Navchaa · A. Bulgan
Department of Mathematics, School of Arts and Sciences, National University of Mongolia, University street 1, Building 1, Room 116, Ulaanbaatar, Mongolia
e-mail: amarzaya@num.edu.mn

D. Tumenbayar
e-mail: tumenbayar@num.edu.mn

T. Navchaa
e-mail: navchaa@smcs.num.edu.mn

A. Bulgan
e-mail: bulgan_amar@yahoo.com

B. Burmaa
The ONE Foundation, Khan Uul District, Narkhan hothon, Narkhan town house, Mahatma Gandi street, Ulaanbaatar, Mongolia
e-mail: burmaa@one.mn

D. Porter
Ontario Online Learning Consortium (eCampusOntario), 372 Bay Street, 14th Floor, Toronto, Ontario M52W9, Canada
e-mail: davidp@ecampusontario.ca

L. Munkhtuya
Office of ICT and Distance Education, Mongolan National University of Education, Baga Toiruu-14, 210648 Ulaanbaatar, Mongolia
e-mail: munkhtuya@msue.edu.mn

© Springer Nature Singapore Pte Ltd. 2020
R. Huang et al. (eds.), *Current State of Open Educational Resources in the "Belt and Road" Countries*, Lecture Notes in Educational Technology,
https://doi.org/10.1007/978-981-15-3040-1_6

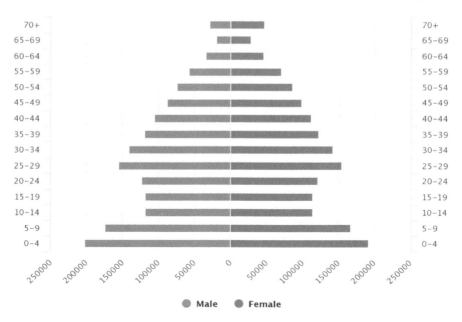

Fig. 1 Population demographic pyramid for Mongolia

The population demographic pyramid of Mongolia by age and gender is shown in Fig. 1 (National Statistical Office of Mongolia, 2017). The figure shows a larger portion of the young generation under 35 years old in total population.

The country is divided administratively into 21 provinces (**aimags**) and the capital city Ulaanbaatar. Each aimag is divided into subprovinces or districts which are called **soums in Mongolian**. Ulaanbaatar city is divided into 9 districts. The total number of soums is 329.

The education system of the country is composed of preschool, primary school, secondary school, high school, and university education. In total, there are 729 primary, secondary, and high schools in the country and 96 higher education institutions. Most of the HEIs are small sized and 18 of these institutions are stated owned. The school enrollment rates are high in all levels of education with low literacy rates. According to UNESCO 2010, total number of illiterate members of population aged 15–24 is 9,000 and total number of illiterate members of the population aged over 15 years old is about 30,000. However, there are not enough sources of evidence to conclude the quality of education system of the country. The country is no longer participating in international comparative educational assessment projects like PISA and TIMSS.

In the tables that follow, we provide information about the education system of Mongolia (Tables 1, 2 and 3).

The Parliament of Mongolia regulates education-related matters through approving laws related to education, and the Ministry of Education approves procedures

Table 1 Enrollment rate by education levels. This table provides enrollment data for Primary and Secondary education from the National Statistics Office of Mongolia (2017)

Primary		Secondary		High school		Tertiary	
Total	Female	Total	Female	Total	Female	Total	Female
98.6	98.5	103.3	104.2	100.29	100.61	64.56	75.31

Table 2 Number of teachers (elementary, secondary, and upper secondary school) by school years

	2015–2016	2016–2017	2017–2018
Total	28,490	28,889	29,242
Female	23,120	23,479	23,876
Male	5,370	5,410	5,366

and regulatory frameworks, consistent with laws passed by parliament and assures everyday activities of schools and kindergartens. The school principals are appointed by the heads of Aimags or Districts.

2 Current Situation with OER in Mongolia

As previously stated, Mongolia is the country with lowest population density in the world. This creates many problems in planning, delivering, and effectively financing education of all levels. Successfully developed and effectively delivered OER will help to ease these problems and will be an advantageous for keeping traditional nomadic lifestyle while scoping with the global educated world.

In *Guidelines for Open Educational Resources (OER) in Higher Education* (Commonwealth of Learning, 2011), the report defined key guidelines for governments to promote OER developments in higher education as follows.

a. Support the use of OER through their policy-making role in higher education.
b. Consider adopting open licensing frameworks.
c. Consider adopting open standards.
d. Contribute to raising awareness of key OER issues.
e. Promote national ICT/connectivity strategies.
f. Support the sustainable development and sharing of quality learning materials.

In upcoming subsections, while supposing these guidelines are also applicable for all levels of education, we will review whether these guidelines are reflected in Mongolian OER development.

Table 3 Age and gender of teachers (elementary, secondary, and upper secondary school) by school years

	First year		1–5 years		6–10 years		11–15 years		16–20 years		21–25 years		Above 25 years	
	Total	Female	Total	Female	Total	Female	Total	Female	Total	Female	Total	Female	Total	Female
2016–2017	1,732	1,411	9,287	7,262	5,866	4,680	4,576	3,846	1,732	1,411	9,287	7,262	5,866	4,680
2017–2018	1,675	1,350	9,405	7,225	5,892	4,706	4,348	3,691	1,675	1,350	9,405	7,225	5,892	4,706

2.1 Infrastructure

"Sustainable development goals for Mongolia – 2030" was the only recent long-term policy document which outlined development objectives in various sectors of the country including education and the ICT sector. It included ambitious goals such as the development and utilization of infrastructure, improving access, removing the digital divide, and enabling public access to broadband. Moreover, it created various opportunities to infuse Open Educational Resources (OER) into both compulsory and higher education, and also into lifelong learning.

The development of infrastructure is one of the pillars to promote the usage and development of OER in Mongolia.

Infrastructural resources, besides the availability of personal computers and mobile phones, also included access to the Internet, the World Wide Web, email, and presentation software. For some indicators, results from the school level survey from the National Statistical Office between 2015 and 2017 are shown in the following Table 4 (National Statistical Office of Mongolia, 2017).

The data in the second row of the table may seem high in comparing with some other underdeveloped countries. However, the average speed of the Internet is not satisfactory and heads of the preuniversity level schools might not understand the importance of Internet connectivity for both students and teachers.

About 25,000 (85%) school teachers (including primary, lower, and upper secondary) received laptop computers through the "Teacher's Development" subprogram of the "New Century Education" program in 2015. Through this project the Mongolian government also supplied 1–2 computer laboratories for each school nationwide. The total number of these laboratory computers is 11,000. In the planning and implementation phase of this project, the government did not emphasize the importance of software licensing, and currently the licenses of software are expiring and need extension. Moreover, through this project, all schools and local education agencies received smart-boards and projectors. Also, a data center for the education sector was created as a result of this project and 122 schools in Ulaanbaatar and 69 schools from the centers of aimags were connected to the Internet with a GPON broadband cable. Moreover 350 schools from 334 soums were also connected to the Internet with broadband connections. The schools were also provided with wireless Internet connection equipment.

The number of smartphone users reached 1.9 million in 2015 with an increase of 1.8% from 2014. But this number rose sharply to 3.3 million in 2017 which is much

Table 4 Some infrastructure indicators

	Indicators	2015 (%)	2016 (%)	2017 (%)
1	Connected to electricity	96.6	96.6	96.6
2	The internet is available for educational purposes	67.8	68.4	68.4
3	Schools equipped with computers for learning purposes	94.8	95.4	95.4

higher than the world average number for smartphone users per 100 people; it is 2.3 times higher. There are 75 companies providing Internet services in Mongolia.

By 2017, the total number of Internet users was 2.9 million. The average Internet service connectivity speed is more than 2 Mbps in Ulaanbaatar, Darkhan, and Erdenet cities, and between 300 Kbps and 2 Mbps in other areas. The total number of computers in the country is 617,703.

Since the main source for Internet connection is smartphones, stakeholders need to focus on producing OER which are consistent with smartphones.

The International Telecommunication Union, a United Nations specialized agency for information and communication technologies uses the so-called ICT development index which is calculated using 11 indicators. The indicators are grouped into three subindexes: access, use, and capacity. Based on these indexes, Mongolia ranked 91th out of 167 countries in 2017, compared to ranking 97th in 2010, advancing a few places up the rankings. Comparing this level of development indicator to 2010, the ICT access subindex has increased by 1.48 points, while the usage subindex increased by 4.2 points, and the capacity subindex increased by 0.67 points respectively. Specifically, the capacity subindex has advanced 19 places in development priority and is ranked 33rd. It is also ranked 13th out of the 40 countries in the Asia Pacific region. In the Global Information Technology Report 2015, Mongolia ranked 61th with 4.2 points out of 143 countries in the "Networked ReadinessIndex."

The main players providing soft infrastructures for OER are the Ministry of Education, Culture, Science, and Sports (MECSS), the Institute of Teachers Professional Development (ITPD), the National Center for Lifelong Education (NCLE), and the Institute of Education Research (IE). We will discuss their products in section about Resources.

In 2015, through a development project implemented by the Asian Development Bank, MECS founded a distance education center based at the Mongolian State University of Education. This center has subcenters in rural universities including Dornod University, a sub-branch of MSUE in Arkhangai province, a sub-branch of NUM in Zavkhan province and at KhovdUniversity. The main objective of this center is to build the capacity of rural teachers through distance education, to disseminate methodologies of online teaching and learning, and to provide rural teachers with recent information related to education.

Our survey concerning the infrastructure of the main state universities shows that universities pay high importance to Internet connectivity and the speed of connection depends on the financial ability of universities. The average Internet speed of state universities is 2 megabits per second. It also shows that universities use their own developed student–teacher management systems. Some universities use free or open-source software systems like Google Classroom and Moodle. Moreover, all state-owned universities are using learning management systems.

2.2   *Policy*

2.2.1   Policy for Development of Infrastructure to Support OER

During the period of 1999–2015, the government of Mongolia initiated various development policies, programs, and strategic plans in order to support the development of the information and communications technology (ICT) sector and successfully implemented them.

"The Education Master Plan 2006–2015" and "ICT Vision 2021 in Education" emphasized the use of ICT for teacher development (Government of Mongolia, 2006; ICT and Post Authority of Mongolia, 2011). Between 2012 and 2016, the government of Mongolia approved a policy to improve the continuous professional development of teachers through a national teacher training platform (Information and Communication Technology, Education Policy, 2012–2016, 2012). Further, the Education Policy Action Plan (2012–2016) also implemented a program to renew teacher training programs in accordance with the latest ICT development and OER, as well as new education standards and curriculum (Ministry of Education Culture Science and Sports, 2012).

In 2015, the Parliament passed the policy document titled "Policy of the State on Education, 2014–2024" which states that the Government will support the development of open education resources and ICT for Education. Parallel with this policy, MECSS established a web-portal for promoting the accumulation of OER and interactive learning content.

In 2016, "ONE Mongolia" an open educational national program, 2016–2024, was approved by the Government of Mongolia. Designed as an open educational national program, it has supported the use of OER, raising awareness of OER and open licensing. Derived from this vision, the framework of the Open Education ONE Mongolia national program has been implemented around three pillars at the beginning stage: the ONE Academy, the ONE School, and the ONE Language in a multilingual approach that is an essential component of OER development in Mongolia.

"Sustainable Development Vision for Mongolia – 2030" is a policy document that has outlined development objectives in the ICT sector such as development and utilization of infrastructure, improving access, removing the digital divide, and enabling public access to broadband. The following are the objectives of the ICT specified in this development concept (Parliament of Mongolia, 2016).

Phase I (2016–2020): 70% of the total population will be connected to high-speed Internet networks. They will benefit from the same price and tariffs regardless of location and information flow transmitted through high-speed information network connecting Asia and Europe, which will increase 10-fold.

Phase II (2021–2025): 90% of the total population will be connected to high-speed Internet networks. 70% of the rural population will use broadband Internet services, and not less than 50% of public services will be provided to citizens online.

Phase III (2026–2030): 95% of the total population will be connected to high-speed Internet networks, and not less than 85% of public services will be provided to citizens online, and a national satellite will be launched and utilized.

In order to sustain the effectiveness of this policy, the Parliament of Mongolia passed a law ensuring that criteria for each of the Phases must be checked periodically and reported. According to NSO, the goals for 2017 of Phase I are fulfilled. This means that 67% of the total population is already connected to a high-speed Internet network.

2.3 Resources

The development and accumulation of OER relies heavily on financing. We can classify sources of financing for OER in Mongolia into four types: government supported, institutions supported, private initiatives and international initiatives, and cooperation.

We review the situation for all levels of education in the sections that follow.

2.3.1   At the Elementary, Secondary, and Upper Secondary School Level (School Level)

The guiding policy for the Ministry of Education is to finance the development of OER by teachers, private initiators, and companies and make the resources free for the public based on the Creative Commons principles.[1]

To be precise, the Ministry of Education publishes and prints textbooks for all grades and subjects and owns the copyright. Since 2013, the government of Mongolia decided to make all textbooks used in elementary, secondary, and high schools available online for the public. Currently 168 textbooks are available online for students, teachers, parents, schools, and other stakeholders. During the 2013–2014 school year the Ministry of Education financed complete lesson packages for Mathematics and Natural Science for each grade of the secondary and high school levels. All these materials were developed jointly by school teachers and some private companies. Currently open educational resources on more than 140 interactive packages of Math, Physics, Chemistry, and Biology for grade 8–12 students are available in the Mongolian language on the website. Each package contains theoretical introductions, interactive examples, assessment materials, and ancillary resources. The website also contains numerous video lesson packages and handbooks for elementary school teachers. Preparation of these video lessons and teacher handbooks was financed by the JICA project. The second phase of this project was started in 2018 and will continue until 2022.

---

[1]https://econtent.edu.mn/content/library.html.

The Institute of Education, the only state-financed education research institute, also develops teaching guides of all subjects for all grades and publishes them on its website.

Another key source of OER for Mongolian teachers and students is the teachers' development site of ITPD. The core idea of this project is that the registered teachers can upload their own lessons or OER on the page and other teachers can use, share, comment, download, and edit these OER. The basic statistics related to the teachers is also available. This site has 25,841 open resources from 20 subjects, classified into grade levels. This project started in 2013 and access has reached to 333,370 users (https://teacher.itpd.mn). Teachers also vote for the best lessons online and the best lessons were chosen in each year. This portal site is currently the most popular site for Mongolian teachers. We will give brief discussion of our research result on the usage of this site in later sections.

The Education Evaluation Center (EEC) prepares and publishes all high-stakes examinations for elementary, secondary, and high school preparatory materials on its site eec.mn. Currently the Center created an item bank consisting of more than 17 thousand items and teachers can use the items freely. All of the noted webpages are sponsored by the Ministry of Education.

Parallel with the availability of resources previously noted, other governments and educational community initiatives are also activating. Jointly with the ONE foundation team and school teachers, university teachers, university preservice students and staff from some preservice teacher institutes translated Khan Academy video lessons and online exercises into Mongolian under the financial support of MECS. Elementary and secondary school math, history, computer science, and biology subjects have been successfully translated with Mongolian voices and subtitles and are widely used by both students and teachers. The main advantage of these free lessons is that they are available from YouTube and can be reviewed, commented, and shared by users. Those videos are also supplemented with interactive exercises and a personalized learning dashboard that empowers learners to study at their own pace in and outside of the classroom.

The most surprising outcome of this activity is that besides the students in Mongolia, students living in 16 countries from Asia, Australia, Europe, and North America used these videos and reviewed them. This underscores the importance of OER to learners and educators.

Here we give a brief summary of these lessons (Table 5).

Other evidence of successful OER initiatives includes the activities from the Mongolian Institute of GeoGebra. The institute is an independent group of voluntary teachers, educators, and students with aims to promote and support the use of the open mathematical software-GeoGebra and disseminate OER produced using this software. Since 2012, the Institute is becoming a translator of a Mongolian version of GeoGebra and is keeping the software up to date. The Institute also supports research on the impact of use of OER made by using GeoGebra and other open-source software by organizing a research conference called, "Open Education."

One of the important criteria to become a one of the Asia's Top 100 universities is to have a learning management system (LMS) and its infusion into the everyday

Table 5 A brief summary of Khan academy video lessons in Mongolian

	Biology	Teacher essentials	World history	Computer science	Mathematics	All
Number of videos	59	3	78	15	936	1091
Duration time (min)	821	10	736	51	4156	5774
Watch time (min)	14,150		198,742	1577	20,191	242,570
Views	5379	966	36,690	761	15,575	64,003

teaching and learning activities. By extending and renewing data from Suvdmaa, Banzragch, and Saizmaa (2016), we cite general information on LMS development and other supporting infrastructure and resource elements from the main universities in Mongolia (Table 6).

From this, we can see the picture of current situation of OER implementation among the main universities.

Since 2016, the Ministry of Education has financed free access to world-known scientific resources including EBSCO for state-owned universities. As all free access goes through university libraries, the initiative makes libraries of universities the big players in OER distribution. As a consequence, students and professors are able to connect to prestigious academic journals, reviews, and educational resources.

Professors and lecturers from the National University of Mongolia and the Mongolian State University of Arts and Culture are participating in the Korean UNESCO-UNITWIN OCW/OER initiative hosted by Handong Global University. "The initiative will provide a platform for instructors to upload their materials, allocate monetary funds for instructors willing to participate, and offer training on teaching with digital media and intellectual property." (Source: UNESCO-UNITWIN OCW/OER, Handong Global University home https://www.uuooi.org/english). Professors upload their lesson packages prepared in the Mongolian language and make them available for their students. However, the number of professors who participate in this initiative is small.

We conclude this subsection with the following observations.

1. For universities which have educational resources, it's hard to say that the resources are open for all. Usually, access to the materials is limited to only the students of that university.
2. The quality of lesson materials not satisfactory from both methodological and technological point of view. Universities need to improve the capacity of staff and faculty in these directions.
3. The mechanisms for continuous improvement are not yet established for all the above mentioned systems.
4. The development of materials and resources is in the early stage. It will require further contributions from professors and organizations.

Table 6 Summary of University policies on resources

Name of institution	IPRs policy or strategy	E-learning policy or guideline	Center of faculty development	Resources
Mongolian National University	Yes, University guideline on IPRs, August 31, 2012	No	Center for faculty development and online instructional design	Started mooc.num.edu.mn
Mongolian University for Science and Technology	Yes, University guideline on IPRs, October 23, 2012	Started as "E-learning program" from 2007.05.03 Approved "Regulation for E open university and library service of MUST" in 2010 Distance education handbook for master students approved in 2014	"E-open institute" emust.edu.mn 2010.01.28	E-OI (E-open institute) platform, about 400 e-lesson packages Also started Mooc.edu.mn
Mongolian University of Education	Yes, University guideline on IPRs, February 21, 2018	Regulation for library services, 2017.11	Distance Learning Center 2017.09 Teacher Development Center 2018.04	
Mongolian University of Life Sciences	Has extension center since 2006 for IPRs	No	No	Undergraduate 668 lesson packs, master level 147, Ph.D. 110 lessons
Mongolian National University of Health Sciences	Yes, University guideline on IPRs and technology transfer, 2013	Regulation for e-learning, 2016.11	E-learning center 2015.09 Teacher development center 2014.10.06	E-learning platform based on Moodle and Edex. Reading materials, online handbooks, assessment tools are available

2.4   Open Licenses

In reality, the volume and speed for the accumulation of OER resources for elementary, secondary, and high schools is low and there is a need for more contributions from the Ministry of Education, teachers, and administrators.

As stated previously, the Ministry of Education has purchased resources and has made them freely available for students, teachers, and schools especially during the period between 2012 and 2016. However, because of current financial difficulties this idea has no longer been supported in the most recent two years by the government or parliament.

Creative Commons licenses for OER have been adopted in Mongolia since 2011. Over the past eight years, the ONE (Open Network for Education) Foundation of Mongolia and DREAM IT funded by the IDRC.ca (Canada) project have been active in capacity-building initiatives to introduce and demonstrate a range of OER practices.

The ONE Foundation supports open education and open knowledge, posited open educational research, innovation, and socioeconomic impact.

The ONE Foundation is implementing the ONE Mongolia national program and other OER programs with the goal of supporting Mongolia's emergence as a learning nation with a knowledge economy based on open development principles.

DREAM IT (Development Research to Empower All Mongolians Through Information Technology) conducted a series of applied research projects over five years, between 2009 and 2013, and has been significant to Mongolia for the opportunities to researchers and development workers from many universities, government, and non-government organizations, to freely explore the potential of ICTs and OER to contribute to the country's socioeconomic development (www.dreamit.mn).

"A National Seminar on Open Educational Resources," organized by *DREAM IT*, was held in Ulaanbaatar in October 2010. This seminar introduced Mongolian educators and government officials to OER worldwide and provided opportunities for in-depth discussion about the merits and mechanics of open education principles and practices. A follow-up workshop was held in September 2011 where there was a general discussion on open publishing, open data, and open government in addition to OER.

Spurred on by the 2012 UNESCO OER Declaration, Dr. D. Enkhbat, a former member of parliament and his team, laid out their vision for an Open Network for Education (*ONE*) *Mongolia*, at the July 2012 national seminar. This included the structural components that would be needed for Mongolia to join the ranks of other nations supporting OER development. The ONE Mongolia proposal received enthusiastic support from many of the educators who attended the national seminar. The ambitious sub-projects led by ONE Mongolia enabled Mongolian students, teachers, parents, and the public to use open video lessons in Mongolian. In another sub-project, ONE Mongolia provided classroom tools powered by Google Education, including Google Drive, Forum, Sites, and Gmail to universities and schools in Mongolia, without any costs and complexities that come with maintaining hardware and software.

At the May 30, 2013 national seminar, the *ONE Foundation* announced the signing of the Creative Commons Mongolia Affiliate Memorandum of Understanding (MOU) and the team officially launched the *ONE Mongolia, ONE Academy*, and *ONE Student* websites.

This signing of the Creative Commons Mongolia Affiliate MOU marked a historic step in the growing movement for OER (www.creativecommons.mn).

The ONE Foundation, combined with consulting expertise from Dr. David Porter of BCcampus (https://bccampus.ca/) and financial support from IDRC.ca contributed significantly to all these historic milestones.

At the *ONE* Foundation, over 150 English language and 50 Mongolian language video lessons have been made openly available through its website using a Creative Commons (CC) attribution share-alike license (CC-BY-SA). The video lessons can be viewed at https://www.one.mn.

As a commencement of the Creative Commons Mongolia Affiliate, preschool (from the book "Deciding Age") and 1st and 2nd grade education materials and newly published 8 volumes Mongolian dictionary were uploaded as OER under Creative commons licenses.

Moreover, ONE Mongolia is working hard on developing a Mongolian online dictionary under CC license. The work demonstrates a significant movement toward open licensing in Mongolia.

The ONE Foundation is working continuously on getting more involved with the Creative Commons community and supporting collaborations and partnerships to maximize government investments in education, including the sustainable development and distribution of educational materials and the sharing of digital resources by the public.

In the last three years, the ONE Foundation has succeeded at raising awareness and building capacity about the concept of Creative Commons and open educational resources (OER).

2.5 Curriculum and Teaching Methodology

A new curriculum was developed for the primary level in 2013 and piloted in 2014, and for the lower secondary and preschool levels the new curricula were prepared in 2014 and piloted in 2015. Upper secondary curricula were developed in 2015 and piloted from 2016. However new curricula adopted for preschool, primary, and secondary level educations do not yet define through policies, programs, or instructions, how OER can be integrated into teaching. But having infrastructures for OER at certain levels and the accumulation of OER in Mongolia is advantageous and gives some hope for the future. Moreover, teaching instructions and textbooks for each subject at each level are openly available for students, teachers, and parents. These resources will support the implementation of the approved curriculum. Open lessons and resources provided by ITPD and Moodle-based online training for preschool and school teachers working at the 1st, 5th, 10th, and 15th years are very important tools for teachers to develop continuously in their workplace, understand changes and challenges of curricula, and implement the curricula.

A common theme in the open educational resource literature was that educators were still at the early stages of awareness and adoption of these resources (Kelly,

2014; McGreal, Anderson, & Conrad, 2015; Rolfe, 2012). Many educators were described in the study as unknowingly using open resources (such as images, Wiki articles, and other openly licensed Internet resources) without necessarily labeling them OER (Allen & Seaman, 2014). The skills of teacher to find useful resources and use of these materials for their needs are fundamental for integration of OER in teaching. For this reason, at the beginning of the school year 2018–2019 we studied opportunities for teachers to find OER in their mother language and how they might use the OER. The survey covered 598 teachers of various subjects.

If we look at the locations of teachers:

- 45.8% were rural teachers,
- 29.2% were teachers from centers of provinces
- 25.0% were from Ulaanbaatar.

Age of respondents was:

- 11.2% (67) younger than 25 years old, (Rolfe, 2012)
- 25.1% (150) between 25 and 29,
- 34.3% (205) between 30 and 39,
- 20.4% (122) between 40 and 49,
- 8.2% (49) older than 50.

Respondents assessed possibilities to find useful OER from following sources with scores between 1 and 5 (1 = Impossible, 2 = Less, 3 = Neutral, 4 = possible, 5 = very possible). The sources are:

1. Facebook,
2. Google,
3. Slide Share, Prezi,
4. Blogs,
5. YouTube,
6. Website of ITPD,
7. Website of MIE,
8. MECS site econtent.edu.mn, and
9. Website of EEC.

Here we summarize the result of responses to this question in the following Fig. 2.

In order to give a general picture, the percentage of teachers who rated from 1 to 5 shown in the following table. Here we abbreviated Facebook, Google, Slide Share or Prezi, Blogs, YouTube, Website of ITPD, Website of MIE, MECS site econtent.edu.mn, and Website of EEC as R1, R2, R3, R4, R5, R6, R7, R8, and R9, respectively (Table 7).

From the table, we can see that percentage of teachers who answered impossible to find useful OER is less than 8% except for the case of Blogs. On the other hand, the percentage of teachers who answered it is possible or very possible is more than 40% except for the case of Blogs. Here we can see that teachers are able and can find useful OER in their mother language and they mostly use Google (60.9%), ITPD site, (54.5%), YouTube (49.7%), EECs site (47%), and SlideShare (46%).

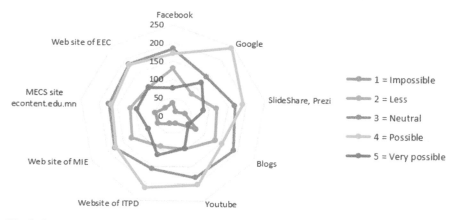

Fig. 2 Level of use of sources

Table 7 Level of usage for sources (N = 598)

	Sources	Percent (n) (rate 1) (%)	Percent (n) (rate = 2) (%)	Percent (n) (rate = 3) (%)	Percent (n) (rate = 4) (%)	Percent (n) (rate = 5) (%)
R1	Facebook	5.9 (35)	21.7 (130)	30.8 (184)	28.6 (171)	12.7 (76)
R2	Google	2.3 (14)	13.2 (79)	23.4 (140)	40.8 (244)	20.1 (120)
R3	SlideShare	5.5 (33)	20.1 (120)	28.3 (169)	31.9 (191)	14 (84)
R4	Blog	12.2 (73)	22.2 (133)	31.6 (189)	25.6 (153)	8.2 (49)
R5	YouTube	3.8 (23)	16.1 (96)	30.3 (181)	33.8 (202)	15.9 (95)
R6	Website of ITPD	4.0 (24)	15.1 (90)	26.1 (156)	35.3 (211)	19.2 (115)
R7	Website of MIE	7.4 (44)	20.9 (125)	29.8 (178)	29.3 (175)	12.5 (75)
R8	Website of MECSS	7.9 (47)	19.2 (115)	28.9 (173)	27.6 (165)	16.2 (97)
R9	Website of EEC	4.8 (29)	16.9 (101)	30.8 (184)	30.3 (181)	16.7 (100)

Looking at the average usage ranking of each source, the ranking of teachers under the age of 35 is the highest (See Appendix 1). So, we tested the difference in the average rank of usage of the source based on the age of the teacher. In order to clarify these differences, we used Kruskal–Wallis test and the following tables show results of this analysis (Table 8).

As a results of Kruskal–Wallis test, the average rank of use for SlideShare, blog, websites of ITPD, and MECS the differences are statistically significantly depending on the age of the teacher. However, the mean rank of use for Facebook, Google, YouTube, web sites of EEC, and MIE is still high for younger teachers, but there is

Table 8 Analysis of age differences for using sources

	R1	R2	R3	R4	R5	R6	R7	R8	R9
Chi-square	3.79	8.97	24.16	16.60	7.33	16.27	7.62	14.79	7.81
Df	4	4	4	4	4	4	4	4	4
Asymp. sig	0.435	0.062	0.000	0.002	0.119	0.003	0.106	0.005	0.099

df Degrees of freedom, *Asymp. sig* Asymptotic significance

no significant difference. Thus, although the average ranking used for some sources varies with age, there is the advantage that the teachers use many popular sources to find useful information in the Mongolian language.

Previous studies concluded that the lack of educational resources is often problematic in locations and along with some groups. Rural communities generally have poorer physical infrastructure and Internet connectivity. Teachers in urban areas have more opportunities for teacher professional development and are thus better placed to develop new pedagogical knowledge and skills. They are also more likely to have access to personal digital devices and computer labs in which to practice technologically enabled educational innovation.

We compared the average usage rankings to identify spatial differences in teacher usage rankings for each source. As a results of comparative studies, SlideShare, Blogs, and YouTube will have a higher rank for UB and province center teachers. For other sources, rank of use is not different depending on location. It is important for teachers to use the most popular information sources to obtain information in their own language regardless of location.

We also asked whether teachers search and use OER in foreign languages. The responses were never 14.2% (85), less 30.5% (182), sometimes 32.5% (194), good 18.8% (112), well 4.0% (24). From this, 77.2% of the teachers evaluated moderate or less, and 22.8% evaluated as good or very good. The average ranking of use OER in foreign languages depends on the location, which is 196.55 for UB teachers, 177.78 for province center teachers, and 143.47 for teachers from soums. To check whether the average rank varies depending on the location, the Kruskal–Wallis test results show (Chi-square $= 18.43$, df $= 2$, p $= 0.00$) the difference.

Few studies focused on teachers' usage of OER in teaching and learning. In order to check the level of use of OER in teaching practices we used several questions with 5 responses where $1 =$ Don't use, $2 =$ Less, $3 =$ Neutral, $4 =$ Good, $5 =$ Very good. Questions are following:

To improve theoretical knowledge (TU1), to improve teaching methodology (TU2), to understand change in curriculum (TU3), to assess students (TU4), to prepare lesson resources (TU5), to use resources directly in the lessons (TU6). The responses of teachers are shown in the following Fig. 3.

We provide a general picture of how teachers use OER in their lessons in the following Table 9.

From this table, we can see that percentage of responses 1 (don't use) is very low or less than 6%. On the other hand, total percentage of responses 4 and 5 is more than 40%. The percentage of teachers who use OER in less or medium level is in between 37.3 and 53.2%. The mean rank of using OER in order to improve theoretical knowledge is 172.08 for teachers from UB, 180.4 for teachers from province teachers, and 148.78 for teachers from soums. (Appendix 2). In other words, the ranks are high for teachers from UB and province centers (Chi-square $= 8.65$, df $= 2$, p $= 0.013$). The mean ranks for other types of use of OER are almost the same not depending on the locations of teachers. Hence, we can say that teachers use OER in their teaching activities independent from their location of living and this is also advantageous from the point of view of geography and population density of Mongolia.

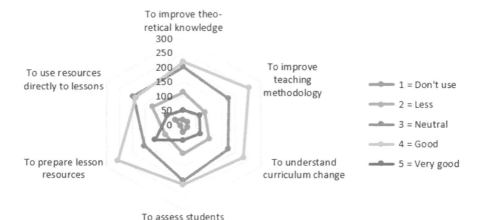

Fig. 3 Integration of OER into teaching practices

Table 9 Ways that OER is integrated into teaching practices (N = 598)

Code	Statement	Percent (n) (rate 1) (%)	Percent (n) (rate = 2) (%)	Percent (n) (rate = 3) (%)	Percent (n) (rate = 4) (%)	Percent (n) (rate = 5) (%)
TU1	To improve theoretical knowledge	2.7 (16)	18.7 (112)	33.4 (200)	36.5 (218)	8.4 (50)
TU2	To improve teaching methodology	2.7 (16)	14 (84)	29.8 (178)	42.8 (256)	10.5 (63)
TU3	To understand curriculum change	3.0 (18)	17.1 (102)	29.4 (176)	39.3 (235)	11 (66)
TU4	To assess students	4.7 (28)	17.2 (103)	33.1 (198)	35.5 (212)	9.4 (56)
TU5	To prepare lesson resources	1.7 (10)	11.7 (70)	25.4 (152)	42.6 (255)	18.4 (110)
TU6	To use resources directly to lessons	5.4 (32)	20.2 (121)	32.8 (196)	31.1 (186)	10.4 (62)

2.6 Outcomes

There was a lack of evidence of the effectiveness of OER. Educators considering a shift in their practice were interested in evidence about whether or not OER resulted

Table 10 Level of engagement with OER (N = 597)

Code	Responses	Percent (n) (%)
E1	Once a week	1.5 (9)
E2	Once every two weeks	12.4 (74)
E3	Once a month	31.8 (190)
E4	Once a period	33.2 (198)
E5	Never	20.9 (125)

in improved learner and teacher outcomes. The advantages of the usage of OER are manifold.

At the beginning of the school year 2018–2019, we studied levels of teachers' OER engagement, beliefs about using OER and perceived advantages. The survey conducted 598 teachers. In order to check the level of OER engagement we used a question "How often do you use OER for classes?" with 5 responses where 1 = once a week, 2 = once every two weeks, 3 = once a month, 4 = once a period, 5 = never. One of the 598 teachers who participated in the survey did not respond and the survey results are shown in the following table. Here we abbreviated once a week, once every two weeks, once a month, once a period, and never as E1, E2, E3, E4, and E5, respectively (Table 10).

From this table, we note that percentage of responses 5 (never) is 20.9% (125). Also, we can see that the percentage of responses 1 (once a week) and 2 (once every two weeks) is 13.9% (83), of responses 3 (once a month) and 4 (once a period) is 65% (388). So, we conclude that teachers' frequency of OER use is low. Teachers' goals have a significant impact on their motivation and engagement. The low frequency may depend on the purpose of the teacher. For example, there may be goals such as only career advancement and taking part in a competition or contest. On the other hand, there may be little support from management and school. There are currently no studies on factors affecting the optimal use of OER and OER adoption. Therefore, further research is needed to implement policies and programs to improve public interest, attitudes, knowledge, and understanding about OER.

What advantages do you see in using OER for you and your students?

In order to clarify teachers' beliefs about the work-related advantages in using OER we used 5 questions with 5-Likert scale. The result of the response is shown in the following Fig. 4.

In order to get picture on teachers' beliefs about work-related advantages in using OER in their lessons, here we compared percentage of responses 1 (strongly disagree) and 2 (disagree) against the percentage of responses 4 (agree) and 5 (strongly agree). Table 11 shows the percentage of teachers who rated 1 and 2; 3; also 4 and 5. The used statements are abbreviated as WRB1, WRB2, WRB3, WRB4, and WRB5.

From this table, we can see that the percentage of responses 1 (strongly disagree) and 2 (disagree) is 13–23.9%. Also, we can see that percentage of responses 3 (neutral) is 30.1–38.1. %, percentage of responses 4 (agree) and 5 (strongly agree) is 38–55.4%. For a statement "Gives possibilities to scope with each students pace"

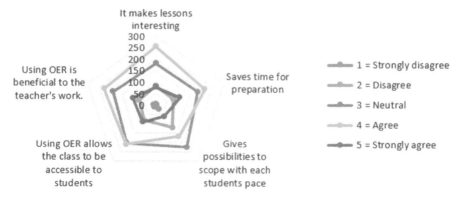

Fig. 4 Teacher's beliefs about using OER

Table 11 Teachers' beliefs about work-related advantages (N = 598)

Code	Statement	Percent (n) (1 and 2) (%)	Percent (n) (3) (%)	Percent (n) (4 and 5) (%)
WRB1	It makes lessons interesting	14.5 (87)	30.1 (180)	55.4 (331)
WRB2	Saves time for preparation	14.2 (85)	31.5 (188)	54.3 (325)
WRB3	Gives possibilities to scope with each student's pace	23.9 (143)	38.1 (228)	38.0 (227)
WRB4	Using OER allows the class to be accessible to students	15.1 (90)	34.6 (207)	50.3 (301)
WRB5	Using OER is beneficial to the teacher's work	13.04 (78)	31.94 (191)	55.02 (329)

percentage of responses 1 and 2 is higher and percentage of responses 4 and 5 is lower.

In order to clarify teachers' beliefs about the student-related advantages in using OER we used 4 questions with 5-Likert scale. The result of the response is shown in the following Fig. 5.

Table 12 shows the percentage of teachers who rated 1 and 2; 3; also 4 and 5. The used statements are abbreviated as SRB1, SRB2, SRB3, and SRB4.

From this table, we can see that the percentage of responses 1 (strongly disagree) and 2 (disagree) for all questions is between 10.0 and 18.6%. Also we can see that percentage of responses 3 (neutral) is 32.1–37.1%, percentage of responses 4 (agree) and 5 (strongly agree) is 44.3–54.9%. For a statement "OER provides to completing

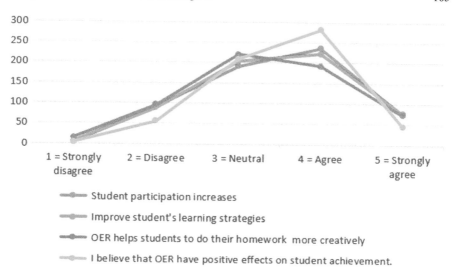

Fig. 5 Teachers' beliefs about students learning and motivation

Table 12 Teachers' belief about students' learning and motivation (N = 598)

Code	Statement	Percent (n) (1 and 2) (%)	Percent (n) (3) (%)	Percent (n) (4 and 5) (%)
SRB1	Student participation increases	15.9 (95)	32.1 (192)	52.0% (311)
SRB2	Improve student's learning strategies	15.7 (94)	34.3 (205)	50.0 (299)
SRB3	OER helps students to do their homework more creatively	18.6 (111)	37.1 (222)	44.3 (265)
SRB4	I believe that OER have positive effects on student achievement	10.0 (60)	35.1 (210)	54.9 (328)

their homework more creatively," the percentage of responses 1 and 2 is higher and percentage of responses 4 and 5 is lower.

If we look at the mean rank of OER integrating into teaching practices, teacher beliefs regarding the use of OER by engagement levels, the ranking for teachers with high engagement is highest (See Appendices 3, 4, and 5). So we studied the average ranking differences which are OER integrating into teaching practices and the teachers' beliefs about using OER at the teachers' engagement levels. In order to

Table 13 Analysis of mean rank differences for OER integrating into teaching practices

	TU1	TU2	TU3	TU4	TU5	TU6
Chi-square	80.4	119.2	81.3	84.3	116.2	76.9
Df	4	4	4	4	4	4
Asymp. sig	0.000	0.000	0.000	0.000	0.000	0.000

clarify these differences, we used Kruskal–Wallis test and the following tables show results of these analyses (Tables 13 and 14).

As a results of Kruskal–Wallis tests, the average rank of all the characteristics that are integrated into teacher training and the teacher's beliefs regarding to the use OER are statistically significantly depending on the engagement level of the teacher. In other words, all the characteristics of the teacher are higher with the higher involved teachers. Therefore, it is important for program to provide comprehensive OER teaching materials to the teacher and to focus on improving attitudes and awareness toward all levels of the OER community.

At the international level, much research has been done on the relationship between OER integrated teaching methodology and student characteristics (student's attitude toward learning, motivation, learning strategy). However, in Mongolia, this type of research is not enough. In the future, studies on attitudes, beliefs, awareness of the students on OER, factors affecting student characteristics, and relationships among these variables are necessary.

2.7 Stakeholders

In this section, we analyze the situation of Mongolia from the point of view McGill, Currier, Duncan, and Douglas (2008).

According to these authors, OER stakeholders can be classified into the following groups:

- The global community (affected by cultural, language, and political issues)
- The national community (sometimes significant investment by Government)
- Educational institutions (not one homogenous community but several)
- Subject communities (including employers and professional bodies)
- Individuals supporting learning and teaching (teachers, librarians, learning technologists, educational developers)
- Learners (enrolled and global).

Our research team has examined the advantages of OER to these stakeholders. Conversely, in this Section we try to define who are the main representatives of these groups in Mongolia and review their current type contribution and rough estimation of degrees of contribution to the development of OER in Mongolia. By the development

Table 14 Analysis of mean rank differences for teachers' beliefs about using OER

	WRB1	WRB2	WRB3	WRB4	WRB5	SRB1	SRB2	SRB3	SRB4
Chi-square	113.4	105.6	79.7	112.6	136.2	131.1	133.7	116.6	134.1
df	4	4	4	4	4	4	4	4	4
Asymp. sig	0.000	0.000	0.000	0.000	0.000	0.000	0.000	0.000	0.000

of OER we mean production, use, support, and other types of activities which support the OER.

In order to define the degree of contribution we defined the following rubrics.

1. No evidence of involvement or contribution
2. Has an evidence of involvement or contribution
3. Have many evidences of contribution and received feedbacks
4. Full of evidence of contribution, received feedback and makes improvement based on feedbacks
5. Full of evidence of contribution, received feedback and makes regular improvement based on feedbacks.

The scores are assigned to each of the stakeholders rather than representatives for certain types of activities (Table 15).

The table shows that the educational institutions including MECSS and ITPD are playing fundamental role in the development of OER in Mongolia. And, since the average score is not less than 3, we conclude that overall degree of supports of each stakeholder is not in high level and needs measures to increase these levels of supports.

2.8 Impact

Many studies have been done on how ICT-based learning affects student learning approaches and attitudes. First, we cite some results of these studies.

Some researchers investigated differences between students' self-regulated learning strategies which are cognitive learning strategies (rehearsal, organization, elaboration, critical thinking), metacognitive learning strategies, time-resource management strategies (time and study environment strategies, peer learning strategies, help seeking strategies) in traditional and nontraditional mathematics classrooms (Davaanyam & Tserendorj, 2015). The research was done in 2014 and 131 students participated in this study. The results of the study implied that students who participated in an ICT-based Mathematics course had more effective use of various learning strategies including organization, elaboration, and critical thinking. Students in both traditional and nontraditional classrooms used rehearsal strategies more frequently, but there was no significant difference. Also, this research found that students who participated in the ICT-based course used more desirable metacognitive learning strategies and more effectively managed the learning environment and created study schedules and sought help more often than students who participated in the traditional classroom. This research implied that if teachers effectively manage their teaching strategies in the ICT-based Mathematics course then students may use more powerful cognitive, metacognitive learning strategies, and more appropriate time and resource management strategies.

An empirical study was conducted with more than 500 primary school teachers from diverse locations across the country and looked at two aspects of education

Table 15 Degree of supports of stakeholders

Stakeholders	Representatives	Type of support/activities	Degree of support
The global community	Global providers of OER, e.g., MIT OCW	Provision of OER Enhancement of sustainability of OER development New ideas	NA
The national community	NGOs	Provision of OER Enhancement of sustainability of OER development New ideas	2 2 1
Educational institutions	MECS Institute of Education Institute of Teacher Professional Development Universities Schools Teacher development centers	Enhance the sustainability of OER development Provision of OER Use and effective feedback to developers	3 2 1
Subject communities	Subject teachers' communities Student communities of certain subjects Education researchers	Participation of development of OER Use and effective feedback	2 2
Individuals supporting, learning, and teaching		Enhancement of sustainability of OER development	1
Learners	Elementary school students Secondary and high school students University students Adult learners	Use and give feedback to producers	2

practices, teacher training activities and practical ICT experiences at school level, and investigated their relationships to three domains of perceived self-efficacy, confidence, competency, and satisfaction, within the primary school teachers in Mongolia (Yamamoto & Yamaguchi, 2016). The study found that school-based training is associated with higher self-efficacy among different levels of teacher training activities. The study also found that positive institutional attitude toward ICT-integrated education is important for teachers' high self-efficacy. Two points are suggested as implications of the study. First, planning ICT-related trainings at school level, especially employing peer learning, should be a priority. Second, including training sessions for school managements to provide them with a broad understanding of the pedagogical value of ICT is a critical strategy.

Few studies have been conducted about OER in the Mongolian context. Here we introduce the results of research on how the influence of teachers' beliefs about using OER affects their teaching practices. The survey was conducted with 598 teachers in the first period of 2018–2019. 15 questions with 5-Likert scales used in 2.5 and 2.6 are used here.

For these questions, we considered the results of factor analysis. Measurement of sampling adequacy coefficient KMO = 0.966, chi-square = 8570.88, df = 105, p < 0.001, the main diagonal element of the anti-correlation matrix is 0.947–0.985. So, the results of the factor analysis are reliable. Questionnaires by factor analysis are divided into three subscales. There are 6 questions on the "Use of OER" subscale, which are to identify the use of OER in their teaching-related activities. The "beliefs about work-related advantages" subscale consist of five questions and identifies the teachers' beliefs about work-related advantages when using OER. And, the "student related beliefs" subscale consists of four questions and identifies the teachers' beliefs about student-related advantages when using OER. The following table shows results of this analysis (Tables 16 and 17).

The following table shows results of descriptive statistics for these variables and correlations between predictors and dependent variables.

Descriptive statistical results showed that the mean and standard deviation of "use of OER" are M = 3.38, SD = 0.86, "work related benefit" are M = 3.48, SD = 0.85, "student related beliefs" are 3.45, SD = 0.80. From the results of the correlational analysis, we can see that there is a high correlation between predictor and dependent variables, predictor and another predictor variable. These are "Work related advantages" and "Use of OER" (r = 0.823), "Student-related advantages"

Table 16 Range of factor coefficients and eigenvalues

Subscales	Items code	Factor loadings (eigenvalues)
Use of OER	TU1, TU2, TU3, TU4, TU5, TU6	0.663–0.759 (10.15)
Work-related advantages (WRB)	WRB1, WRB2, WRB3, WRB4, WTRB5	0.645–0.752 (1.02)
Student-related advantages (SRB)	SRB1, SRB2, SRB3, SRB4	0.698–0.779 (1.01)

Table 17 Results of descriptive statistics and correlational analysis

	Mean	S.D	Use of OER	WRB	SRB
Use of OER	3.38	0.86	1.000		
WRB	3.48	0.85	0.823[a]	1.000	
SRB	3.45	0.80	0.743[a]	0.844[a]	1.000

[a]Correlation is significant at the 0.01 level

and "Use of OER" (r = 0.743), "Work-related advantages" and "Student-related advantages" (r = 0.844).

In order to check whether predictor variables affect the dependent variable we used the following three models:

$$\text{Model 1. Using OER} = a0 + B1 * WRB + e1$$
$$\text{Model 2. Using OER} = b0 + B2 * SRB + e2$$
$$\text{Model 3. Using OER} = c0 + B1 * WRB + B2 * SRB + e3$$

Models fits are shown in the following Table 18.

From this table, we can see that teacher beliefs about work-related advantages and student-related advantages can be predicting 68 and 55% of variance of the dependent variable. For Model 3, the table shows that 69% of the variance in *using OER* can be predicted from two predictor variables combined. Model 3 explains the highest variance in *using OER*. For each model, the regression coefficients and the significant levels are shown in the following Table 19.

Table 19 shows that for each model, predictor variables are statistically significant in contributing to the model. But, model 3 has multicollinearity because of 1-R square = 0.31 > Tolerance (0.29). So, Model 3 is not suitable model for this situation. Therefore, we used following equation for this situation.

$$\text{Model 1. Using OER} = 0.49 + 0.83 * WRB + e$$
$$\text{Model 2. Using OER} = 0.64 + 0.79 * SRB + e$$

From these results, we can conclude that teacher beliefs about work-related advantages and student-related advantages influence positively on the use of OER in

Table 18 Model fit

	R	R square	Adjusted R square	df1	df2	F	Sig
Model 1	0.82	0.68	0.68	1	596	1251.63	0.000
Model 2	0.74	0.55	0.55	1	596	734.21	0.000
Model 3	0.83	0.69	0.69	2	595	648.72	0.000

Table 19 Regression coefficients

	Constant	B1 (SE)		B2 (SE)		t	Sig	Tolerance
Model 1	0.49	0.83 (0.02)	0.82	–	–	35.38	0.000	1
Model 2	0.64	–	–	0.79 (0.03)	0.74	27.09	0.000	1
Model 3	0.37	0.69 (0.04)	0.68	0.18 (0.05)	0.17	15.90 3.93	0.000 0.000	0.29

teaching-related activities. In other words, this study found that teachers' positive beliefs about work-related advantages and student-related advantages are important for teacher's use of OER in teaching practices.

There are gaps in research on the use and adaptation of OER and impacts of using OER on students' characters, behaviors, or teachers' attitudes. Policymakers should promote and fund evidence-based research for policy and practice on how OER are produced and how they are used in specific contexts and by specific actors in the education system (teachers, instructors, and learners).

3   Discussion and Conclusion

We give our conclusions and proposals for future work for each of the factors.

3.1   Infrastructure

The infrastructure of most schools is ready for the usage of OER for students and teachers. Some preparatory measures like change of attitudes toward OER are needed.

From the data in 2.1, we can see that main source of the Internet usage is smart and mobile phones. And hence OER developers and providers should focus on OER materials which are suitable for smartphones and mobile devices.

As stated previously, some software licensing for schools and teachers is expiring. The government of Mongolia should provide an open licensing policy to sustain the usage of software and computers for both teachers and students.

3.2   Policy

Looking back in the most recent 10–20 years, we can conclude that parliament and government's focus on policy has been centered mostly on ICT infrastructure rather than financing of OER and establishing open licensing. The next stage of policy-making should close this policy gap in shortest possible time period with a systematic plan of action.

Even with policy established, the implementation of the policies is not satisfactory or some have noted begun or remain only as "paper policies." For example, the policies for providing open licensing and open standards are still not in place and are awaiting effective solutions.

Table 20 Level of supports for schools and universities

Sectors of education	Types of support for OER			
	Government	Institutional	Private initiative	International initiative and cooperation
Elementary	High	No	Medium	Medium
Secondary	High	No	Medium	Medium
Upper secondary	High	No	Medium	Medium
University	No	Less	Less	Less

3.3   Resources

We begin our conclusion by giving the following table which will help to get overall vision of the system (Table 20).

Governments' share is high in support of developing OER at the school level. The government and parliament must seek ways to increase support from other stakeholders.

The development of OER in universities is still low and needs more focus. Universities are capable of creating an interuniversity online community like Coursera for Mongolian students. On the other hand, if the English proficiency level of Mongolian students rises to international English user level, it would be beneficial both for students and universities to be using globally developed OER.

The mechanisms and policies that sustain the development of OER are not yet set in the country.

Most part of the educational resources of universities are still not open to the public. Administrative bodies and the government of Mongolia must seek ways to make these resources open to the public. Universities also need to collaborate in order to speed up the accumulation of open educational resources for service to the public.

3.4   Curriculum and Teaching Methodology

The use of OER in order to integrate curriculum and teaching methodologies has several opportunities, advantages, and disadvantages.

Opportunities and advantages.

– Lower density of population and sparsely distributed in a large land area.
– Younger average age of population implies also younger average age of teachers (about 73% of teachers are working less than 15 years).
– Infrastructure of OER is set for a specific level and the country is still continuing the policy to develop the infrastructure.

– Most parts of the population are using smartphones and connecting to the Internet via smartphones.
– Accumulation and duration of OER is the result of government, institutional, and private initiatives to date.
– Teachers tend to use OER from various sources in specific education levels.
– Teachers tend to use OER in their teaching activities at specific levels.

Disadvantages.

– Uneven, disorganized supply
– Incompatible policies and lack of incentives (OER and curriculum, teaching and learning)
– Lack of OER standards
– Use of OER in foreign languages is low
– Limited proof of effectiveness
– Less attractiveness of public interest, awareness, and understanding
– Sufficiency of technology, equipment's, and the Internet is still in question especially in rural communities.

Looking into opportunities, advantages, and disadvantages the MECSS needs to emphasize on the following issues.

– To organize activities in order to provide complete OER for basic subjects in preschools, schools, and basic courses in universities.
– Supportive policies that remove restrictions on OER funding and implementation and that provide incentives for OER adoption
– OER sustainably integrated into education
– Adoption of OER that improve teaching and learning
– OER adapts to new transformations in technology (e.g., mobile phones, tablets, etc.)
– See OER as one strong tool to defeat poverty in the country.

3.5 Outcome

Based on our survey results we conclude that it is important to initiate an ambitious national project which will supply comprehensive OER teaching materials for pre-university school teachers and implement policy on improving positive attitudes and awareness toward OER in the wider communities in the country.

At the international level, much research has been done on the relationship between OER-integrated teaching methodology and student characteristics (student's attitude toward learning, motivation, learning strategy). However, for the case of Mongolia, this type of research is not enough. In the future, studies on attitudes, beliefs, awareness of the students on OER, factors affecting student characteristics, and relationships among these variables are crucial.

3.6 Stakeholders

Educational institutions including MECSS and ITPD are the main engines for the development of OER for school teachers and students in Mongolia. But the overall degree of support for each stakeholder group to develop OER is not high enough and this should be a key point of focus for future.

3.7 Impact

There are gaps in research on use and adaptation of OER and impacts of using OER on students' characters, behaviors, or teachers' attitudes. Policymakers should promote and fund evidence-based research for policy and practice on how OER are produced and how they are used in specific contexts and by certain actors in the education system (teachers, instructors, and learners).

Acknowledgements If you wish to acknowledge persons who contributed or sponsoring agencies, do so here in this optional section.

Appendix 1: Average Ranking of Using Sources by Age

	Age	N	Mean rank		Age	N	Mean rank
R1	1.00	67	320.04	R6	1.00	67	292.89
	2.00	150	298.22		2.00	150	326.34
	3.00	205	299.88		3.00	205	303.46
	4.00	122	292.52		4.00	122	282.61
	5.00	49	260.86		5.00	49	221.58
	Total	593			Total	593	
R2	1.00	67	306.64	R7	1.00	67	309.13
	2.00	150	316.37		2.00	150	314.77
	3.00	205	305.21		3.00	205	299.53
	4.00	122	268.70		4.00	122	285.26
	5.00	49	260.59		5.00	49	244.64
	Total	593			Total	593	
R3	1.00	67	340.21	R8	1.00	67	314.63
	2.00	150	332.52		2.00	150	319.40

(continued)

(continued)

	Age	N	Mean rank		Age	N	Mean rank
	3.00	205	292.51		3.00	205	298.82
	4.00	122	262.91		4.00	122	288.32
	5.00	49	232.82		5.00	49	218.30
	Total	593			Total	593	
R4	1.00	67	314.87	R9	1.00	67	318.34
	2.00	150	325.97		2.00	150	311.76
	3.00	205	301.73		3.00	205	301.93
	4.00	122	270.52		4.00	122	276.48
	5.00	49	230.03		5.00	49	253.11
	Total	593			Total	593	
R5	1.00	67	318.63				
	2.00	150	310.60				
	3.00	205	295.90				
	4.00	122	291.39				
	5.00	49	244.32				
	Total	593					

Appendix 2: Average Ranking of OER Integrating into Teaching Practices by Locations

	Locations	N	Mean rank		Locations	N	Mean rank
TU1	1.00	149	329.77	TU4	1.00	150	319.03
	2.00	174	276.98		2.00	174	280.08
	3.00	274	296.25		3.00	274	301.14
	Total	597			Total	598	
TU2	1.00	150	312.96	TU5	1.00	150	303.53
	2.00	174	282.75		2.00	174	302.14
	3.00	274	302.77		3.00	274	295.62
	Total	598			Total	598	
TU3	1.00	150	304.72	TU6	1.00	150	314.25
	2.00	174	286.90		2.00	174	292.01
	3.00	274	304.64		3.00	274	296.18
	Total	598			Total	598	

Appendix 3: Average Ranking of OER Integrating into Teaching Practices by Engagement Levels

	Engagement level	N	Mean rank		Engagement level	N	Mean rank
TU1	1.00	125	364.30	TU4	1.00	125	355.00
	2.00	197	339.14		2.00	198	351.22
	3.00	192	259.67		3.00	192	254.81
	4.00	74	211.04		4.00	74	208.59
	5.00	9	75.61		5.00	9	91.61
	Total	597			Total	598	
TU2	1.00	125	372.55	TU5	1.00	125	372.62
	2.00	198	356.50		2.00	198	353.26
	3.00	192	245.80		3.00	192	249.51
	4.00	74	188.28		4.00	74	191.35
	5.00	9	91.06		5.00	9	56.83
	Total	598			Total	598	
TU3	1.00	125	357.61	TU6	1.00	125	350.24
	2.00	198	346.44		2.00	198	346.72
	3.00	192	257.46		3.00	192	264.64
	4.00	74	211.47		4.00	74	206.04
	5.00	9	80.39		5.00	9	68.11
	Total	598			Total	598	

Appendix 4: Average Ranking of Teachers' Beliefs About Work-Related Advantages by Engagement Levels

	Engagement level	N	Mean rank		Engagement level	N	Mean rank
WRB1	1.00	125	385.05	WRB4	1.00	125	378.93
	2.00	198	343.91		2.00	198	348.97
	3.00	192	247.29		3.00	192	248.89
	4.00	74	198.24		4.00	74	190.01

(continued)

(continued)

	Engagement level	N	Mean rank		Engagement level	N	Mean rank
	5.00	9	80.50		5.00	9	87.83
	Total	598			Total	598	
WRB2	1.00	125	375.02	WRB5	1.00	125	396.06
	2.00	198	345.96		2.00	198	346.79
	3.00	192	255.14		3.00	192	243.64
	4.00	74	191.11		4.00	74	182.29
	5.00	9	66.11		5.00	9	73.50
	Total	598			Total	598	
WRB3	1.00	125	367.49				
	2.00	198	339.32				
	3.00	192	256.55				
	4.00	74	215.40				
	5.00	9	86.89				
	Total	598					

Appendix 5: Average Ranking of Teachers' Beliefs About Student-Related Advantages by Engagement Levels

	Engagement level	N	Mean rank		Engagement level	N	Mean rank
SRB1	1.00	125	391.50	SRB3	1.00	125	385.49
	2.00	198	342.64		2.00	198	345.17
	3.00	192	254.99		3.00	192	249.70
	4.00	74	174.50		4.00	74	187.92
	5.00	9	49.94		5.00	9	80.22
	Total	598			Total	598	
SRB2	1.00	125	395.62	SRB4	1.00	125	391.09
	2.00	198	345.85		2.00	198	346.75
	3.00	192	243.23		3.00	192	244.96
	4.00 advantages	74	187.37		4.00	74	184.04
	5.00	9	67.28		5.00	9	100.83
	Total	598			Total	598	

References

Allen, I. E., & Seaman, J. (2014). Opening the curriculum: Open educational resources in U.S. higher education. Babson Survey Research Group.

Commonwealth of Learning. (2011). Guidelines for open educational resources (OER) in higher education. UNESCO.

Davaanyam, T., & Tserendorj, N. (2015). Students' self-regulated learning strategies in traditional and non-traditional classroom: A comparative study. *Research in Mathematical Education, 19*, 81–88.

Government of Mongolia. (2006). Education Master Plan 2006–2015. Ulaanbaatar.

ICT and Post Authority of Mongolia. (2011). *The white paper on ICT development of Mongolia*. Mongolia: Ulaanbaatar.

Kelly, H. (2014). A path analysis of educator perceptions of open educational resources using the technology acceptance model. *The International Review of Research in Open and Distributed Learning, 15*(2), 26–42.

McGill, L., Currier, S., Duncan, C., & Douglas, P. (2008). Good intentions: Improving the evidence base in support of sharing and learning materials. Joint Information Systems Committee (JISC).

McGreal, R., Anderson, T., & Conrad, D. (2015). Open educational resources in Canada in 2015. *International Review of Research in Open and Distributed Learning, 16*(5), 161–175.

Ministry of Education Culture and Science. (2012). *Information and communication technology in education*. Mongolia: Ulaanbaatar.

Ministry of Education Culture Science and Sports. (2012). *Action plan of the information and communication technology in education policy, 2012–2016*. Mongolia: Ulaanbaatar.

National Statistical Office of Mongolia. (2017). Mongolian statistical information service. Retrieved from https://www.1212.mn/.

Parliament of Mongolia. (2016). *Sustainable development vision of Mongolia—2030*. Mongolia: Ulaanbaatar.

Partnership on Measuring ICT for Development. (2016). Core List of ICT indicators. Retrieved from https://www.itu.int/en/ITU-D/Statistics/Pages/intlcoop/partnership/default.aspx.

Rolfe, V. (2012). Open educational resources: Staff attitudes and awareness. *Research in Learning Technology, 20*(1).

Suvdmaa, T., Banzragch, O., & Saizmaa, T. (2016). E-learning in Mongolian Higher Education. *International Review of Research in Open and Distributed Learning, 17*(2).

UNESCO Institute of Statistics. (2017). Retrieved from UNESCO Institute of Statistics. https://uis.unesco.org/en/country/MN.

Yamamoto, Y., & Yamaguchi, S. (2016). A study on teacher's self-efficacy for promoting ICT integrated education in primary schools in Mongolia. *Journal of International Cooperation in Education, 18*(2), 1–15.

A. Amarzaya is an Associate Professor at the Department of Mathematics, School of Arts and Science, National University of Mongolia, Mongolia. He acquired his Masters and Bachelors degree from National University of Mongolia, Mathematics and Computer Science School, Mongolia. He defended his Ph.D. degree at Tokyo Metropolitan University, Japan. His research interests are in Education, Differential Geometry and Manifold theory.

D. Tumenbayar is an Associate Professor at the Department of Mathematics, School of Arts and Science, National University of Mongolia, Mongolia. She acquired her Masters degree and Undergraduate degrees from National University of Mongolia, Mathematics and Computer Science School, Mongolia. She defended her Ph.D. degree at Chonbuk National University, Korea. Her research interests are in Educational Curriculum Development, Educational Assessment, and Lesson study.

T. Navchaa is a Lecturer at the Department of Mathematics, School of Arts and Science, National University of Mongolia, Mongolia. She acquired his Masters and Bachelor degree from National University of Mongolia, Mathematics and Computer Science School, Mongolia. Her research interests are in Integration of ICT into Teaching and Learning.

B. Burmaa is CEO of the ONE Foundation and Director of MN Domain Registry, Datacom. Her areas of responsibilities are open education, open licensing, international relationship, research and development and human resource capacity building. B. Burmaa is an expert over 23 years of experience in information technology and open education resources. She was project coordinator of the DREAM IT research project funded by IDRC, Canada from 2008 to 2013. Her research interests are open education, ICT policy and information technology in the educational sector.

David Porter is the CEO of eCampusOntario, the primary face of the Ontario Online Learning Consortium (OOLC), a not-for-profit corporation whose membership is composed of all publicly-funded colleges and universities in Ontario, Canada. He is a long-time advocate for the advantages of adapting new technology to deliver educational opportunities, and has been involved in open and distance learning since the 1990s, at both the K-12 and higher education levels. David was formerly Associate VP Educational Support and Innovation at the British Columbia Institute of Technology. Prior to that appointment, David was the Executive Director of BCcampus. During his term at BCcampus, David and his team engineered Canada's first government funded open textbook program, a leading-edge development in higher education in 2012. David has also worked as a project leader and consultant for international open and distance learning projects, most recently in Mongolia, Malaysia, and Vietnam. He is a co-editor of the International Journal of E-Learning and Distance Education (IJEDE.ca), an open access journal published on behalf of the Canadian Network for Innovation in Education (CNIE).

L. Munkhtuya (Associate Professor) is a director at the Office of ICT and Distance Education, Mongolian National University of Education, Mongolia. She acquired his Bachelor degree from MNUE, and Maters degree from MULS. She defended her Ph.D. degree at Mongolian National University of Education, Mongolia. Munkhtuya has worked as a project team member for distance learning projects, recently in Mongolia. Her research interests are in ICT in Education, Informatics, Blended Learning and Lesson Study.

Chapter 7
Open Educational Resources in Morocco

**Imane Zaatri, Sofia Margoum, Rachid Bendaoud, Ilham Laaziz El Malti,
Daniel Burgos and Khalid Berrada**

1 Case Overview on the Educational System in Morocco

Open Educational Resources (OER) has reached a significant level of development
and diversification in the last decade to the point of becoming a component in higher
education transformation. The term OER was coined at UNESCO's, 2002 Forum on
Open Courseware and designates "teaching, learning and research materials in any
medium, digital or otherwise, that reside in the public domain or have been released
under an open license that permits no-cost access, use, adaptation and redistribution
by others with no or limited restrictions" (UNESCO, 2002). Open licensing is built
within the existing framework of intellectual property rights as defined by relevant
international conventions and respects the authorship of the work (UNESCO, 2012).

In the past years, there have been many activities in the area of OER, including the
Paris OER Declaration which was drafted in the world OER congress that UNESCO
convened in Paris in June 2012, which results in some other declaration thereafter in
other countries.

I. Zaatri · S. Margoum · R. Bendaoud · K. Berrada (✉)
Trans ERIE - Faculty of Sciences Semlalia, Cadi Ayyad University, 2390 Marrakech, BP, Morocco
e-mail: berrada@uca.ac.ma

R. Bendaoud
e-mail: bendaoud@uca.ac.ma

D. Burgos
Research Institute for Innovation & Technology in Education (UNIR iTED), Universidad
Internacional de La Rioja (UNIR), Avenida de la Paz, 137, 26006 Logroño, Spain
e-mail: daniel.burgos@unir.net

I. L. El Malti
Ministère de l'Education Nationale et de la Formation Professionnelle, de l'Enseignement
Supérieur et de la Recherche Scientifique, Avenue Ennasr - Bab Rouah, Rabat, Morocco
e-mail: ilham.laaziz@men.gov.ma

© Springer Nature Singapore Pte Ltd. 2020
R. Huang et al. (eds.), *Current State of Open Educational Resources
in the "Belt and Road" Countries*, Lecture Notes in Educational Technology,
https://doi.org/10.1007/978-981-15-3040-1_7

Located northwest of Africa, Morocco has 35,669,497 of population. The capital is Rabat and the official languages are Arabic and Tamazight. Currently, it is estimated that there are 18.3 million Internet users, which represents a 56% penetration rate in the population (HCP Morocco, 2018).

The higher education system in Morocco comprises 13 public universities, 8 private universities, and 211 private Higher education institutes and schools.

Higher education in Morocco regulated by statute No 01–00, in the responsibility of the state, which provides for the planning, organization, development, regulation, and guidance of the system.

As part of the new educational reform, Moroccan universities have adopted the LMD system according to the Bologna process in 2003. The system of Licence's, master's, and doctoral degrees now prevails throughout the university structures.

Master's degrees were introduced in Morocco at the start of the 2006/2007 academic year the new centers for doctoral studies established in 2008, became operational in 2009. The studies are thus based on 3 grades:

- *Licence degree (6 semesters)*
- *Master's (10 semesters)*
- *Ph.D. (3 years after the master).*

2 Current Situation of OER

Morocco is among the most active of the South Mediterranean countries in the OER movement. In 2005 the Moroccan government adopted a strategy to make ICT accessible in all public schools to improve the quality of teaching: infrastructure, teacher training and the development of pedagogical content was also part of this national program.

2.1 Infrastructure

The ministry of national education created the National Laboratory of Digital Resources, which produces and collates digital educational resources, some of which are OER.

There are also several projects in this field in Morocco. For example, the Korea International Cooperation Industry project produces digital resources that are free to access and use for scientific disciplines at the secondary education level in partnership with Al Akhawayn University in Morocco.

There is also a Unit for the Promotion of Software and Open Educational Resources at the Moroccan-Korean Centre of ICT Training. The center was created in 2011 with the main objective of promoting the use of software and OER to support the national policy of widespread use of these technologies through the GENeralization of Information Technologies and Communication in Education (GENIE) program by offering very low-cost, and often free, ICT solutions. Since 2006 the GENIE program for secondary school incorporates OER, and the strategy was adopted by the National Laboratory of Digital Resources of the Ministry of Education, where a reference to OER is presented in draft ministerial notes regarding validation and certification of digital resources that are in development (Berrada, Benelrhali, & Laaziz, 2019).

2.2 OER Policy in Morocco

During the Morocco OER Strategy Forum organized at Cadi Ayyad University in December 2016, a consortium of universities launched a declaration named "OER Morocco declaration". This declaration is addressed the Moroccan Government, education agencies, schools, middle schools, high schools, universities, the third sector, and all organizations and individuals involved in teaching and learning including galleries, libraries, archives and museums (OER Morocco declaration, 2016).

Two considerations guide this declaration. First, Open Education can expand access to education, knowledge transfer, social inclusion, and create a culture of collaboration and sharing. Second, there is a sound economic case for Open Education: releasing publicly funded educational resources under open licenses represents an investment return on public spending. This policy outlines the vision of Moroccan universities toward Open Education (OE) in every step (Fig. 1).

These 9 pillars are considered the backbone of Open Education, and furthermore (Burgos, 2017), Open Science, to the matter. Every region that is capable of significant

Fig. 1 The 9 considered pillars for open education

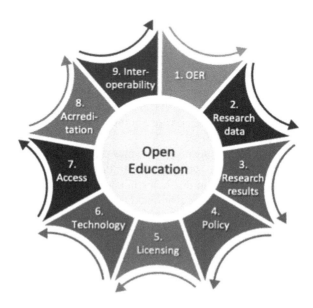

progress with them will support significantly the future of OE. Just content is not enough to ensure access or open licensing, for instance (Jahn & Tullney, 2016; Schimmer, Geschuhn, & Vogler, 2015).

The policy provides a combination of general guidelines to adopt OE in Higher Education by teachers and students so that they can use, reuse, create, share, and publish contents, services, and good practices inside and outside the university.

The next step forward is to join up these initiatives and develop policy support and guidance to enable the culture shift required to embed Open Education across all sectors of Moroccan education. To facilitate this development, several recommendations are proposed in the Declaration.

The strategic priorities of the policy lean on various fronts: from the release of OER by the university, the integration of OER produced by others into the university, the creation of OER, the awareness of OE into the society and the open access to data and research results, among other measures.

2.3 Open License

A license, in general, is a document that specifies what can and cannot be done with work. It grants permissions and states restrictions. An open license is a license agreement that describes the conditions under which the holder of the intellectual property grants the users to perform a variety of uses for his intellectual or artistic works. Through open licenses, authors grant permission for users to reproduce, adapt, or distribute the work, with the accompanying requirement that any resulting copies or adaptations are also bound by the same licensing agreement.

There are many open licenses developed for different areas of knowledge. However, when it comes to open educational resources the most typical and common open licenses used are Creative Commons Licenses (Downes, 2007; Wong, 2017).

Creative Commons (CC) license provides a legal framework for more flexible intellectual property rights than copyright. The CC license aims to eliminate, or at least reduce, the brakes that hinder the dissemination of knowledge and culture on a large scale. In particular, that enable the free distribution of an otherwise copyrighted "work". The CC licenses are a composition of the following four conditions (source: wikipedia.org) (Fig. 2).

Thanks to the OpenMed Erasmus + project, nearly 70 teachers received a 4-month training program. We were able to distinguish between Copyright, Open Licenses, and Public domain; this helps in choosing and using the proper creative commons licenses that fit the educational content.

There is also an important distinction to make between Open, Universal and Free. Every content can provide a combination of these features and be still valid. Further, there is no binary approach toward openness: either completely open or not

Icon	Right	Description
	Attribution (BY)	Licensees may copy, distribute, display and perform the work and make derivative works and remixes based on it only if they give the author or licensor the credits (attribution) in the manner specified by these.
	Share-alike (SA)	Licensees may distribute derivative works only under a license identical ("not more restrictive") to the license that governs the original work. (See also copyleft.) Without share-alike, derivative works might be sublicensed with compatible but more restrictive license clauses, e.g. CC BY to CC BY-NC.)
	Non-commercial (NC)	Licensees may copy, distribute, display, and perform the work and make derivative works and remixes based on it only for non-commercial purposes.
	No Derivative Works (ND)	Licensees may copy, distribute, display and perform only verbatim copies of the work, not derivative works and remixes based on it.

Fig. 2 Description of the LCC conditions

open at all. The variety of nuances[1] allows for exploitation and implementation of resources based on the rights assigned by the author and the owner, the needs from the practitioner and the constraints of the educational context (e.g. academic program or regional accreditation) (McAndrew, 2010).

2.4   Resources

The pilot experience of the Cadi Ayyad University of Marrakech, running since 2013 with the launch of a UC@MOOC platform, allowed students to benefit from free educational materials open to a huge public (Idrissi Jouicha et al., 2020). The UC@MOOC initiative consists of scripting, producing, and distributing videos of courses, tutorials and practical work of the courses taught at the University. Thus, 560 video units were made so far. The number of visitors who log on to the platform https://mooc.uca.ma continues to grow (>8 million visitors and more than 79,000 followers), as well as the reading time (several decades) and the average module (>80 years watching).

Thanks to this project, the university was able to offer students hybrid pedagogy for some available modules. Some modules have even been tested in reverse class mode (Idrissi Jouicha, Margoum, Bendaoud, & Berrada, 2018).

In the second stage of the project, greater attention was given to the educational scenario to offer complete and accredited training in hybrid mode. Still based on these videos, inverted classroom teachings have been successfully developed.

Courses and directed work are previewed and face-to-face time is used to complete their learning. Learners have the opportunity to discuss with their teachers the difficulties encountered and optimize their face-to-face training. The UCA project team

---

[1]BURGOS, D. (2016) 50 shades of openness. Retrieved June the 12th, 2019 from https://research.unir.net/blog/50-shades-of-openness/.

is currently working on the implementation of in-line diplomacy training courses (30% face-to-face) with the help and support of the teacher-researchers in the sectors involved. Today, these contents are hosted on the OpenEdex platform at https://ucamooc.uca.ma.

On the other hand, let's mention an initiative that targets high school and college students. Since 2010, the Ministry of National Education has launched the implementation of the educational platform Taalim.ma in partnership with Microsoft. It complements the implementation of internal and external communication systems and the development of ICT (https://www.taalim.ma). The Taalim.ma portal project is part of this process and aims to:

- *Have a more structured flow of information and richer communication between the different members of the educational community.*
- *Contribute to the development of a more efficient education system in which all the actors will be able to collaborate better and work better.*
- *Promote the exchange of good practices within the educational community.*

The National Laboratory of Digital Resources as an entity attached to the GENIE Program direction, in charge of Digital Resources, has put in place a procedure for the validation and labeling of open educational resources that are produced by the actors of the educational system (Procedure called V@REN). It aims to promote the culture of innovation, sharing, and recognition for Moroccan teachers to encourage them to produce OER.

Participation sessions are organized throughout the year. Multidisciplinary E-commissions have been set up for the monitoring, supervision, evaluation, validation, and labeling of the creations of educational actors.

The Moroccan-Korean Training Center in ICT in Education (CMCF-TICE) organizes training and distance learning sessions (GENIE-MOOC, CompracTICE, ScolarTICE …) dedicated to the use and development of OER. One hundred trainees' projects on OER are available on the portal taalimetice.ma.

An important project is started in collaboration with the laboratory of digital resources around the production of OER kits based on enriched videos with an interactive environment (Exercises, summaries, activities, simulations, animations around a concept), aiming at school tutoring in different disciplines.

In order to reinforce this component of the OER, and to open up on the international initiatives, the direction of the GENIE program is adhered to the Open Educational Resources initiative led by ALECSO, in order to exploit, to exchange, to share, and to produce OER on the platform MAROC-OER-ALECSO, TELMIDTICE, and TAALIMTICE.

The inspectors have done the first task. It focused on the collection, selection, evaluation, and validation of OER for scientific disciplines (Maths-PC). It aims to share and make available to the Moroccan teaching community the OER on both TAALIMTICE and TELMIDTICE spaces.

In parallel, a project is underway aimed at assembling and designing an editorial policy for producing OER. This project will provide the education system with a database of OER-DNL (scientific disciplines taught in French), to enrich the courses' database in TELMIDTICE.

To encourage the use and production of free digital resources, a UNESCO repository has been shared and regulation of the production and dissemination of digital resources has been popularized through the ministerial notes organizing the competition of the production of OER. This is the culture of resources' dissemination and uses under the Creative Commons License (CC). Thanks to this platform, the pedagogical body will be able to receive ICT information regularly, the purpose provided by the National Laboratory of Digital Resources is to access all the digital resources acquired or developed by the program of generalization of ICT for education in Morocco (GENIE).

In Higher Education, Morocco created an innovative initiative called MUN (Maroc Université Numérique) that has been started in 2019 with the support of the Ministry of Higher Education and the French Embassy in Morocco and partnership of FUN (France Université Numérique) (https://www.mun.ma). Currently, this platform is starting with 49-selected free access MOOCs in various fields. This numerical openness can only be beneficial since it will make it possible to overcome several difficulties encountered by the students and will also contribute to solving the linguistic problem, but also that of the massification by reducing the numbers in the amphitheaters. MUN is now becoming the very innovative Open and freely Morocco Higher education platform dedicated to a very large public in June 2019.

2.5 Curriculum and Teaching Methodology

The Ministry of National Education, Higher Education, Executive Training and Scientific Research is responsible for applying government policy in the realm of education. Its structure is highly centralized. It consists of a large Department for Higher Education, another for School Education, a Standing Committee for Curricula, and sixteen Regional Academies of Education and Training (AREFS). These Academies have important powers, the result of the new decentralization policy that Morocco intends to implement. In turn, the Academies are organized into Provincial Delegations of Education that correspond to the administrative divisions of provinces and prefectures. They are responsible for educational affairs, both administratively and pedagogically (Elmasrar, 2015).

2.5.1 Pre-primary Education

Pre-primary education is aimed at children between 4 and 6 years of age. Its objective is to facilitate the physical, cognitive, and affective development of the child, encouraging autonomy and socialization by developing sensory, motor, imaginative, and expressive skills, among others, and to provide an initiation into basic religious, ethical, and civic values; to engage in elementary practical and artistic activities, such as drawing, painting, music, and so on; and activities to prepare for reading and writing in Arabic, through a command of spoken Arabic and based on the child's mother tongue.

Basic Education.

Basic education is compulsory from 6 to 15 years of age. It begins with Primary Education for pupils of 6–12 and is structured in two cycles:
   The First Cycle lasts for two years, from 6 to 8 years old. Its main objective is to consolidate and expand on what was learned in the pre-primary stage.
   The Intermediate Cycle lasts for four years, from 8 to 12 years of age. It aims to develop the children's capabilities, by exploring what was learned at earlier levels in more depth, especially religious, ethical, and civic questions; developing their comprehension and expressive skills in Arabic; learning to read, write and express themselves in a first foreign language.

2.5.2   Secondary Education

Secondary education is organized in two independent cycles: compulsory collegial education and qualifying secondary education (post-compulsory). At the end of the three-year Collegial Education, the Brevet d'Enseignement Collégial (BEC)—a certificate enabling progress to the next educational cycle—may be awarded. Qualifying Secondary Education consists of three types of training—general, technical, and vocational—with two corresponding types of Baccalaureate: a general one and a technological-vocational one, each with different specialties and a brief period of vocational training.

2.5.3   Higher Education

After independence in 1956, the Moroccan government laid down the strategic objectives of educational policy. These goals are mainly: Moroccanization, unification, generalization, Arabization, and centralization.
   Indeed, the Scientific Centre for Higher Studies and training was transformed into Science Faculty according to the Dahir of 1959. The first university created in Morocco was Mohammed V University in Rabat. It was founded in 1957 to train the executives in public administration and education. However, the academic year 1959–1960 has known a limited number of students (3300) and professors (150).
   During the sixties and the seventies of the twentieth century, Morocco has chosen to integrate the global economy. It has therefore adopted an educational policy based on the creation of academic institutions, equality between the two sexes, the spread of scholarships, and free access to education. This policy has influenced the total

number of enrolled students as well as teachers in the academic year 1979–1980 which exceeded 74,500 students and 2171 teachers including 391 women (18%).

During the 80s, Morocco has undergone radical changes in the economic and social levels, which prompted it to adopt new education strategies that relate higher education to the socio-economic sector by creating engineering schools, graduate schools of technology, and private institutions for higher education. Indeed, the number of teachers was approximately 6187 of which 1349 females (22%) and the number of students was around 198,054 in the academic year 1989–1990.

Like the other periods, the 1990s witnessed a significant extension of institutions but with more emphasis on the creation of science and technology faculties, management and commerce schools (ENCG), multidisciplinary faculties as well as focusing on the training and the qualification of the human resources. The year 1997 was marked by a reform that mainly affected the postgraduate training by the Decree N°2- 96–796 of February 19, 1997.

The Higher Diploma for Advanced Studies (DESA) and the Doctorate of State were therefore introduced. The access to the DESA and DESS is selective and teachers who are accredited researchers by the Ministry of higher education for four years propose the program.

The Ministry of Education in Morocco has adopted a new reform to adapt its educational system with the international systems. It has developed a new law 01.00 that was enacted on March 3, 2000 by the parliament.

This law granted autonomy (pedagogical, administrative, and financial) to the university. It has reformed the educational architecture into cycles, modules, and courses and it allowed the university's openness to the outside world.

Starting from the academic year 2003–2004, the LMD system (Licence, Master, and Doctorate) has been implemented in the Moroccan university. It was not until the academic year 2006–2007 that "the universities start to introduce masters to consider the implementation of the doctoral training The reform has started to regulate access to the technical institutions (FST, EST, and ENCG). For the first time, in the academic year 2006–2007, universities will conduct an assessment and accreditation of BAs (licenses) undertaken in 2003. They were preparing, besides, to introduce the doctoral schools, which were expected to open later in the academic year 2007–2008. In the same vein, it was anticipated also to start the reform within the engineering schools" (Kouam, 2006).

This was achieved during the academic year 2008–2009 with the new form of doctoral cycle and centers.

In the current structure of the Moroccan educational system, the academic year has two semesters. The semester is composed of 14–16 weeks of instruction and assessment, which is about 300–360 h of learning according to stream. The license (BA) cycle consists of six semesters and passing the first four semesters ends up obtaining DEUG or DEUP certificate. The master program consists of four semesters after the license while the doctoral cycle lasts three years minimum and five years maximum.

The reform has set a number of objectives:

- *Enable students who wish to pursue their graduate studies to develop the required skills and training.*
- *Enable students who wish to get access to the labor market to get the prerequisite skills to facilitate their insertion.*
- *Improve the performance of the educational system.*
- *Respond to the constraints and evolution of the socio-economic environment.*
- *Provide and develop methodological, linguistic, and communicative skills.*
- *Establish a progressive career guidance system.*
- *Prepare for insertion into the socio-economic environment.*
- *Transmit and convey fundamental cultural values.*

In this regard, Moroccan have been invited to start the reconquest of reason and common values that are the basics to enhance a space for conviviality and social ties where the words of dignity, justice, and freedom would be expressed in the same manner and combined with the same requirements, whatever are our origins, cultures, and spirituality.

Distance learning is significantly increasing in Morocco in both public and private universities. The increased availability and functionality of information technology (IT) had brought new teaching tools to the Moroccan market, including mobile phones, video-conferencing, e-mail, discussion forums, chat software, and document sharing.

Morocco's finance ministry recently decided to integrate a dedicated distance learning service into its organizational structure.

The Ministry of National Education had begun work on an interactive television system (TVI), which aims to provide remote training for teachers across the Kingdom. The E-learning Centre is dealing with E-learning and is supervising distance learning on the use of ICT for university teachers of the Maghreb (Algeria, Tunisia, and Morocco).

Additionally, The MUN (Maroc Université Numérique) was launched in July 2016 as a collaboration between Morocco's Ministry of Higher Education and FUN (France University Numérique) in order to face the massification of Higher Education and to encourage online production of quality learning.

Today, with the expansion of the Internet and the high demand for training needs including ICT-based learning, we are witnessing a new generation of educational content in MOOC format or their derived forms (SPOC, …) at the level of institutions of higher education, as well as departments and training centers. Several structuring projects have emerged and position Morocco as a leader and innovator in this new way of learning and training.

The OpenMed project an Erasmus plus (https://openmedproject.eu) which aims among its objectives to further widen this field of production of educational resources to eventually implement an open system of education and free access at the level of the North Africa and Middle East region (MENA).

The contribution of the Universities Cadi Ayyad of Marrakech and Ibn Zohr of Agadir to the OpenMed project (2015–2018) first focused on a study of the state of play of initiatives in the field of open education in these universities. This study made it possible to inform about the work carried out or in progress and whose objective is to facilitate the adoption of OEP by Moroccan universities.

2.6 Outcome

The implementation of open education within the university is first and foremost a desire to change pedagogical practices in the same institution. This change also requires a commitment from all components: teachers, administrators and students. The problem is not limited to offering material resources and technical solutions, which are often surmountable, but rather resides in the management of change and the resumption to an open environment for the sharing of open educational resources and the establishment of free educational practices.

The multiple experiments conducted within Cadi Ayyad University as well as for most of the Moroccan universities have shown great interest from the main user, who is the student.

The student arrives at higher education to enrich his knowledge and develop his know-how, knowing that the world of digital offers him already and all the necessary without moving to the university. We must provide him with added value by taking advantage of the classroom teaching available and provided by our teacher-researchers and flexibility and interactive learning that will help him to take advantage of the time available throughout his training.

UCA as a partner in the OpenMed project has made a firm commitment to implement all the results of this project and places open education today among its priority actions. As a result, the establishment of the Innovation Center for Open Education (CIEO) within the CIP (Centre for pedagogical innovation) is an opportunity for research professors to broaden the sharing of their productions with a view to improving the quality of media produced, that learning (Berrada, 2018).

The Cadi Ayyad University, aware of the essential role of making open education a strategic issue to improve learning at university and to cope with the effects of massification and linguistic difficulties encountered by our students, recommends integrating the elements key to the success of Open Education among its priorities. Thus, it was decided to:

– *Organize ongoing training for UCA pedagogical staff on Open Education;*
– *Organize thematic training schools on education open annually;*
– *Engage in the development of cooperation projects with its partners and OpenMed partners for the creation of networks for a better exchange;*
– *Put the CIOE (CIP) at the service of institutions for their support in the production of OER and to increase staff awareness of the benefits of open education;*
– *Launch a thesis subject on open education within the Trans ERIE project team to carry out research in this direction.*

2.7   Stakeholders

Openness in Higher Education seems to be common sense for equal and democratic access to knowledge. Stimulating supply and demand for high-quality OERs is essential for modernizing education. If universities really want to find more resources to invest in better teaching and research, it is essential that the open sharing of resources be encouraged. Knowledge must be shared and spread, teachers encouraged to network and collaborate on course development and institutions discouraged from fragmentation and all producing their own slight variations on the same course.

Nevertheless, the adoption of open practices in Morocco is not well exploited. According to the Survey on Governments' Open Educational Resources (OER) Policies (Commonwealth of Learning and UNESCO, June 2012), the obstacle to OER adoption in the Arabic countries is Language and Cultural diversity according to the 33% of the respondent (against the 8.2% of the total across all responses). To succeed in all these aspects, stakeholders should play an important role in supporting initiatives at all levels. However, the essential stakeholders that come to mind in developing OER should include students, faculty members, librarians, bookstores, and publishers. It might even be easy to think of additional stakeholders at the campus level—distance learning, registrar's office, etc. When my library is working on OER initiatives, these are the stakeholders we think of too. We don't often enough think about open education stakeholders beyond the academic community. There are actually many more potential stakeholders that work on public interest issues.

Although many stakeholders in the educational arena support OER and open access, their use in education in South Mediterranean countries, has not yet reached a critical mass. Most teachers use ICTs mainly to prepare their teaching, rather than to work together and with their students during lessons or connecting classrooms.

Even when OER, and most generally distance education, is actually implemented, the focus remains on building more access to digital contents and too little consideration is given to whether this really fills in the knowledge gap of learners and the needs of the labor market. Many HEIs in South Mediterranean countries do not yet participate in OER initiatives, not all educators and students are aware of the benefits and pitfalls of OER and fragmentation of approaches and interoperability is registered.

2.8   Impact

Several actions and initiatives were put in place after the adoption of strategies to open up university education, among these actions:

Action 1: Integration of Training Modules in UCA's continuing education for the benefit of UCA's young research teachers (mandatory training). Six modules are offered face-to-face:

M1   Agree to Open His Course and His Teachings and Introduction to REL.

M2   Identify Open Licenses that You Would Apply to Your Course
M3   Use OER in Your Course/teaching
M4   Locate OER in the Context of Your Course
M5   Develop an Open Learning Plan and Share It
M6   Presentation of an LMS Platform and Planned Activities.

Certificates in the form of badges will be given to the participants.

Action 2: Organize annually a summer school on open education in Morocco for about 70 teacher-researchers in the presence of experts. The first school is scheduled for next November in Marrakech.

Action 3: Participate in conferences and communicate research results under development by a doctoral student from the Trans ERIE UCA Marrakech team. Several works have already been presented in national and international conferences.

Action 4: Assembly of a new project on Open Education for Morocco and member states of Islamic countries in partnership with UNIR and UNIMED.

The project entitled "ISESCO Open Education" accepted for funding. The first coordination meeting was held in Rabat in March 2019 at ISESCO Headquarters.

Action 5: Development of a MOOC "Open Educational Resources" for the national platform "Maroc Université Numérique" with support from the Ministry of Supervision.

100% of the MOOC REL is inspired by the OpenMed project and is produced with the participation of:

– *Cadi Ayyad University (UCA), Morocco*
– *Ibn Zohr University, Morocco*
– *Universidad Internacional de La Rioja (UNIR), Spain*
– *Coventry University, United Kingdom*
– *University of Seville, Spain*
– *UNIMED, Italy*
– *Politecnico University of Turin, Italy.*

Action 6: "FORMAREL" project of the CIP-UCA which obtained a grant from the AUF in April 2019 and which consists of the establishment of a training of trainers' platform on the OER for educators of the national education in Morocco. FORMAREL is part of the "APPRENDRE" call for projects from the Agence Universitaire de la Francophonie.

3   Discussion and Conclusion

The overall vision of the regional OER agenda is that the opening of education and the sharing of academic content can lead to improved networking, collaboration, and integration of education systems (ES), through comprehensive development and creation of relevant interrelated content platforms inside and outside institutions. In addition, the adoption of OER and OEP is aimed at ensuring greater accessibility to ES and at diversifying the channels and ways of learning and updating learners' knowledge.

In summary, Open Education can truly change the educational systems and make it better, more accessible and relevant, and all the features for a global knowledge-sharing society.

Acknowledgements The authors would like to thank the European Commission for supporting the Erasmus + OpenMed project which was the start of structured actions in Open Education in Morocco since 2016. Special thanks are also given to UNIMED Italy, UNIR Spain and all OpenMed partners for their contribution and for sharing activities among the consortium. We are also very grateful to all colleagues at Moroccan universities, especially Professor Ahmed Al Makari, for supporting Open Education actions we were developing together in Morocco and for his support of the OER Morocco declaration.

References

Berrada, K. (2018). *Institutional Roadmap for Open Education*. Report at Cadi Ayyad University. https://openmedproject.eu/wp-content/uploads/OpenMed_IR_UCA.pdf.

Berrada, K., Benelrhali, A., & Laaziz, I. (2019). *An overview on teaching informatics/Computer science and ICT in Morocco at National education level*. Retrieved from https://www.researchgate.net/publication/330994753.

Burgos, D. (Ed.) (2017). Open Education Policy. UNIR: Logroño, La Rioja (Spain). Open Access from https://bit.ly/unir-openpolicy (English) and https://bit.ly/unir-educacionabierta (español).

Downes, S. (2007). Models for sustainable open educational resources. *Interdisciplinary Journal of Knowledge and Learning Objects*, *3*. Retrieved from http://ijklo.org/Volume3/IJKLOv3p029-044Downes.pdf.

Elmasrar, K. (2015). The current university reforms in Morocco: The present situation of labour faculty of letters and human sciences. *International Journal of Humanities and Social Science, 5*(9), 182–188.

Haut Commissariat au Plan. Le Maroc en chiffres 2018. https://www.hcp.ma/downloads/Maroc-en-chiffres_t13053.html.

Idrissi Jouicha, A., Berrada, K., Bendaoud, R., Machwate, S., Miraoui, A., & Burgos, D. (2020). Starting MOOCs in African University: The experience of Cadi Ayyad University, process, review, recommendations, and prospects. *IEEE Access, 8*, 17477–17488.

Idrissi Jouicha, A., Margoum, S., Bendaoud, R., & Berrada, K. (2018). UC@MOOC's effectiveness by producing open educational resources. *International Journal of Interactive Multimedia and Artificial Intelligence*, *5*(2).

Jahn, N., & Tullney, M. (2016). A study of institutional spending on open access publication fees in Germany. *PeerJ, 4*, e2323.

Kouam, M. (2006). – État d'avancement de la réforme au Maroc, in Actes de la rencontre des recteurs et présidents d'université des pays du Maghreb et des conférences francophones de l'union européenne intitulée vers un espace euro-maghrébin solidaire, des 1er et 2 décembre 2006 à Tunis.

McAndrew, P. (2010). Defining openness: Updating the concept of 'open' for a connected world. *Journal of Interactive Media in Education, 2010*(10), 1–13.

OER Morocco declaration, Marrakech 2016. https://www.change.org/p/universites-declaration-du-maroc-sur-les-ressources-educatives-libres-oer-morocco-declaration.

Schimmer, R., Geschuhn, K. K., & Vogler, A. (2015). Disrupting the subscription journals' business model for the necessary large-scale transformation to open access. *Max Planck Digital Library*, Munich. https://doi.org/10.17617/1.3.

UNESCO Final report. *Forum on the Impact of Open Courseware for Higher Education in Developing Countries.* UNESCO, Paris, 1–3 July 2002. https://unesdoc.unesco.org/ark:/48223/pf0000128515.

UNESCO Paris OER Declaration. (2012). World Open Educational Ressources (OER) Congress, Paris. https://en.unesco.org/oer/paris-declaration.

Wong, E. Y. (2017). e-Print Archive: arXiv. org. *Technical Services Quarterly, 34*(1), 111–113.

Imane Zaatri is a Ph.D. Student at Cadi Ayyad University (UCA). She is a Master's Degree in Engineering and Technology for Education and Training and involved in developing research on Open Educational Resources.

Sofia Margoum is a Ph.D. Student at Cadi Ayyad University (UCA). She is a holder of a Master's Degree in physics, chemistry, and analysis of materials. She is developing research on the implementation of Micro-Computer Based-Laboratory and OER at Trans ERIE group of research of UCA. She is also contributing to the join MOOC on Societal Implication on Neurosciences between UCA and Bordeaux University in France. She is participating in many Erasmus plus projects and has published papers in related fields.

Rachid Bendaoud is professor of physics in charge of e-Learning at Cadi Ayyad University. He holds a Ph.D. in physics from Toulouse University (France) and the International Master in e-Learning from Kurt Bush Institute (Switzerland). He is the Joint-Director of Trans ERIE (Transdisciplinary Research group on Educative Innovation and member of Centre for pedagogical innovation. He is working on MOOCs, blended learning, open education, and one of developers of UC@MOOC initiative at Cadi Ayyad University. He works as an instructor for professors-researchers in e-Learning and is also a consultant in educational techniques and teaching methods with university institutions. He coordinated about fifteen projects funded by IRD, OIF, CNRST and currently by AUF, which deals with the training of trainers in open education. He is also team member of several Erasmus plus projects at Cadi Ayyad University, including the OpenMed project, Opening up Education in South-Mediterranean countries.

Ilham Laaziz is professor of Chemistry. She is Director of GENIE program at Ministry of National Education, Professional Training, Higher Education and Scientific Research. She has obtained her State Doctorate in Applied Sciences (1997) from Mohammadia School of Engineers—Mohamed V University in Rabat Agdal and a Ph.D. in Materials Chemistry (1990) of the Ecole Nationale Supérieure de Chimie de Montpellier. She was leading the collection and processing of information in the National Documentation Centre (1993–1999) at the Ministry of Planning. She was the head of Program and direction of research in the DRSCU MESFCRS (2000–2002). She was the chief of the Division of Technological Development (2002–2006). Management programs targeted to strengthening the links between universities and industry (Interface structures, RDT, RGI, incubators network) (1999–2006). Acting Director CNIPE (2006–2007). She was a program Director mainstreaming of ICT in education (since April 2007). She was member of the Board and Secretary General of the Moroccan Association for support and assistance for the mentally handicapped (AMSAHM 1997–2003). General Secretary of the Association for Human Development (Hassanate) since 2009. She is also member of the Moroccan Society of Membranes and Desalination (WSSD). Author of several articles, publications, reports and books.

Daniel Burgos works as Vice-rector for Knowledge Transfer and Technology at Universidad Internacional de La Rioja (UNIR). In addition, he holds the UNESCO Chair on eLearning and the ICDE Chair in Open Educational Resources. He works also as Director of the Research Institute for Innovation and Technology in Education (UNIR iTED). Previously, he worked in Atos and the Open University of The Netherlands. His interests are mainly focused on Educational Technology and Innovation: Adaptive/Personalised and Informal eLearning, Learning Analytics, Social Networks, eGames, and eLearning Specifications. He has published over 100 scientific papers, 15 books and 16 special issues on indexed journals. He is or has been involved in +50 European and Worldwide R&D projects, with a practical implementation approach.

He is a visiting professor at Coventry University (UK), Universidad Nacional de Colombia (UNAL, Colombia), Universidad de las Fuerzas Armadas (ESPE, Ecuador) and An-Najah University (Palestine). He has been chair (2016, 2018) and vice-chair (2015, 2017) of the international jury for the UNESCO King Hamad Bin Isa Al Khalifa Prize for the Use of ICTs in Education. He holds degrees in Communication (Ph.D.), Computer Science (Dr. Ing), Education (Ph.D.), Anthropology (Ph.D.), Business Administration (DBA) and Artificial Intelligence (MIT, postgraduate).

Khalid Berrada is professor of physics. He is director of the centre for pedagogical innovation and UNESCO Chairholder on "Teaching physics by doing" since 2010. He was the founder and president of the Moroccan Society of Applied Physics 2006–2011. He has been Chair of international conferences on Physics, education and optics (ALOP2006, ICPE2007, GUMP2008, IWOP2010, CNTE2012, IMDM2013, IsyDMA2016, RUN2015, ExAO2013, CINU2016, CINE2018, TiceMed2018, etc.). He has authored (or co-authored) many research papers and has been member of many national and international conference and meeting committees. He has organized and facilitated many active learning workshops in Morocco, Tunisia, Algeria, India, Zambia, Philippines and Cameroon. He is also one of the developers of the successful French edition program of UNESCO Active Learning in Optics and Photonics and has facilitated many workshops in Morocco on Micro-computer based laboratories. Currently, he is coordinating the UC@MOOC project created in 2013 at Cadi Ayyad University. He is also coordinating and contributing to many Erasmus plus projects at Cadi Ayyad University: OpenMed, EXPERES, MericNET, InSIDE, EduBioMed, FORMAREL AUF, … Currently, he is leading a Group of research on Educative innovation at UCA (Trans ERIE) and the Morocco Declaration on Open Education since 2016.

Chapter 8
Open Educational Resources in Palestine

High Hopes Promising Solutions

Jamil Itmazi

1 Case Overview

It is important to remember that Palestine is located in the Middle East between the Jordan River and the Mediterranean Sea. The territory of historical Palestine is greater than the territory of the Palestinian Authority (the State of Palestine). In order to limit the scope of this chapter, the information and issues concerning the West Bank (Without Israeli settlements), the Gaza Strip, and the city of Jerusalem. See Fig. 1: Palestine People and land from 1946 to 2010 (PNC, 2019).

The State of Palestine had an estimated population of about 4.95 million people in 2017 with 38.9% of the population under the age of 15 (PCPS, 2019). The country is divided into two physically separated geographic regions, the West Bank, and the Gaza Strip.

In Palestine's education system, compulsory basic education includes Grades 1 to 10 and this is divided into the preparatory stage (Grade 1–4) and the empowerment stage (Grade 5–10). Secondary education covers Grades 11 and 12. It is worth mentioning that, Ministry of Higher Education and Scientific Research are mainly responsible for the governance of 49 higher education institutions. There are 15 universities and 16 technical colleges (which mainly offer four-year courses). Additionally, there are 18 community colleges (that mainly offer two-year diploma courses in technical and commercial specializations). The number of students enrolled in Palestinian higher education institutions for the academic year (2016/2017) was 218,415 students, (MOEHE, 2019).

J. Itmazi (✉)
Palestine Ahliya University, P.O.Box: 1041, Bethlehem, West Bank, Palestine
e-mail: j.itmazi@gmail.com
URL: https://sites.google.com/site/jamilitmazi

© Springer Nature Singapore Pte Ltd. 2020
R. Huang et al. (eds.), *Current State of Open Educational Resources in the "Belt and Road" Countries*, Lecture Notes in Educational Technology,
https://doi.org/10.1007/978-981-15-3040-1_8

Fig. 1 Palestinian loss of land 1946–2010

2 Current Situation of OER

2.1 Infrastructure

It is well known that infrastructure is very important for adopting and using OERs.

"An appropriate OER-based IT infrastructure is required for the proper operation and management of the concerned open and distance learning institutions (ODLIs). The IT infrastructure should further help in proper dissemination, sharing, and utilization of OER so as to provide good quality course/programme content, e-content, instructional processes, web-based systems, and others." (Khanna & Basak, 2013).

OER Infrastructure needs software, hardware, and service. In Palestine, "Israel has controlled the Palestinian ICT infrastructure, hindering its development and Palestinians' digital rights including recent mass surveillance and monitoring of Palestinian content online… More than a decade after the Palestinians made the initial request for the release of Third Generation (3G) frequencies; the service became available for Palestinian customers in the West Bank in early 2018… Israel's control of the ICT infrastructure and flow of information has allowed it to limit and violate Palestinians' digital rights, specifically the rights to access the internet, privacy and freedom of expression," (7amleh, 2018).

A study about how higher education institutions are selecting and using technology platforms for the creation and delivery of Open Educational Resources (OER) found that the "institutions are most commonly using existing tools like the Learning Management System (LMS) to deliver OER." (Nyland, 2018).

In general, Palestine needs to improve the ICT infrastructure; they need to have rights to operate 4th generation of mobile networks as well as 5G. In the official (governmental) level, we do not have any proof of formal support to OERs initiative.

Most of Palestinian higher education institutions publish their resources (open and close) within local digital libraries, databases, and repositories. The majority of these digital libraries allow free access to their resources, but the licenses of these resources are mostly free not OERs, for example, you cannot translate or adapt the resource.

Some of Palestinian higher education institutions rely on some international platform to disseminate, share, and utilize its resources.

2.2 Policy

Open educational resource policies (OER policies) are principles or tenets adopted by governing bodies in support of the use of open content—specifically open educational resources (OER)—and practices in educational institutions. Such policies are emerging increasingly at the national, state/province, and local levels (CERI, 2007).

Creative Commons defines (OER) policies as "legislation, institutional policies, and/or funder mandates that lead to the creation, increased use, and/or support for improving OER." (CC, 2019).

Creative Commons hosts a crowdsourced Open Policy Registry. As of early 2013, there were 66 OER policies in the registry, the OER Policy Registry was moved in fall 2018 to the OER World Map (https://oerworldmap.org/oerpolicies), it currently contains 157 of proposed open education policies from around the world.

"Open education policies are formal regulations regarding support, funding, adoption, and use of open educational resources (OER) and/or open education practices (OEP). Such policies are designed to support the creation, adoption, and sharing of OER and the design and integration of OEP into programs of study. Open education policies underscore the viability and value of OER in teaching and learning and can help inculcate OEP at colleges and universities. The development of open education policies will help to move OER and OEP from the periphery to the center of education practice. This publication is one in a three-part series designed to provide a point of departure for conversations about all aspects of open education: content, Practices and Policies," (EDUCAUSE, 2018).

In the Arab States (Palestine included), it was noted that there are insufficient open digital contents in the Arabic language. In fact, all the Arabic contents in the web are less than 3% of the global contents. In addition, the lack of political strategies or action plans from the Arab Ministries was noted as an obstacle to OER construction and application.

In the Arab States, we find "ALECSO OER Community" which consists of 22 Member States (one of them is Palestine State). The creation and sharing of OER is in line with ALECSO's goal to enhance the fields of education, culture, and science at regional and national levels, and to foster coordination between Arab states thereon. ALECSO is pursuing the creation and adoption of OER in a two-part process. The first part of the project, involved cooperation with regional and international organizations, awareness-raising and capacity-building activities, along with the development of manuals and guidelines concerning the use, development, and sharing of OERs. The ALECSO OER hub is now being established to allow Arab countries to share, develop, and disseminate OERs, and that facilitates access to these resources (ALECSO, 2019).

The Palestinian ministry of education and Higher Education (MOEHE) has some initiatives and projects related to e-Learning and smart learning. In 2008, e-Learning project was implemented to support education by using laptops and internal networks. Although the utilization of galaxy 3 started, the students need to be in planned time and to be in a specific place. In 2016, some public schools started to implement Smart Learning projects.

At Palestinian national level, there is no explicit OERs polices. The OER Commons Platform, a dynamic digital library and network owned and operated by the Institute for the Study of Knowledge Management in Education (ISKME), stated that "There is no Country Champion for Palestinian territories, yet," (OERWORLDMAP, 2019).

2.3 Resources

Some of Palestinian higher education institutions rely on some international platform to dissemination, sharing, and utilization its resources while the majority of them publish their resources (open and close) within local digital libraries, databases, and repositories. The majority of these digital libraries allow open access or free access. Mostly, the related resources are not OERs, although they are free of charge.

Table 1 shows that there are good quantities of published resources from Palestinian higher education institutions. It is important to change the policies and licenses of these resources from closed access to open access.

Table 1 summarized the Palestinian local digital libraries, databases, and repositories in the main Palestinian higher education institutions as an example of Palestinian Resources.

Table 1 Digital libraries, databases, and repositories in some Palestinian higher education institutions

University/Home page	Resources: Thesis, Books, Researches, and more	Open Access to Journal/s articles	e-Learning site
Al-Azhar University–Gaza www.alazhar.edu.ps	https://alazhar.edu.ps/library/ marchive.asp	Journal of Al-Azhar University–Gaza: Natural Sciences: www.alazhar.edu.ps/ journal/prevNature.asp and Human Sciences: www.alazhar.edu.ps/ journal/prevHuman.asp	http://moodle.alazhar.edu.ps/ login/index.php
Al-Aqsa University www.alaqsa.edu.ps	https://bit.ly/2XMPgH3	Journal of Al-Aqsa University–Gaza Natural Sciences and Natural Sciences: https://bit.ly/2XYvH2T	
Al-Istiqlal University www.pass.ps		Al-Istiqlal University research Journal: http://dsr.alistiqlal.edu.ps/page-2-ar.html	
Al-Quds Open University (QOU) www.qou.edu	• www.qou.edu/ar/sciresearch.do • MOOCs: http://ecourse.ps • OSOL repository for digital content: OSOL is an open access digital repository offered by Al-Quds open university to capture, store, organize, index, preserve, and provide access to its digital assets and intellectual output, such as QOU's scientific journals, scholarly papers, thesis, articles, projects, books, digital learning content, smart courses, and others • https://dspace.qou.edu/handle/194/2506	• Palestinian Journal of Open Education. • Journal of Al-Quds Open University for Research & Studies. • Researches on e-Learning. • Researches on Open Education. https://journals.qou.edu/	→ e-Learning → Digital content repository → e-Courses → QOU Slideshare → QOU Tube https://elearning.qou.edu/

(continued)

Table 1 (continued)

University/Home page	Resources: Thesis, Books, Researches, and more	Open Access to Journal/s articles	e-Learning site
AL-Quds University www.alquds.edu	https://dspace.alquds.edu		https://eclass.alquds.edu/
An-Najah National University www.najah.edu	• https://scholar.najah.edu/theses • An-Najah National University in Palestine Offered Its First MOOC Called "Discover Palestine" Which Describes the Country's History, Heritage, Culture, and Archaeology: https://elc.najah.edu/node/304 • Conferences Papers: https://scholar.najah.edu/conferences	An-Najah University Journal for Research—Humanities An-Najah University Journal for research—Medical and Health Sciences An-Najah University Journal for Research—Natural Sciences https://scholar.najah.edu/journals	https://elc.najah.edu/
Bethlehem University www.bethlehem.edu	www.bethlehem.edu/institutes/library	Bethlehem University Journal: www.jstor.org/journal/bethunivj	https://eclass.bethlehem.edu
Birzeit University www.birzeit.edu	http://library.birzeit.edu/librarya/bzu-ths/bzu-ths.php https://ritaj.birzeit.edu/instructor/publications/public/		https://itc.birzeit.edu
Hebron University www.hebron.edu	http://elearning.hebron.edu/enrol/index.php?id=274	Hebron University Research Journal: www.hebron.edu/index.php/jour-archive.html	http://elearning.hebron.edu

(continued)

Table 1 (continued)

University/Home page	Resources: Thesis, Books, Researches, and more	Open Access to Journal/s articles	e-Learning site
Islamic University of Gaza (IUG) www.iugaza.edu.ps	http://library.iugaza.edu.ps/thesis.aspx https://library.iugaza.edu.ps/browse_ thesis.aspx http://lectures.iugaza.edu.ps/	• Islamic University of Gaza Journal: • IUG Journal of Islamic Studies • IUG Journal of Humanities Research • IUG Journal of Economics and Business • IUG Journal of Educational and Psychology Sciences • IUG Journal for Natural • http://journals.iugaza.edu.ps	http://elearning.iugaza.edu.ps
Palestine Polytechnic University (PPU) www.ppu.edu	DSpace at PPU is a digital repository of original research produced at Palestine Polytechnic University. The repository contains scientific papers, staff publications, student projects, master theses, and electronic materials: http://scholar.ppu.edu/	Palestine Journal of Mathematics http://pjm.ppu.edu/	http://eclass.ppu.edu/
Palestinian Technical University—Kadoori, www. ptuk.edu.ps	The Digital Repository of Palestine Technical University: https://scholar.ptuk.edu.ps Videos: www.youtube.com/user/ptukmerc/ featured	Palestine Technical University Research Journal: https://ptuk.edu.ps/ptuk_journal	http://moodle.ptuk.edu.ps
The Arab American University (AAUP) www.aauj.edu		Journal of the Arab American University: www.aaup.edu/Research/Journals/Journal-Arab-American-University/Archive	
University of Palestine http://up.edu.ps	DSpace University of Palestine Repository: http://dspace.up.edu.ps/jspui	Journal of Palestine University https://bit.ly/30zmICY	http://upinar.edu.ps

2.4   Curriculum and Teaching Methodology

We mentioned that (MOEHE) have some initiatives and projects related to e-Learning and smart learning. In 2008, e-Learning project was implemented to support education by using laptops and internal networks and in 2016, some public schools started to implement Smart Learning project.

Even though schools had tablets, the students can only make use of these devices in limited time. Teachers developed their teaching methods by using these devices outside the classroom and in the break time during the school day. With the emergence of low-cost embedded sensors and more importantly, sensor-equipped smart mobile devices, the MOEHE implemented the digitalization of education initiative with the help of national organization such as Paltel, PSD (Partners for Sustainable Development), and local communities. Some international organizations are involved in this initiative by supporting schools with interactive projectors (AMIDEAST, USA; Belgian Cooperation Council; China) and professional development of teachers (AMIDEAST).

Recently in Palestine, the SL paradigm, which combines u-Learning and social learning, has emerged since 2016. The evolution of Smart Learning is expected to improve the educational environment to an advanced level regarding devices, networks, education programs, etc. However, discussions on Smart Learning have just begun in Palestine, and the related studies are insufficient. The smart learning project in Palestine now includes 50 middle schools as a pilot project. In the coming years the project will be carried over the country. At the beginning of the academic year 2015–2016, some public schools started to implement Smart Learning Project (SLP) in grade fifth and sixth aiming to replace the teaching and learning practices in the traditional classroom with the best technological practices (Khlaif and Farid 2018).

2.5   Outcome

The outcome of OERs in Palestine could be discussed within 3 areas:

Projects OERs Related
The OpenMed project, supported by the Erasmus + Capacity-Building in Higher Education program of the European Union, had been launched during 2015–2018 to widen participation and adoption of Open Educational Resources (OER) and Open Educational Practices (OEP) as a bottom-up approach to support the modernization of the Higher Education sector in the South-Mediterranean. The project involved an international consortium composed of five partners from Europe and nine from South-Mediterranean Countries. Two of the partners are Palestinian universities:

- BZU, Birzeit University,
- ANNU, An-Najah National University,

OpenMed raised awareness and facilitated the adoption of Open Educational Resources (OER) and Open Educational Practices (OEP) in the South-Mediterranean countries, with a particular focus on higher education in Egypt, Jordan, Morocco, and Palestine (OPENMED, 2019).

Within this project, on April 20, 2017, Birzeit University hosted the Palestine OER Strategy Forum, a national seminar aimed at gathering together educators and managers from higher education institutions in Palestine, expected to analyze challenges and priorities for opening up Higher Education in Palestine, outlining possible strategic actions to maximize the benefits of Open Education Practices and Open Educational Resources for university course development (OPENMED, 2017a).

The "Recommendations from the External Quality Expert" in (The Palestine OER Strategy Forum) recommended to ensure that there is leadership and guidance to ensure that every university can participate actively in developing Open Education strategies and programs, and to ensure that the national agenda is guided by the principles, which make Open Education in Palestine a unique case. "It is also important that they present their cases to the ministry and to senior management toward persuading them about the importance of promoting and supporting Open Educational developments, developing a national strategy, as these are key to enhance quality education and to promote good practices." (OPENMED, 2017b).

A course (Open Education: fundamentals and approaches) had been developed in English, Arabic, and French as one of the outcomes of this project.

See https://course.openmedproject.eu.

Researches OERs Related

Some researches related to OERs from Palestinian academics are selected as examples in this domain:

1. A study entitled "The philosophy of MOOCs and the feasibility of employing it in higher education institutions with respect of quality of education and freedom of use." (Shaqour, 2013).

   Abstract: The study reviews one of the current teaching trends in higher education, namely; Massive Open Online Courses (MOOCs) and the feasibility of employing them in institutions of higher education in the light of the quality of education and freedom of use. It highlights the necessity of activating the role of technology in raising the quality of higher education and the urgent need for that because of the current societal changes. And reviews the theoretical foundations adopted by this type of courses and their impact on the quality of higher education. The current study has highlighted the intellectual property—related aspects of these courses for both the teacher and the learner and the educational institution. The study concluded with a number of recommendations, including encouraging educational institutions to be opened to MOOCs and take advantage of them through seminars, lectures, and workshops and to work collaboratively to support the design and deployment of this type of courses and training of teachers in educational institutions on strategies of design and development of these courses.

2. A study entitled "Trends in Faculty Use of Open Educational Resources in Higher Education: A Case Study of Palestine Ahliya University." (Okkeh & Itmazi, 2015).

    Abstract: The most important issue of rapid change in the field of teaching is the emergence of OERs during the last decade which described as a revolution in the field of learning and teaching. There are many great initiatives in the world to adopt this concept, e.g., some universities offering all its courses with all their resources and materials online and freely and openly, imposes the managers of Arabic universities, besides Arabic educational and training institutions keeping pace with these developments, as well as making plans always to continuously integrate modern technologies in accomplishing their tasks in teaching and research, due to its great benefits in terms of improving the effectiveness of teaching and learning, as well as the achievement of justice and equality of educational opportunity and raise the institution profile.

    This study is founded upon the direction of Palestine Ahliya University to encourage the use of these resources, to explore the trends of faculty members toward the use of OERs in higher education. It used the descriptive approach and it used a designed questionnaire as a tool to get the data from faculty members. The study sample chosen randomly consisted of 67 faculty members of Palestine Ahliya University. The results showed that there were no statistically significant differences at significance level ($\alpha = 0.05$) in the trends of faculty members in the use of OERs in university education due to the following variables: Gender, college, years of experience, age, published research, degree, full-time working, the daily use of Internet, and English language proficiency.

3. A study entitled "The importance for adoption of Open Educational Resources in Arab Education and Training Institutions." (Itmazi, 2015).

    Abstract: The rapid change in the world in all fields, especially the developments of OERs and particularly the digital ones, imposes the managers of Arabic universities, besides educational and training institutions keeping pace with these developments, as well as making plans always to continuously integrate modern technologies in accomplishing their tasks in teaching and research. It is no longer acceptable to continue accomplishing tasks with techniques and resources that belong to the nineties of the last century. Also, it is important to realize that when the rate of change inside an institution becomes slower than the rate of change outside, the end is in sight.

    This study provides an introduction of OERs, clarifies that Arabs and Muslims scholars were the founders and builders of OERs, mentions its components and explains its degree of openness with a focus on accessibility for disabilities, in particular the economic disabilities which deployed in Arab countries. Moreover presents a summary of the latest trend in electronic courses: the MOOCs which are often emerge from OERs, mentions its sources and platforms, also, it lists the open licenses. In the last, upon our research and experience, a road map has been proposed which shows how to adopt initiatives of OERs in Arab Education and Training Institutions within a clear and flexible framework which illustrates the main issues of the plan and takes into account the specificity of these institutions.

4. A study entitled "Reflection on MOOC design in Palestine." (Affouneh, Wimpenny, Ghodieh, Alsaud, & Obaid, 2018).

Abstract: This paper will share Discover Palestine, an interdisciplinary Massive Online Open Course (MOOC) and the first MOOC to be created in Palestine, by the e-Learning Centre, Faculty from the Department of Geography, and Department of Tourism and Archaeology from An-Najah National University in Palestine. The paper traces the process of development of the Discover Palestine MOOC from its early inception as a cross institutional online course, to its current delivery, and engagement with a global and diverse group of learners. Using a descriptive case study design and thematic analysis, the reflective experiences of four course team members involved as facilitators/designers in the design and delivery of the MOOC are shared. Three key themes, namely, "Informing pedagogies including delivery methods," "A commitment to a national cause," and "Teacher presence," are presented and contextualized with data evidence. The findings share not only the hurdles the Discover Palestine team had to navigate during the MOOC development, but more importantly, how academic collaborations promoting open education practices offer powerful tools for the reciprocal exchange of knowledge, not least in shifting mindsets, and offering opportunities for shared fields of understanding to be realized in revealing creative, cultural practices, as well as lost histories.

5. A book entitled "Open Educational Resources: Usage, sharing and Adoption." (Itmazi & Essalmi, 2019).

The book includes ten chapters, which have explained the OERs from a practical and technical point of view, simplified their concepts and highlighted their licenses, and areas of use by non-specialists. It also highlighted the presentation of the most famous Arab and international OERs platforms, also showed e-Learning systems and types which used by modern universities, explained the ways to develop and to build OER, how to adopt, privatize, publish, and share the available resources according to their licenses.

This book is intended for all those interested in e-Learning and interested in digital, open and smart education, and interested in the tools, resources and OERs.

2.6 Stakeholders

The OERs Stakeholders may have much in common among international communities, but it is useful to discover the groups of OERs Stakeholders in Palestine.

The following lists the main groups of OERs Stakeholders in Palestine:

- The international community.
- The national community and government.
- Educational Institutions.
- Subject communities, e.g., employers and professional bodies

- Teaching staffs, tutors, supervisors, librarians, learning technologists, and educational developers.
- Learners and students.

2.7 Impact

It is nice to mention here what Atenas (2017) wrote about Open Education in Palestine (A tool for liberation):

This year (2017), and thanks to the OpenMed Project, we had the opportunity to travel to Palestine, to the West Bank, to visit the project partners and participate at the Palestine OER strategy Forum. Due to its political history, this trip has let us thinking about why we need a stronger commitment toward promoting Open Education …

The day of the OpenMed—Palestine OER strategy forum started with a presentation on *Open Education for Palestine* by Professor Marwan Tarazi, Director of the Centre for Continuing Education who stated that *Open Education is a tool for liberation*. He mentioned that under the current occupation, openness becomes essential to Palestine at philosophical level, and that the educators in Palestine need to open up"…

His presentation let us thinking, why we do what we do, in the way we do it. At personal level, I do believe in Openness [Open Education, Open Data, Open Access, Open Science, Open Government, and Open Policies], yes, but I never considered openness as a tool for liberation, I always thought about it as a human right, as an instrument for social justice, or a tool for active citizenship, but his words were inspiring, because sometimes the concept of liberation has to do with becoming free from colonial and dominant perspectives, when we do work with communities in countries at the so-called "global south," we must are use an approach that supports the development of strategies for opening up education, science, and governance accordingly to their own culture and history (Atenas, 2017).

3 Discussion and Conclusion

The awareness about OERs in Palestine is in its infancy. At the governmental level, the initiatives, projects, and related plans are weak despite the existence of great potentials and broad possibilities for better doing.

Regards to institutions, including universities and institutes, there is better progress than the official level, especially universities of Birzeit University and An-Najah National University, who participated in a large project (The OpenMed project), which benefit the movement of OERS in Palestine in more than one area. An-Najah National University developed the first course of MOOCs (Discover Palestine). In addition, Al-Quds Open University is a pioneer of open education in Palestine and even in the Arab world. It has a platform that includes a number of open courses and many OERs. It is clear that Al-Quds Open University, which is located in all major cities in the West Bank and Gaza, is clearly interested in OERs.

At the level of individuals and academics, it is well known of necessity for greater awareness of OERs despite the existence of some relevant literature and research. However, the Arab digital content is weak (not exceeding 3% of the global content), including educational content and there is a lack of scientific research in Arabic.

OERs are important to world in terms of justice, sharing, openness, etc. as well as the Arab world (including Palestine). Nowadays, the Arab educational institutions have a difficult situation at the level of educational contents, cooperation, and participation among them, since these institutions were produce and export knowledge a—in the past—but now they are importing it. The educational sector is aware of the limited availability of Arabic contents either educational or others. These digital resources will help our students and researchers access knowledge after these resources being translated to Arabic, adapted, and customized. In addition, In addition, it could be divided, composition as well as modified to make the most benefit of them.

As for the importance of OERs to the people of Palestine in particular, they suffer from unique problems resulted from the Israeli occupation:

- Movement problems: the lives of Palestinian peoples are filled with checkpoints, walls, patrols, military posts, and heavy restrictions on freedom of movement in addition to the difficulty of travel between the West Bank and Gaza as well as between both of them and between Jerusalem and/or Palestinian territories occupied in 1948.
- Construction problems: in most areas of the West Bank (C area) Thus hampering the provision of educational and technological services infrastructure and the expansion of universities and laboratories.
- Technological problems:
- The Israeli occupation hinders technological progress. It impedes the import of equipment and hardware, controls frequencies and prevents Palestinian ICT companies form offer 4th generation of mobile networks as well as 5G.
- Problems of impoverishment as Israel's actions lead to impoverishment of people and thus affect universities and students.

These numerous and unique problems are specific to Palestine case. e-Learning may contribute to alleviating some of these problems in Palestine, However, e-Learning requires modern and advanced learning courses and contents. Happily, this is available in OERs. In fact, OERs nowadays represent a revolution in the world of educational resources, and they are changing the educational landscape in general and providing a strong opportunity for everyone to benefit from formal and informal education. OERs can be adapted, privatized, and translated into Arabic. In addition, it can divide, compose, and modify until they are fully utilized.

The area of OERs may be a valuable opportunity to help our students, researchers, and all those seeking knowledge.

The rapid change in education systems, methods, and techniques in the global educational and training institutions, including Arab and Palestinian ones, requires the management of these institutions to keep abreast of these developments and to design plans to integrate modern technologies into their systems. Needless to say, the institution that fails to adapt to this age will be doomed to darkness or to extinction.

OERs for Palestinian researchers, students, and educational and training institutions are one of the ways to free themselves from the handicaps imposed on the Palestinian people.

References

7amleh. (2018). The Arab Center for the Advancement of Social Media. In *Connection Interrupted: Israel's Control of the Palestinian ICT Infrastructure and Its Impact on Digital Rights*. Retrieved on July 11, 2019 from, https://7amleh.org/wp-content/uploads/2019/01/Report_7amleh_English_final.pdf.

Affouneh, S., Wimpenny, K., Ghodieh, A., Alsaud, L., & Obaid, A. (2018). Reflection on MOOC design in Palestine. *The International Review of Research in Open and Distributed Learning, 19* (2), 22–36. www.irrodl.org/index.php/irrodl/article/view/3469/4610.

ALECSO. (2019). About the ALECSO OER community, OER commons. *ASKME*. Retrieved on July 14, 2019 from, www.oercommons.org/hubs/ALECSO.

Atenas, J. (2017). *Open education in Palestine: A tool for liberation*, On October 18, 2017. Retrieved on July 3, 2019 from, https://education.okfn.org/open-education-in-palestine-a-tool-for-liberation/.

CC. (2019). *OER policy registry. Creative commons*. Retrieved on July 14, 2019 from, https://oerworldmap.org/oerpolicies.

CERI. (2007). Giving knowledge for free: the emergence of open educational resources. In *Centre for Educational Research and Innovation (CERI), OECD*. Retrieved on July 14, 2019 from, www.oecd.org/edu/ceri/38654317.pdf.

EDUCAUSE. (2018). *7 things you should know about open education: policies*. August 13, 2018. Retrieved on June 29, 2019, https://library.educause.edu/resources/2018/8/7-things-you-should-know-about-open-education-policies.

Itmazi, J. (2015). The importance for adoption of open educational resources in Arab Education and Training Institutions. *Arab Journal of Information: a special Edition: ICT in education, issued by the Arab Organization for Education, Culture and Science-ALECSO, 25*. www.alecso.org/newsite/2015-04-01-12-13-13/2015-04-02-11-41-03/isdarat/233111/2015/ictineducation.html.

Itmazi, J., & Essalmi, F. (2019). Open educational resources: usage, sharing and adoption. ISBN: 978-9973-15-404-0, Published by Science and Research Department of The Arab League Education, Culture and Science Organization (ALECSO) in Tunisia. April 2019 (p. 224). Language: Arabic. Available free, http://ossl.alecso.org/doc/OER_BOOK.pdf.

Khanna, P., & Basak, P.C. (2013). An OER architecture framework: need and design. *The International Review of Research in Open and Distributed Learning, 14* (1), 65–83. https://doi.org/10.19173/irrodl.v14i1.1355.

Khlaif, Z.N., Farid, S. (2018). Transforming learning for the smart learning paradigm: lessons learned from the Palestinian initiative. *Springer Berlin Heidelberg, 5* (12). https://doi.org/10.1186/s40561-018-0059-9.

MOEHE. (2019). *Ministry of Higher Education and Scientific Research, facts and figures*. June 20, 2019, www.mohe.pna.ps/moehe/factsandfigures.

Nyland, R. (2018). The infrastructure of openness: results from a multi-institutional survey on OER platforms. *International Journal of Open Educational Resources, 1* (1). https://doi.org/10.18278/ijoer.1.1.3.

OERWORLDMAP. (2019). *OER WORLD MAP. Palestinian territories.* Retrieved on July 14, 2019 from, https://oerworldmap.org/country/ps.

Okkeh, M., & Itmazi, I. (2015). Trends in faculty use of open educational resources in higher education: a case study of Palestine Ahliya University. *Cybrarians Journal, 37,* 1–37. ISSN: 1687-2215. Arabic language (Online Version): http://journal.cybrarians.info.

OPENMED. (2017a). *The Palestine OER national Strategy Forum. Birzeit University,* 20 April 2017. Retrieved on July 14, 2019 from, https://openmedproject.eu/results/national-oer-strategy-forums/palestine.

OPENMED. (2017b). OpenMed—*Opening up Education in SouthMediterranean countries. D2.2— Strategy Forum Seminars.* May 2017. Retrieved on July 14, 2019 from, https://openmedproject.eu/wp-content/uploads/D2.2_National-Strategy-Forums.pdf.

OPENMED. (2019). *WELCOME TO OPENMED!. The OpenMed project, Erasmus + Capacity Building in Higher Education programme of the European Union.* Retrieved on July 14, 2019 from, https://openmedproject.eu.

PCPS. (2019). *The Palestinian Central Bureau of Statistics, Main Statistical Indicators in the West Bank and Gaza Strip,* 20 June 2019. www.pcbs.gov.ps/Portals/_Rainbow/StatInd/StatisticalMainIndicators_E.htm.

PNC. (2019). *Palestine National Council, Palestine People and land (palestinian-loss-of-land-1946–2010).* June 20, 2019, www.palestinepnc.org/en/news/item/14-palestine-people-and-land-palestinian-loss-of-land-1946-2010.

Shaqour, A. (2013). The philosophy of MOOCs and the feasibility of employing it in higher education institutions with respect of quality of education and freedom of use. In © *Communications of the Arab Computer Society,* vol. 6, No. 2. December 2013, ISSN 2090-102X. Arabic language.

Jamil Itmazi is Associate Professor; The dean of e-Learning and the former dean of Scientific Research at Palestine Ahliya University in Bethlehem—Palestinian. He holds Ph.D. in Computer Sciences, specifically in the development of e-Learning software, from the Granada University, Spain, 2005. Dr. Itmazi is an active researcher; He has published more than 50 papers in international journals and conferences, in addition to12 books, and numerous articles in newspapers. He has also been interviewed many times by media. His research interests include but are not limited to the following areas: e-Learning systems, Open Educational Resources (OER), Learning Management Systems, Recommendation Systems and Open-Source Systems. He also enjoys participating in a wide-range of IT-related projects.

Chapter 9
Open Educational Resources in Romania

Gabriela Grosseck, Carmen Holotescu and Diana Andone

1 Case Overview

State profile. Romania is a country located at the intersection of Central and South-eastern Europe, north of the Balkan Peninsula, on the Lower Danube, within and outside the Carpathian arch, bordering on the Black Sea. Almost all the Danube Delta is located within its territory. It shares borders with Hungary, Serbia, Ukraine, Republic of Moldova, and Bulgaria. Romania has the 9th largest territory and the 7th largest population (with 19.50 million resident population) among the European Union (EU) member states. Its capital and largest city is Bucharest with more than 2 million people.

With the fall of the Iron Curtain in 1989, Romania started a series of political and economic reforms. Thus, since December 1989, Romania has pursued a policy of strengthening relations with the West in general, more specifically with the United States and the EU. It joined the North Atlantic Treaty Organization (NATO) on March 29, 2004 and the EU on January 1, 2007. Between January–June 2019 Romania held the presidency of the Council of the European Union (https://www.romania2019.eu).

G. Grosseck (✉)
Department of Psychology, West University of Timișoara, 4 Bd Vasile Pârvan, office 233, Timișoara, România
e-mail: gabriela.grosseck@e-uvt.ro

C. Holotescu
Faculty of Engineering, "Ioan Slavici" University of Timișoara, 144 Păunescu Podeanu str, Timișoara, România
e-mail: carmenholotescu@gmail.com

D. Andone
e-learning Center, Politehnica University of Timișoara, 2 Bl. Vasile Pârvan, IV Floor, Timișoara, România
e-mail: diana.andone@cm.upt.ro

© Springer Nature Singapore Pte Ltd. 2020
R. Huang et al. (eds.), *Current State of Open Educational Resources in the "Belt and Road" Countries*, Lecture Notes in Educational Technology, https://doi.org/10.1007/978-981-15-3040-1_9

151

General Situation of Educational Development. Since the Romanian Revolution of 1989, the Romanian educational system has been in a continuous process of reform that has received mixed criticism. Romania's education system is centralized, both horizontally and vertically. All key responsibilities for education strategy, policy, and delivery are concentrated within the Ministry of National Education (www.edu.ro). The 2011 Education Law (MEN, 2011) defined the current organization and operation of the education system and it consists of the following levels: early childhood (0–6 years), primary education, including the preparatory class and grades I–IV, secondary education (V–XII/XIII classes, general, vocational, and technological), vocational education (lasting 6 months to 2 years), pre-university tertiary education, including post-secondary education. There also exists a semi-legal, informal private tutoring system used mostly during secondary school, which has prospered during the communist regime.

Higher education is aligned with the European Higher Education Area, the Bologna Agreement (Curaj et al., 2015). As a result, most bachelor's programs take 3 years to complete. However, some programs last longer—for example, some technical fields, medicine, law, and architecture. Master's programs take 2 years beyond the bachelor's degree. Master's programs are a prerequisite for admission to Ph.D. programs. Romania has a large higher education sector with 54 public universities and approximately 40 accredited private universities. Among them, "Alexandru Ioan Cuza" University of Iași, Babeș-Bolyai University of Cluj-Napoca, University of Bucharest, and West University of Timișoara have been included in the QS World University Rankings' top 800 and Shanghai Top Rankings.

Even though "the education system does not sufficiently prepare people for employment and better social integration" (EC COMM SWD (2019), 1022) there is a particular sector were Romania has a fastest-growing rate, namely—the Information and Communication Technology (ICT) sector. Romania is the leader in Europe, and sixth in the world, in terms of the number of certified ICT specialists, with density rates per 1,000 inhabitants greater than in the United States or Russia (Digital McKinsey, 2018). There are almost 100,000 specialists in the ICT sector. Approximately 5,000 of the 30,000 engineers graduating every year in Romania are trained in ICT (NIS, 2019). According to Microsoft (who acquired since 2003 the Romanian Antivirus Technology Bitdefender), Romania has a clear potential in ICT, an area in which Romanian students, researchers, and entrepreneurs excel. Its western-oriented culture and the high educational degree of its youth bring Romania forward as a huge potential market (the second largest software producer in Eastern Europe) (Eurostat, 2018). In terms of ICT outsourcing services Romania is ranked in the third place worldwide successfully challenging India.

Currently, Romania controls 5% of the offshore software development market and is the third leading country (after India and China) among software exporters (World Bank, 2018).

However, despite all the scientific achievements through time, there is a growing gap between how Romania perceives itself and how it ranks in research and innovation compared to other European countries. On the one hand, Romania is home to new cutting-edge research infrastructure projects (such as the large Extreme Light Infrastructure—Nuclear Physics infrastructure project, at Măgurele or the International

Center for Advanced Studies on River Delta Sea Systems at Tulcea, a pan-European research infrastructure dedicated to interdisciplinary studies of large-river systems), and, on the other hand, it is *a modest innovator*, as the Communication from the Commission to the European Commision (2019) notes. At the beginning of 2019, Romania still ranks on the last place among the 28 EU member states for the spending on research and development (RD), and is one of the few European countries that reduced their RD spending during the last decade. More worryingly, Romania's innovation performance has deteriorated since 2011 in every region, including the most dynamic ones.

2 Current Situation of OER

Over the last two decades the impact of technology can be seen in every field of education. More and more emerging technologies are shaping our practices, emphasizing on the idea of openness in education, Open Educational Resources (OER), Open Education Practices (OEPs), or Massive Open Online Courses (MOOCs) have already made their headlines in education.

According to Inamorato dos Santos, Punie and Mũnoz (2016), Open Education (OE) is an umbrella term which implies different understandings through time. More specifically, they refer to OE as a "mode of realizing education, often enabled by digital technologies, aiming to widen access and participation to everyone, by removing barriers and making learning accessible, abundant, and customizable for all. It offers multiple ways of teaching and learning, building and sharing knowledge, as well as a variety of access routes to formal and non-formal education, bridging them". In a nutshell, OE means access to content, courses, support, assessment, and certification in ways that are flexible and accommodate diverse needs. Barriers, as regards, for example entry or cost, are reduced or eliminated.

There are two key concepts of Open Education: *Open Educational Resources* and *Massive Open Online Courses*.

In 2002, at the "Forum on the Impact of Open Courseware for Higher Education in Developing Countries", UNESCO brought for the first time to the public attention the term of *Open Educational Resources*. The OER was defined as any teaching, learning, and research materials that are freely and openly available to be used, shared, combined, adapted, or expanded by teachers, educators, students, and independent learners, without an accompanying need to pay royalties or license fees (UNESCO, 2002). In 2019, UNESCO proposed an updated definition of OER: Open Educational Resources are teaching, learning, and research materials in any medium that may be composed of copyrightable materials released under an open license, materials not protected by copyright, materials for which copyright protection has expired, or a combination of the foregoing.

Open Educational Practices are closely related to OER and are defined as a whole "range of practices around the creation, use and management of OER with the intent to improve quality and innovate education" (OPAL, 2011). A broad perspective of the notion of "openness" can be found in Conole (2013), "covering each major phase of the education life cycle, namely, design, delivery, evaluation and research".

A decade ago, education was challenged by a new paradigm, the *Massive Open Online Courses*, which have brought innovation at all levels, aiming to respond to the most pressing learning needs, generated by the new development policies and the rapid evolution of technology.

It has already been noticed in the literature that every letter in the MOOC acronym is negotiable. Therefore, the MOOC definition embraced by the majority of scholars and researchers and adopted as an operational definition by the authors is the one proposed by the partners of three important European projects (HOME,[1] ECO project,[2] OpenupEd[3]) as: *Massive Open Online Courses* are "courses designed for large numbers of participants, that can be accessed by anyone anywhere as long as they have an internet connection, are open to everyone without entry qualifications, and offer a full/complete course experience online for free" (OpenupEd, 2015).

As we shall see later in the chapter, in Romania the paradigm of OE has been strongly promoted in the last 5 years by individuals and civil society organizations. Their proposals for action for opening up education did/does not require major legislative changes or a new "reform" but are compatible with elements of the current strategic programs. However, it is necessary to re-prioritize the construction of specific projects.

2.1 Infrastructure

With the information and communications technology (ICT) sector accounting for 6% of the Romanian GDP in 2016, the country ranks fourth among 28 European Union (EU) countries regarding these criteria, as specified by GISWatch Report (2016). There are two major hubs in Bucharest and Cluj, but important ICT investments are registered in other cities.

With a download speed of 21.8 Mbps, Romania has dropped from fifth to 37th, in a ranking of internet speeds around the world in 2019.[4] In 2018, the average download speed was 38.6 and 21.33 Mbps in 2017 (18th position).

There were 14,387,477 Internet users in December 2018, representing 73.8% of population, according to Internet World Stats.[5] This means an important increase comparing with the penetration of 62.8% in 2017 and the doubling in 6 years of the percentage of 39.2% reported in 2012.

---

[1] https://home.eadtu.eu.

[2] https://project.ecolearning.eu.

[3] https://www.openuped.eu/.

[4] Cable (2019). *Worldwide Broadband Speed League*. Retrieved from https://www.cable.co.uk/broadband/speed/worldwide-speed-league/.

[5] Internet World Stats, *Usage and Population Statistics*. Retrieved from https://www.internetworldstats.com/europa.htm.

Digital inclusion has been a high priority on the Romanian ICT and Education Ministries agenda. Developing the ICT infrastructure and internet connection for the Romanian education institutions, training teachers, developing quality online resources, and providing access to online learning spaces were the core goals of the following major programs (Holotescu, 2012):

(a) EUR200 Program was launched in 2004, and by 2011, it helped 200 thousand students from low-income families purchase computers (GISWatch, 2011).

(b) SEI Program (Sistem Educational Informatizat/IT-Based Educational System[6]): carried out during 2001–2009, the project was implemented by the Ministry of Education in partnership with Siveco (https://siveco.ro), a company specialized in e-learning, HP Romania, and IBM Romania, under the Romanian Government Strategy in the field of information and computer-aided education. It has equipped all the Romanian schools with 15,000 laboratories with 10–25 computers each, with the latest technology and with internet connection, trained teachers, and developed digital lessons. In 2012 the number of students per school computer was 4.6, better than the worldwide average value (OECD, 2015).

SEI covers the following major activities in the education sector:

- *Education*. AeL (from Advanced e-learning) is the core of the SEI program, offering support for teaching and learning, testing and evaluation, content management, and training programs for more than 140,000 teachers;
- *Communication and collaboration* on a national education portal (https://www.portal.edu.ro), forums, newsletters, training sessions, and educational initiatives.

Users and beneficiaries (almost 7 million) are situated at all levels of the education system: local, regional, and national level, being teachers, students, parents, managers, operators, policy-makers, and the general public.

(c) RoEduNet (Romanian National Research and Education Network, https://www.roedu.net): was initiated in 1993 and represents the Romania's research and education network, that connects universities, schools, research centers, and cultural institutions across the country.

(d) Knowledge Economy Project (KEP): KEP was implemented by the Ministry of Communication and Informational Society in partnership with the Ministry of Education, between 2005–2013, and was funded by the World Bank. During the project 255 rural/disadvantaged communities from 38 counties, addressing over 1,8 million people (8% of Romania's population), got internet access, and supported small business development and content creation. The schools of these communities were the beneficiaries of ICT infrastructure, training of teachers, and inclusion of new technologies in education. The project was awarded with the European Commission's Inclusion medal in 2008, in the Geographical Inclusion section.

(e) Wireless Campus: is a project funded with European funds in July 2019, through which 4,500 secondary schools will be provided with wireless equipment, and in (at least) 2,000 educational institutions will be created the technical infrastructure

---

[6]IT Based Educational System ("SEI"), https://portal.edu.ro/index.php/articles/c11/en.

necessary to use OER and Web 2.0 in education. The total value of the signed contract is 45 million euros, and the implementation period is of 3 years, during which over one million students and teachers are estimated to benefit from the project results. The objectives of this project are within those of the European Agenda "Communication on Opening Up Education", adopted by the European Commission in 2013, involving all stakeholders, from educational institutions, decision-makers, teachers, schools, parents, and children, through a series of concrete actions within four pillars: learning environments and open educational resources, connectivity and concerted actions to take advantage of the opportunities of the digital revolution in education and training.
(f) IT system for educational management[7]: was launched on September 10, 2019 and will be implemented in three years, for increasing the performance of compulsory education by reducing absenteeism, violence and school dropout, being integrated with the Electronic Catalog systems. It will be used by the management of schools, by teachers, by pupils, but also by parents, creating, at the same time, accountability on all the parties involved through the access to all information regarding evaluation and truancy.
(g) Digital platform for OER—Virtual Library: was launched in the same day with the previous one, being financed using European funds, the total value being nearly 100 million euro. With an implementation length of 2 years, the digital platform with host open educational resources, mainly for the gymnasium cycle of education. For an efficient use of this instrument in the classroom, the project implies also the equipping of 5,400 schools with multimedia kits and the training of 4,000 teachers.

At the Central and Eastern Europe Innovation Roundtable event (21 January 2019), organized in Warsaw, the Secretary of the State with the Ministry of Communications and Information Society (MCSI) said that "the development of the ICT sector is one of the Romanian government's priorities",[8] the focus being placed on the implementation of 5G technologies, cloud services, Internet of Things (IoT), and Artificial Intelligence (AI). Moreover, in the context of Romania's Presidency of the Council of the EU, the Digital Assembly 2019[9] was organized in partnership with the European Commission and MCSI (Ministry of Communication and Information Society), in June 2019, in Bucharest. The event brought together high-level representatives and stakeholders from EU member states, who discussed European digital policies and the implications of the latest technological developments.

---

[7]Agerpres (2019). *Financing contracts for projects regarding electronic catalogue and virtual library*, Retrieved from https://www.agerpres.ro/english/2019/09/10/financing-contracts-for-projects-regarding-electronic-catalogue-and-virtual-library-signed-at-gov-t--367212.

[8]News release MCSI (23 January 2019). *Participarea secretarului de stat Ionuţ–Valeriu Andrei la Central and Eastern Europe Innovation Roundtable*, Retrieved from https://www.comunicatii.gov.ro/participarea-secretarului-de-stat-ionut-valeriu-andrei-la-central-and-eastern-europe-innovation-roundtable/.

[9]Digital Assembly, https://ec.europa.eu/digital-single-market/en/events/digital-assembly-2019.

2.2 Policy

The most important initiatives for policies at national level are mentioned below (Holotescu, 2012; Holotescu and Grosseck, 2018):

- The first proposals at government level related to OER, Web 2.0, collaborative platforms for learning were formulated in a report of the Knowledge based Economy Project (KEP) (Holotescu, 2007); since then, only a few were adopted in official documents.
- The National Strategy on Digital Agenda for Romania 2020 (February 2015) considers the usage of OER and Web 2.0 informal and lifelong learning education as strategic lines of development for ICT in education.[10]
- In the spirit of this agenda, the government program published in 2017 has mentioned the implementation of an e-learning platform and online repositories. In November that year, a project to implement online directories for OER was launched at the level of the counties inspectorates, but the products miss a coordination and quality criteria.[11] However, the Ministry's note does not even offer a standard approach or a guide with criteria for evaluating the materials proposed to be included in the network, which meant for many inspectorates an additional difficulty. As such, there were major differences in how these institutions understood to comply with the new obligation outlined. At the end of 2018, almost all County School Inspectorates (40 out of the 42) had OER sections on their official websites and have implemented procedures to collect and publish OER from teachers (over 5000 resources were submitted by more than 2000 teachers).
- Under the CRED project (CRED: Relevant Curriculum, Open Education for all, https://educred.ro, 2017–2021), the most ambitious project of MEN in the past 10 years, with European funds (see details later), the MEN will deliver training on digital skills and Open Educational Resources for 55,000 teachers, in addition to creating at least 7,200 new OER.
- Since the autumn of 2014, digital textbooks for pre-university education are freely available for download from a section of the Ministry of Education site (https://manuale.edu.ro) (European Commision, 2016). However, the e-books are not published under open licenses and do not use open formats. One very good aspect is that for the first-time pupils with hearing disabilities have digital textbooks tailored to their needs. Also, there are digital textbooks for 26 disciplines in 9 languages of national minorities. The textbooks law was adopted in the spring of 2019, specifying that the digital textbooks become OER.[12]
- *The Educated Romania* (2016–2019) is a project of the Romanian Presidency, conducting a broad public debate on education and research for a set of policies,

---

[10]Digital Agenda for Romania 2014–2020, https://www.comunicatii.gov.ro/agenda-digitala-pentru-romania-2020/.

[11]Nota MEN (2017 4 November). *Rețele de resurse educationale deschise, înființate la nivelul inspectoratelor școlare județene*, Retrieved from .

[12]Senatul României (22 October 2018). *Propunere legislative. Legea manualui școlar*, https://www.senat.ro/Legis/Lista.aspx?cod=21761.

for resettling Romanian society around values and the development of a culture of success based on performance, merit, work, and professionalism (https://www.romaniaeducata.eu).

- In the recent strategic action plan for education, *Education unites us* (2019–2030), the Ministry of Education states a series of measures to reform the education system, among the priorities being the de-bureaucratization and digitalization of the public education service (see for more details https://www.edu.ro/planul-de-ac%C8%9Biune-pentru-educa%C8%9Bie-2019-2030).

2.3   Open License

The Romanian Law on Copyright and Neighboring Rights 8/1996 was adopted in March 1996, being further modified several times, last time in 2019, mainly to adapt it to the EU Acquis Communautaire.[13] The law specifies the attributes of the Romanian Copyright Office (ORDA), established in 1997 (https://www.orda.ro).

The Article 35 of the Romanian Law on Copyright and Neighboring Rights specifies that the educational uses of (some parts of) a work already disclosed to the public are permitted without the author's consent and without payment of remuneration, being mandatory to mention the source and the author's name if it appears on the work used[14]:

- The use of isolated articles or brief excerpts from works in publications, television or radio broadcasts or sound or audiovisual recordings exclusively intended for teaching purposes and also the reproduction for teaching purposes, within the framework of public education or social welfare institutions, of isolated articles or brief extracts from works, to the extent justified by the intended purpose;
- The representation and execution of a work as part of the activities of educational institutions, exclusively for specific purposes and on condition that both the representation or execution and the public's access are free of charge.

Romania is also a member of the Berne Convention for the Protection of Literary and Artistic Works.

On September 2, 2008, the Creative Commons Romania version was launched with the help of ApTI—The Association for Technology and Internet.[15] This launch followed a period of prior work with iCommons, the entity that manages these

---

[13]Legea nr. 8/1996 privind dreptul de autor si drepturile conexe, https://www.euroavocatura.ro/print2.php?print2=lege&idItem=1367.

[14]Romanian Law on Copyright and Neighboring Rights (No. 8 of March 14, 1996), https://www.legi-internet.ro/en/copyright.htm.

[15]Creative Commons Romania, https://creativecommons.org/licenses/by-sa/3.0/ro/.https://wiki.creativecommons.org/Romania.

licenses internationally, which involved the translation of licenses and their adaptation to the Romanian legal framework, a consultation period public, and finally the availability of these licenses in the country.

2.4 Curriculum and Teaching Methodology

According to EC (2017 and 2018) Romania is reforming its primary and secondary curriculum for the first time in almost two decades. In a nutshell here are some highlights drawn out from these documents:

- Plans are underway to train teachers to teach the modernized curriculum. According to the Federation of Education Unions, Romania is the only country in the EU in which unqualified teachers are officially part of the education system—there were 4,500 such teachers in 2017.
- Underachievement in basic skills (digital included) remains one of the highest in the EU. This is due to educational factors and equity challenges. According to OECD (2018), PISA (2018), today 40% of Romanian 15-year-olds still lack the foundation skills needed for lifelong learning and productive employment.
- Access to quality mainstream education is particularly a challenge for students in rural areas and for Roma.
- Funding for education is very low. Romania spends the lowest amount on education in the EU at EUR 248 per capita, compared to an EU average of EUR 1,400, which can be seen as a reflection in the funding which in turn creates a new teacher shortage. Furthermore, teachers in Romania on average earn around EUR 300 per month, which is 10 times less than some of their European counterparts.
- Early school leaving risks remain high, with consequences for the labor market and for economic growth. According to EC (2018a; b) Romania still has among the highest dropout rates in the EU in both primary and lower secondary education. The dropout rate at both levels has increased in the past decade.
- The labor market relevance of higher education is improving, but tertiary educational attainment is the lowest in the EU. Also, there is an urgent need to adopt measures addressing quality and labor market relevance.
- Efforts to introduce dual vocational education and training are underway. Dual VET was launched in 2017 and it is organized at the initiative of interested companies, based on a partnership contract between schools and employers and individual training contracts for students.
- Roma inclusion in education remains a major challenge.
- Adult participation in learning remains low, despite the need for up-skilling.
- Practically, in Romania, at this moment we cannot talk about a consolidated curriculum for the development and exploitation of OER.

Therefore, efforts exist in the work of practitioners in the country, but as we have seen, it has only recently become a necessity to coagulate efforts by establishing the Open Educational Resources Coalition.

However, there is a major preoccupation at the level of the Ministry of Education to introduce OER in the curriculum. In this respect, between 2017–2021, the Ministry of Education runs the "CRED: Relevant Curriculum, Open Education for all" project, financed by the ESF, to support the ongoing curricular reform, with a total budget of EUR 42 million.

The aim of the project is to facilitate the understanding of the new competence-based student-centered curriculum and to modernize teaching practices. The main objectives of the project are to review the curriculum for primary and secondary education and to create open educational resources.

According to DESI, in 2018 Romania ranks last out of the EU-28. Overall, the progress of the country from last year was slow and Romania did not manage to catch up. In most of the DESI dimensions, the digitization of the economy, including digital public services and the digital skills in the population is low. Digitalization is a key challenge if Romanian innovation and competitiveness are to improve.

The findings of a recent nationwide study (Syene, 2018) suggest that a wider training process for teachers for using technology in education would be needed—at least 75% of the respondents noted that teachers are not prepared to use technology in the educational process. Both parents and teachers consider that "the most important entity" that should deal with the integration of new technologies in the classroom is "the Ministry of National Education, through coherent policies and decisions and funding programs". Therefore, through the CRED project, almost 55,000 teachers and 2,500 students will be trained in how to teach the new curriculum and how to adapt teaching and learning processes to the specific needs of students, including students at risk of dropping out. Also, 18 methodological guides on curricular areas will be elaborated to cover all the disciplines foreseen in the new framework plans for primary and secondary education, respectively, 7,200 open educational resources for all disciplines, which are equally accessible to students and teachers from OER centers, but also on an online e-learning platform.

According to MEN, CRED is necessary for the Romanian education system, as a new curriculum was approved for both primary and secondary education, the latter being under implementation. The project achieves all the necessary elements for training for a quality Open Education.

It is clear that we are dealing with a large-scale educational project, maybe the most important MEN project after 1989, with a huge stake: the chance, even the obligation to change the face of the Romanian education in four years by modernizing the teaching methods and the alignment of the education system in our country to those in the other EU states and beyond.

2.5 Outcomes

This section presents projects and initiatives related to OER and MOOCs at regional and institutional levels. As mentioned under the Policy section, a national OER repository is not implemented yet, only collections of OER on the websites of the counties inspectorates. Repositories are expected to be implemented by the CRED project and MEN (Virtual Library) until 2021.

There are several directories and projects for open resources maintained by online communities or private companies, most of them providing open access to digital resources for the pre-university level, and several without clearly specifying open licenses. Some of them are: educational forum of MEN (https://forum.portal.edu.ro), the community of pre-university teachers and the largest portal of educational resources (https://didactic.ro), online community developing good practices facilitated by the project CRED (https://creatorideeducatie.ro), portal of OER created by teachers, a project supported by the Institution of Educational Sciences (https://digitaledu.ro), educational online community of the Mureș County (https://educatie.inmures.ro), online community addressed to primary education sector (https://kidibot.ro), digital education program funded by Orange (https://digitaliada.ro), education through technology portal (https://dacobots.com), platform for publishing educational digital textbooks (https://livresq.com), community for Mathematics contests (https://infoarena.ro), and digital resources projects funded by Vodafone (https://www.scoaladinvaliza.ro and https://civiclabs.ro).

Open educational journals are published on websites such as iTeach platform (https://iteach.ro/experientedidactice), e-learning Romania platform (https://www.elearning.ro), or New Projects (https://revista.newprojects.org).

There are strong communities and events for open source, open access, open data, and open licenses projects.

Also, many projects such as Knowledge based Economy Project (KEP), Moodle Romania, iTeach, ActiveWatch, and CivicLabs[16] have offered training and courses related to open educational pedagogies and media education for teachers in the pre-university system, while DIDATEC trained university teachers for blended learning.[17]

In the following we mention several ongoing institutional and inter-institutional MOOC initiatives developed in the Romanian space, at different educational level and by different educational actors (Holotescu, Andone, and Grosseck, 2016; Holotescu, 2017):

(a) Platforms and MOOCs implemented by academic institutions:

- *UniCampus* (https://unicampus.ro). Started in April 2014 by University Politehnica Timisoara, Unicampus offers MOOCs on a version of Moodle platform based on cMOOCs methodology (Vasiu and Andone, 2014).
- *NOVAMOOC* (https://novamooc.uvt.ro) is a project for development and innovative implementation of MOOCs in Higher Education, run by West University of Timisoara (WUT) during 2015–2017. There were developed

---

[16]Training programs for teachers, https://civiclabs.ro/ro/byproducts/exemple-de-programe-de-formare-a-cadrelor-didactice-din-romania.

[17]Due to the lack of space, for a detailed classification of projects, initiatives and resources related to OER, please refer to the report of the second author in the POERUP project, which presents a map of all the resources available in Romania at this moment.

the MOOCs: Practicing English with Technology, Teaching with OER, Fake news, and Digital storytelling (https://west-university-timisoara.teachable.com).

- *UniBuc Virtual* (https://www.unibuc-virtual.net) by Credis (Department of Distance Learning from Bucharest University) developed and ran three MOOCs for teachers training on a Google Apps-based platform.
- "Critical Thinking MOOC" was developed and ran in 2014 by the Maastricht School of Management Romania on Iversity (https://iversity.org/en/courses/critical-thinking-for-business).
- University "Babes-Bolyai" Cluj-Napoca developed in the eLIADA project materials for four MOOCs (https://eliada.granturi.ubbcluj.ro).

(b) Platforms and MOOCs implemented by *companies and NGOs*:

- *MOOC.ro* (https://mooc.ro) developed by Moodle.ro. Currently, offers two MOOCs about Moodle and Articulate.
- *eStudent* (https://estudent.ro) is a platform that offers MOOCs on psychology, communication, business, geography, and Romanian language. It was developed by APIO (Association of Industrial and Organizational Psychology), CTRL-D (an association created for designers, developers, communication, and advertising people) and university teachers/experts.
- *Startarium* (https://startarium.ro) is a platform nurturing an entrepreneurship ecosystem. It gathers a group of organizations and experts that offer MOOCs, mentoring and crowdfunding around 8,000 potential entrepreneurs, who design and develop their start-up plans using the platform features.
- *Cursera* (https://cursera.ro) developed MOOCs by medical universities, organizations, and hospitals.
- *MOOCs on Udemy*: NGO Management, Association Young Initiative (https://udemy.com/management-ong).
- *MOOC in medical education* offered by Romanian Angel Appeal Foundation (https://raa.ro).

(c) MOOC presence in formal education:

- *MOOC integration in blended academic courses*. Politehnica University of Timisoara was a pioneer by integrating MOOCs in the following courses: "Web Programming" (Holotescu, Grosseck, Cretu, and Naaji, 2014), "Instructional Technologies" (Vasiu and Andone, 2014) and "Embedded Systems" (Bogdan, 2017). There are also such initiatives at "Ioan Slavici" University of Timisoara for the Multimedia, OOP, and Blockchain courses and at West University of Timisoara for "Digital storytelling course", a transversal discipline for all second-year bachelor students, regarding their specializations.
- *Credit (marks) recognition for students' participation in* MOOCs. It involves the students' activity in different projects for some courses at the three universities above.

- *MOOC accreditation* at the Politehnica University of Timisoara: "Digital Marketing" offered by Google (https://atelieruldigital.jaromania.org).
- *Teacher continuing professional development* using MOOCs at "Ioan Slavici" University of Timisoara: participation in MOOCs related to OE, but also to the topics of the taught courses and research.
- *Virtual mobility project*: A summer-day's MOOC, partners Business Faculty, University Babes-Bolyai, Cluj-Napoca Romania, Georgia, and the Netherlands.

(d) Scientific events related to open education:

- Workshops and national conferences organized by the Romanian Coalition for OER.
- Workshops organized by the Politehnica University of Timisoara during the Open Education Week (https://elearning.upt.ro).
- Since 2014, the International Conference "eLSE—e-learning and Software for Education Conference" has a section dedicated to OER and MOOCs, co-chaired by the authors (https://elseconference.eu).
- SMART Conference, coorganized by the authors since 2013, has a special focus on open education (https://academia.edusoft.ro/category/conferences).
- The International "New Trends and Perspectives in Open Education" conference was the first event organized by a higher education institution on Open Education topics (https://novamooc.uvt.ro/?page_id=445).

The projects related to OER and MOOCs represent an important achievement, but to reach the objectives of OE (quality, innovation, and equal access to education), there is the need for better coordination of teacher training projects, resource generation and encouragement of resource reuse, and it is equally useful to attract more actors into the process of producing and reusing content.

2.6 Stakeholders

This section presents the most important institutions and organizations supporting open education initiatives and projects in the country.

Ministry of National Education (Ministerul Educației Naționale, MEN, https://www.edu.ro), along with its strategic partners—Institute of Educational Sciences (ISE, https://www.ise.ro), Teaching Houses and School Inspectorates. As mentioned in the chapter, starting with 2017, MEN has taken concrete steps toward opening up education, stimulating the creation and publication of OER, and reforming the system of designing and acquiring textbooks. In the last national debate on March 5, 2019, "Open Education for the Future: Challenges in the Digital Age", the current Minister of Education, Ecaterina Andronescu, said that the new National Education Law, currently being drafted, has to include as many concrete provisions as possible in order to develop relevant competences, skills and attitudes in the context of digital transformation.

The Ministry of Research and Innovation (Ministerul Cercetării şi Inovării, MCI, https://www.research.gov.ro) is the public body responsible for organizing and coordinating the Romanian RDI system. MCI is also responsible for the development and adoption of the Open Access (OA) national strategy to transpose the developed OA rules into future funding programs for research, mapping of institutional OA practices and policies in Romania. In its efforts to do so, the Ministry benefits from the support of UEFISCDI (the Executive Agency for Higher Education, Research, Development and Innovation Funding, https://uefiscdi.ro), and of two other non-governmental organizations: Center for Public Innovation and Kosson. Its activity is guided by the National RDI Strategy 2014–2020, implemented according to the RDI National Plan 2015–2020.

The **Romanian Coalition for OER** (Coalitia pentru Resurse Educaţionale Deschise România) was launched in October 2013, gathering persons and organizations that support and promote the concepts of open access and OER.[18] The main categories of actions/activities the Coalition carries out are: advocacy and public statements, open content creation, training, sharing best practices, information campaigns, and awareness of the role of open educational resources in various fields. Therefore, the coalition has published guides,[19] has organized different awareness events such as workshops and five National Conferences for Open Education, and formulated concrete OE-related proposals for the government.

The Centre for Public Innovation (Centrul pentru Inovare Publică, CPI, https://www.inovarepublica.ro/) established in 2014 has a mission to build the open society in Romania. As a coordinator of the OER Coalition, CPI has played a substantial role in introducing the concept of OER and open education on the public agenda in Romania. For e.g., in 2016 they successfully managed to include the open education in the Romanian Open Government Partnership Action Plan.[20]

Association for Technology and Internet (ApTI) and Creative Commons Romania. ApTI (https://www.apti.ro) is an independent non-governmental organization (NGO) aiming to support and promote a free and open Internet, where human rights in the digital space are guaranteed and protected. They also contribute on improving digital policies and practices. In relation to OER, ApTI plays a crucial role in providing digital education for Internet users and professional groups. Thus, they were actively involved in carrying out OER-related training for librarians and higher education staff which include awareness campaigns and practical hands-on workshops on open licenses and open educational resources.

---

[18]The Coalition has a solid and active presence on social media (see the Facebook group, https://www.facebook.com/groups/REDRomania/).

[19]For e.g. the COE wrote up the first report on Open Education in the Pre-university Education System in Romania, which was the third in the Open Society Reports series.

[20]CPI is currently holding the secretariat of the Open Data Coalition, a civil society platform advocating for open data and open government in Romania, https://ogp.gov.ro/wp-content/uploads/2018/11/Romania-2018-2020_NAP_EN.pdf.

ApTI has been also involved in the process of translating the Creative Commons licenses in Romanian, adapting them to the Romanian legislation as well as in the promotion of open licenses in Romania.

ApTI is a member of European Digital Rights (EDRI), ICANN's European Regional At-Large Organization (EURALO), and Civil Society Information Society Advisory Council (CSISAC).

2.7 Impact

The number of Open Education and OER initiatives is not so large, but one can note the diversity of projects and of the involved organizations. We appreciate that Romania is active in the OER movement on the following axes/directions:

- Trainings/Courses related to Open Educational Resources and Practices organized for both pre-university and university sectors;
- Proposals at governmental level related to OER—but not yet informal policies; the CRED project, in which one of the partners is MEN, aims to introduce OER in the curriculum;
- National events related to open resources produced by pre-university teachers; national guides (in Romanian language) were published too;
- Directories with open resources (more numerous for pre-university level);
- Projects for MOOCs development and integration at university level and for continuing education;
- Strong communities/events for open source, open access, open data, open culture, open science, and open licenses.

The *drivers* for developing Open Education projects are:

- Researchers and teaching staff, seldom the policy-makers, and managers of the institutions;
- Companies and associations.

The *main barriers* in the Open Education development and adoption could be considered:

- Rigid policies informal education related to curricular systems and assessment practices;
- The lack of possibility to officially accredit online courses, despite an impressive number of projects related to online courses over the last 18 years, and of the policy proposals coming from different organizations (such courses can only be used in a blended approach informal education);
- The lack of OE/OER/MOOCs—related strategies at the national level informal and continuing education;
- Teachers' lack of time and interest to explore, understand, evaluate and use new technologies, OER and MOOCs in the teaching–learning process, despite the projects producing OER in editable formats and with open licenses;

- A slight reluctance to allow students to become creators of open educational resources themselves, even at a declarative level teachers admit that students could also contribute to OER platforms; the idea of a prosumer, both a consumer and a creator of OER, is still seldom applied in the Romanian educational environment;
- A reduced number of training programs for adopting OEPs;
- Lack of incentives, official recognition, and promotion for teachers implementing open educational practices.

The Romanian achievements related to Open Education were also summarized in the EU OpenEdu study of Inamorato dos Santos, Nascimbeni, Bacsich, Atenas, Aceto, Burgos and Punie (2017). Moreover, a recent report found that Romania is the 4th most productive country in OER-related studies, while the authors of this chapter are ranked as top researchers worldwide (Wang, Liu, Li and Gao, 2017).

3 Discussion and Conclusion

3.1 Discussions on Open Education-Related Strategy in Romania

To foster the inclusion of Open Education, OER, and MOOCs in the Romanian educational system, a set of recommendations is proposed below.

The first of them are quoted and updated from the report (Holotescu, 2007) and have not been fully implemented, while some of them are new and original, as derived from our experience (Holotescu et al., 2014; Bogdan, Holotescu, Andone and Grosseck, 2017). Others are quoted and adapted from recent reports of the projects POERUP (POERUP, 2014), OpenEdu (Castaño Muñoz, Punie and Inamorato dos Santos, 2016; Inamorato dos Santos et al., 2016), OpenCred (Witthaus, Inamorato dos Santos, Childs, Tannhauser, Conole, Nkuyubwatsi and Punie, 2016), from recent studies (Patru and Balaji, 2016; Jansen and Konings, 2017; Grech and Camilleri, 2017), from UNESCO Recommendations (2019) and from OER Congress documents (OER AP, 2017). The last was endorsed by ministers and their designated representatives of 20 countries, Romania included.

The recommendations are organized on three levels (Table 1): for policy-makers at national levels, for institutions, and for teachers themselves, because real changes appear from grassroots level.

According to COL (2017), the lack of national policies can limit OE adoption and discourage institutions from engaging in OE activities. The regional consultation in Europe shows the need that OE take the form of a bottom-up movement, focusing at the institutional level, and that national efforts be coordinated through a strategic policy initiative to complement the bottom-up approach.

Table 1 Recommendations for opening up education in Romania

For policy-makers

- The already existing publicly funded educational content should be used more intensively by teachers and students: connections with curricula, the skills they develop should be clearer; encourage and support the sharing of best practices; should be also licensed under CC
- The creation of a repository under CC licenses with the educational projects in which Romanian schools, universities, and educational organizations have participated
- Establish a partnership of the Ministry of Education with publishers, broadcasters, libraries, and cultural institutions to provide open access to their own resources
- Encourage a competitive market to produce educational resources, ensure transparency of supply, and equal opportunities to market actors, based on a set of quality criteria, containing pedagogic, design, accessibility, and openness principles
- Implement an online platform for collaborative production of OER/MOOCs by institutions, teachers, and students, based on open collaborative technologies, presenting open scenarios for learning (Holotescu, 2007)

- Any public outputs from the EC programs (specifically including Erasmus for all) should be made available as open resources under an appropriate license
- Budgets for digital education should include money for developing and maintaining OER/MOOCs
- OER should be allowed on approved materials lists
- Quality agencies in ENQA (the European Association for Quality Assurance in Higher Education) should improve their understanding of new modes of learning (including online distance, OER, and MOOCs) and their impact on quality assurance and recognition
- Encourage Europe-wide validation of the knowledge and competencies developed through online study and informal learning, including but not restricted to OER and MOOCs (POERUP, 2014)

- Promote the use of MOOCs for re-skilling and up-skilling both unemployed people and workers, especially those without employer support to training activities; this would help to reduce the unemployment rate
- Promote digital competence development in both formal education and professional development activities. This could lead to a higher participation rate of individuals in an open education context and, indirectly, to reduced training costs and a greater flexibility in education (Castaño Muñoz et al., 2016)

- Foster dialogue and collaboration between actors in HEI internationalization, student mobility and the validation of non-formal and informal learning (Witthaus et al., 2016)

- The government should support and scale up multi-stakeholder partnerships for efficiency reasons, but also for the benefit of society as a whole (Jansen & Konings, 2017)

- Besides open-licensing policies, the government could support the creation of regional or national centers to finance and promote MOOCs and allied activities (Patru & Balaji, 2016)

- Strategic public–private partnerships are needed in order to fully exploit blockchain in (open) education. The implementations of blockchain technology for education are in initial stages, several organizations are in the initial stages of pilot-testing award of certificates using a blockchain, while others are accepting blockchain-based cryptocurrency payments. The potential of the blockchain in areas such as the issuing of certificates, verification of accreditation pathways, lifelong learning passports, intellectual property management, and data management should be further investigated (Grech and Camilleri, 2017)

(continued)

Table 1 (continued)

For policy-makers

- Sustained investment and educational actions by governments and other key education stakeholders are needed in order to achieve SDG4, in the creation, curation, regular updating, ensuring inclusive and equitable access, and effective use of high-quality materials and programs of study
- Encourage regional and global collaboration and advocacy in the creation, access, use, adaptation
- Redistribution and evaluation of OER can enable governments to optimize their own investments in educational content creation, as well as ICT infrastructure and curation, in ways that will enable them to meet their defined national educational policy priorities more cost-effectively and sustainably (UNESCO, 2019)

For educational institutions

- All teacher training programs should include topics related to OER, MOOCs, open licenses and social media/Web 2.0/collaborative/free tools to create educational materials in a collaborative manner
- Developing open-literacy both for the academic and administrative staff
- Facilitate the sustainable implementation of OER/MOOCs by creating incentives for use and reuse, and funding technical infrastructure to increase access to OER/MOOCs (Holotescu, 2007)

- MOOCs could be adopted for individuals already trained in the efficient use of ICT and online learning; institutions should determine and increase the digital readiness of both teachers and students
- Policies for MOOCs accreditation should be adopted, applied for students, but also for recognition of the teachers' continuous development and for career advancement opportunities (Bogdan et al., 2017)

- Establish strong and ongoing collaborations between schools, universities, and other educational stakeholders involving OER/MOOC projects
- Accessibility should be a priority for all OER/MOOCs, including disability accessibility standards (POERUP, 2014)

- Have a holistic strategy for opening up education that encompasses the 10 dimensions of the OpenEdu framework, making the open education strategy part of the overall institutional strategy
- Explore new practices and welcome changes
- Revise the practices at all levels: mission statement and vision, current organizational management structures and day-to-day policies, and the institution's role in the community and globally (Inamorato dos Santos et al., 2016)

- Validate open learning by offering credentials for MOOCs and free and open online courses
- Provide flexible options for "free elective courses" or "self-study courses" in the curricula, including open learning for study progression
- Join European consortia related to MOOCs and build partnerships with HEIs/employment bodies (Witthaus et al., 2016)

- Build the capacity of users to find, reuse, create and share OER/MOOCs
- Empower educators and learners to develop quality, gender-sensitive, culturally, and linguistically relevant OER/MOOCs appropriate to local cultures and to create local language OER/MOOCs
- Ensure inclusive and equitable access to quality OER/MOOCs (OER AP, 2017)

(continued)

Table 1 (continued)

For policy-makers
• It is important to acknowledge the need for capacity-building among academic institutions in the management of MOOCs and to develop a system of recognition and incentives for the faculty
• The design, development, and delivery of MOOCs can be expensive for an institution; thus, continuous evaluation, reuse, or adaptation of existing or available MOOCs is an important aspect to take into consideration (Patru and Balaji, 2016)
• Adopt different business models in order to develop new projects and to sustain them after the initial funding comes to an end, such as: grants, donations, community-based production, cooperative production consortium, institutional subscriptions, personalized programs/certificates, or corporate training (Grosseck and Holotescu, 2015)

For teachers
• New skills and tasks are required for teachers facilitating blended courses that integrate OER/MOOCs: complex course design and management, OER and MOOCs curation, evaluation of the distributed and collaborative activities of students, facilitation of the local learning community and nurture of its integration in the global communities of MOOCs and many more
• Teachers should be active in communities of practice and attend MOOCs too on topics they themselves teach and also on topics related to new educational technologies and pedagogies. Under these circumstances, each teacher could become a life-long and informed learner
• Teachers should assist and guide students to assess their own learning needs for choosing the OER/MOOCs to use/in which to participate in order to deepen the course topics and for continuing learning (Holotescu et al., 2014)
• Teachers need digital skills to curate MOOCs, to assess MOOC quality and to use learning analytics (Bogdan et al., 2017)

3.2 Conclusions

As a conclusion, at present, there are many OER initiatives in Romania at all educational levels, which are a real gain for teachers and learners, tailoring education as a real engine for change.

Romania does not have a national strategy on open education, only separate measures implemented without a strong consistency. The only national, but insufficient benchmarks on this issue, are contained in the National Strategy on the Digital Agenda for Romania 2020 and in the two National Action Plans (NAP) for 2016–2018 and 2018–2020 of the Open Government Partnership. The NAP 2018–2020 brings a new thing, namely, that the MEN must organize training sessions for teachers to promote open educational resources and inform about copyright. Such a measure is welcome, especially as it is explicitly correlated with the CRED Project.

Therefore, a national strategy for open education is needed, to include both the development of a framework of professional digital competences for teachers, as well as the development of a national initiative on the use of Open Educational Resources. This document must be developed not only in conjunction with the National Education Act, but also with the Digital Agenda of the European Union, the Digital Education Action Plan and other relevant European Commission instruments such as Digital Competence for Citizens (DigComp), for teachers (DigCompEdu) and educational institutions (DigEduOrg).

An example of coherent strategy is "Opening up Slovenia" (https://www.ouslovenia.net), which has built legal mechanisms for implementing open education and for carrying out concrete, cross-dimensional OE projects, consisting in policy actions, capacity-building, services and content, research and development, and supportive environments. Another strategic path can be taken by learning from the experience of the Polish Coalition for Open Education (Śliwowski and Grodecka, 2013).

As specified by the Capetown Open Education Declaration (2017), the Open Education should relate to other open movements and should place the next generation at its core (Capetown, 2017). Also, in order to implement SDG4, "education institutions and programs should be adequately and equitably resourced, books other learning materials, open educational resources and technology that are non-discriminatory, learning conducive, learner friendly, context specific, cost effective and available to all learners – children, youth and adults" (UNESCO, 2019).

The recent Romanian initiatives, the proposal for educational policies made by several educational NGOs[21] and the CRED project, together with the Romanian Coalition for OER could play an important role in shaping the policy of openness. We also believe that the involvement of each teacher is important for mainstreaming Open Education. Also, more focus is needed on information and awareness campaigns targeted at decision-makers, educators, parents as well as pupils and students (Pavel, Manolea, Bucur, Voicu and Constantinescu, 2014).

We hope this work, with an overview of OER and OE, with recommendations on three axes, will be a useful reference for further discussions within and between different institutions and policy-makers in charge of educational policies in the country and worldwide.

References

Bogdan, R. (2017). Integrating MOOCs in embedded systems blended courses. *BRAIN. Broad Research in Artificial Intelligence and Neuroscience, 8*(3), 101–107.

Bogdan, R., Holotescu, C., Andone, D., and Grosseck, G. (2017). How MOOCs are being used for corporate training? *The 13th International Conference eLSE, Bucharest.* Retrieved April 27–28, 2017, from https://www.researchgate.net/publication/316076362_HOW_MOOCS_ARE_BEING_USED_FOR_CORPORATE_TRAINING.

Capetown (2017). The Cape Town Open Education Declaration. Retrieved from https://www.capetowndeclaration.org/read-the-declaration.

Castaño Muñoz, J., Punie, Y., and Inamorato dos Santos, A. (2016). MOOCs in Europe: evidence from pilot surveys with universities and MOOC learners. *JRC policy brief.* Retrieved from https://ec.europa.eu/jrc/sites/jrcsh/files/JRC%20brief%20MOOCs_JRC101956.pdf.

---

[21]SYENE (4 June 2019). Digitalizarea sistemului educaţonal—propuneri de politici publice, Retrieved from https://syene.ro/2019/06/04/digitalizarea-sistemului-educational-propunere-de-politici-publice/.

Centrul pentru Politici Educaționale (2018). Retrieved from https://cpedu.ro/.

COL (2017). *Open Educational Resources: Global Report 2017*. Burnaby: Commonwealth of Learning. Retrieved from https://oasis.col.org/handle/11599/2788.

Conole, G. (2013). *Designing for learning in an open world*. Berlin: Springer.

Curaj, A., Deca, L., Egron-Polak, E., and Salmi, J. (Eds.). (2015). *Higher Education Reform in Romania. Between the Bologna Process and National Challenges*, Springer.

Digital McKinsey (2018). *The rise of Digital Challengers How digitization can become the next growth engine for Central and Eastern Europe. Perspective on Romania*. Retrieved from https://digitalchallengers.mckinsey.com/files/Rise-of-Digital-Challengers_Perspective-on-Romania.pdf.

European Commision (2018a). *Digital Economy and Society Index (DESI). Country Report Romania*. Retrieved from https://ec.europa.eu/information_society/newsroom/image/document/2018-20/ro-desi_2018-country-profile_eng_199394CB-B93B-4B85-C789C5D6A54B83FC_52230.pdf.

European Commission (2018b). *Science, research and innovation performance of the EU 2018 strengthening the foundations for Europe's future*. Retrieved from https://publications.europa.eu/en/publication-detail/-/publication/16907d0f-1d05-11e8-ac73-01aa75ed71a1/.

European Commission (2016). *Education and training monitor 2016—Romania. European commission report*. Retrieved from https://ec.europa.eu/education/sites/education/files/monitor2016-ro_en.pdf.

European Commission (2017). *Education and training monitor. Romania 2017*. Retrieved from https://ec.europa.eu/education/sites/education/files/monitor2017-ro_en.pdf.

European Commision (27.2.2019). *Commission staff working document—Country report romania 2019 including an in-depth review on the prevention and correction of macroeconomic imbalances*. Retrieved from https://ec.europa.eu/info/sites/info/files/file_import/2019-european-semester-country-report-romania_en.pdf.

European Commission (Brussels, 27.2.2019). SWD (2019). 1022 final. *Country report Romania 2019 including an in-depth review on the prevention and correction of macroeconomic imbalances*. Retrieved from https://ec.europa.eu/info/sites/info/files/file_import/2019-european-semester-country-report-romania_en.pdf.

Eurostat (2018). *My country in a bubble, an interactive tool to compare EU countries on several indicators*. Retrieved from https://ec.Europa.eu/eurostat/cache/BubbleChart/?lg=en#tableCode=tin00073.

Global Information Society Watch (2011). *GISWatch report. internet rights and democratisation. Focus on freedom of expression and association online*. Retrieved from https://www.giswatch.org/sites/default/files/gisw11_up_web.pdf.

Global Information Society Watch (2016). *GISWatch report. economic, social and cultural rights and the internet*. Retrieved from https://www.giswatch.org/sites/default/files/Giswatch2016_web.pdf

Grech, A., and Camilleri, A. F. (2017) *Blockchain in Education*. In A. Inamorato dos Santos (Ed.), EUR 28778 EN. https://doi.org/10.2760/60649. Retrieved from https://ec.europa.eu/jrc/en/publication/eur-scientific-and-technical-research-reports/blockchain-education.

Grosseck, G., and Holotescu, C. (2015). *Business model for OER*. OERup project. Retrieved from https://www.oerup.eu/fileadmin/_oerup/dokumente/M6_-_existing_business_models_table.pdf.

Holotescu, C. (2007). *Technical requirements of educational software report. Knowledge economy project*. Retrieved from https://www.scribd.com/doc/189255399/Recommendations-for-Ministry-of-Education-related-to-Open-Educational-Resources-and-Practices.

Holotescu, C. (2012, updated 2016). *OER in Romania. POERUP Project: Policies for OER Uptake Report*. Retrieved from https://poerup.referata.com/wiki/Romania, https://www.researchgate.net/publication/236016012_OER_in_Romania.

Holotescu, C. (2017). *MOOC initiatives in Romania. Workshop "Open Education from theory to practice. OER and MOOCs experiences"*, Timisoara, Romania. Retrieved March 31, 2017, from https://www.slideshare.net/cami13/mooc-initiatives-in-romania.

Holotescu, C., and Grosseck, G. (2018). Towards a MOOC-related strategy in Romania. *BRAIN. Broad Research in Artificial Intelligence and Neuroscience, 9*(2), 99–109. Retrieved from https://www.edusoft.ro/brain/index.php/brain/article/view/822.

Holotescu, C., Andone, D., and Grosseck, G. (2016). MOOCs strategies in Romanian universities. In D. Jansen, & L. Konings (Eds.), *European policy response on MOOC opportunities*. Maastricht: EADTU Publisher. Retrieved from https://home.eadtu.eu/news/111-report-european-policy-response-on-mooc-opportunities.

Holotescu, C., Grosseck, G., Cretu, V., and Naaji, A. (2014). Integrating MOOCs in blended courses. In *The 10th International Conference eLSE, Bucharest* (vol. 4, pp. 243–250). Retrieved April 24–25, 2014, from https://search.proquest.com/openview/d242a855a51d7ea5de208a872a37ffe8/1?pq-origsite=gscholar&cbl=1876338.

Inamorato dos Santos, A. I, Punie, Y. and Mūnoz, J. C. (2016). *Opening up education: a support framework for higher education institutions* (No. JRC101436). Directorate Growth & Innovation and JRC-Seville, Ispra: Joint Research Centre. Retrieved from https://publications.jrc.ec.europa.eu/repository/bitstream/JRC101436/jrc101436.pdf.

Inamorato dos Santos, I. A., Nascimbeni, F., Bacsich, P., Atenas, J., Aceto, S., Burgos, D., and Punie, Y. (2017). Policy approaches to open education. Case studies from 28 EU member states (OpenEdu Policies). *JRC Science Hub*. ISBN: 978-92-79-73495-3.

Jansen, D., and Konings, L. (2017). *MOOC strategies of European institutions. Status report based on a mapping survey conducted in November 2016–February 2017*. Maastricht: EADTU. Retrieved from https://eadtu.eu/home/policy-areas/open-education-and-moocs/publications/413-mooc-strategies-of-european-institutions.

MEN (2011). *Law of national education in Romania*. Retrieved from https://www.edu.ro/sites/default/files/_fi%C8%99iere/Minister/2017/legislatie%20MEN/Legea%20nr.%201_2011_actualizata2018.pdf.

National Institute of Statistics (NIS) (2019). *Romania in figures. Statistical abstract*. Retrieved from https://www.insse.ro/cms/en/tags/romania-figures.

OECD (2015). *Education at a Glance 2015: OECD Indicators*. Paris: OECD Publishing. https://dx.doi.org/10.1787/eag-2015-en.

OECD (2018). *Education at a Glance 2018: OECD Indicators*. Paris: OECD Publishing. https://dx.doi.org/10.1787/eag-2018-en.

OER AP. (2017). *Ljubljana OER action plan, 2nd OER Congress*. Retrieved from https://en.unesco.org/sites/default/files/ljubljana_oer_action_plan_2017.pdf.

OPAL (Open Educational Quality Initiative) (2011). *OEP Guide. Guidelines for open educational practices in organizations*. Retrieved from https://oerworkshop.pbworks.com/w/file/fetch/44605120/OPAL-OEP-guidelines.pdf.

OpenupEd (2015). *Definition massive open online courses*. Retrieved from https://www.openuped.eu/images/docs/Definition_Massive_Open_Online_Courses.pdf.

Patru, M., and Balaji, V. (2016). *Making sense of MOOCs: A Guide for policy-makers in developing countries*. UNESCO and Commonwealth of Learning.

Pavel, V., Manolea, B., Bucur, A., Voicu, O., and Constantinescu, N. (2014). OER: Policy and best practices from Romania. In *The International Scientific Conference e-learning and Software for Education* (Vol. 4, p. 271). Bucharest.

PISA (2018), Romania PISA, https://www.oecd.org/countries/romania/romania-pisa.htm

POERUP project (2014). *Policy advice for universities, schools and colleges*. Deliverable D4.2, 2014. Retrieved from https://www.poerup.info/.

Syene (2018). *Integrarea tehnologiei în sistemul educațional românesc*, Raport elaborat în cadrul proiectului Politici publice pentru educație (EDUPOL). Retrieved from https://syene.ro/wp-content/uploads/2019/Raport_EduTech.pdf.

Śliwowski, K., and Grodecka, K. (2013). *Open educational resources in Poland: challenges and opportunities*. Retrieved from https://iite.unesco.org/pics/publications/en/files/3214727.pdf.

UNESCO (2002). *Forum on the impact of open courseware for higher education in developing countries: final report*. Paris: UNESCO. Retrieved July 1–3, 2002, from https://unesdoc.unesco.org/images/0012/001285/128515e.pdf.

UNESCO (2019). *Recommendation on Open Educational Resources (OER)—Draft.* Retrieved from https://www.oeconsortium.org/2019/06/unesco-draft-recommendation-on-open-educational-resources-oer.

Vasiu, R., and Andone, D. (2014). OER and MOOCs—The Romanian experience. In *International Conference on Web and Open Access to Learning (ICWOAL)* (pp. 1–5). Dubai: IEEE.

Wang, X., Liu, M., Li, Q., and Gao, Y. (2017). A bibliometric analysis of 15 Years of research on open educational resources. In Chen, W. et al. (Eds.), *Proceedings of the 25th International Conference on Computers in Education.* New Zealand: Asia-Pacific Society for Computers in Education. Retrieved from https://icce2017.canterbury.ac.nz/proceedings_main.

Wikipedia (2018). *Romania.* Retrieved from https://en.wikipedia.org/wiki/Romania.

Witthaus, G. R., Inamorato dos Santos, I. A., Childs, M., Tannhauser, A. C., Conole, G., … and Punie, Y. (2016). *Validation of non-formal MOOC-based learning: an analysis of assessment and recognition practices in Europe* (OpenCred). Retrieved from https://publications.jrc.ec.europa.eu/repository/bitstream/JRC96968/lfna27660enn.pdf.

World Bank (2018). *Romania Report.* Report No. 126154-RO. Retrieved May 21, 2018, from https://pubdocs.worldbank.org/en/263771529423124844/Romania-CPF-May-20.pdf.

Gabriela Grosseck is Associate Professor in the Department of Psychology at the West University of Timisoara, Romania. She has expertise in ICT in education (teaching, learning and researching), a solid experience in students'/teachers' training both f2f and online environments. For almost a decade she was an editor-in-chief of Romanian Journal of Social Informatics. An author of many articles in the field of e-learning 2.0, a speaker at different international events, workshop organizer and member of editorial committees (journals and conferences). Her research interests cover main aspects of open education, OER/OEPs and MOOCs, Web 2.0 tools and technologies in higher education, collaborative aspects and proper use of social media (by teachers, students, researchers, policy makers and other educational actors), digital literacy and digital storytelling.

Carmen Holotescu is the Dean of the Faculty of Engineering, also the Director of the Center for Open Education and Blockchain, at "Ioan Slavici" University of Timisoara, Romania. She has conducted innovative research over the last 18 years, in Open Education (OE), conceiving and building Social Media learning spaces and integrating emerging educational technologies, OER and MOOCs in formal/informal learning settings. She has also been involved in many European projects. She is a Certified Online Instructor of University of Maryland University College, USA, acting as Online Tutor for 12 years, between 2002–2013. She wrote over 100 articles and book chapters related to eLearning/Blended Learning/Open Learning, Social Media, OER and MOOCs, Blockchain, having more than 1400 citations. Carmen Holotescu is also the organizer and chair of many national and international conferences, workshops and webinars on OE and Blockchain.

Diana Andone is the Director of the eLearning Center of Politehnica University of Timisoara, responsible for planning and implementing eLearning. Diana Andone holds a Ph.D. in Designing eLearning Spaces for Digital Students with University of Brighton, UK. The publication list comprises 17 books and over 80 papers presented at international conferences. In the last years she was involved in over 30 EU funded projects, recently with a focus in open education, publishing and technologies. She was co-ordinator of the LLL ViCaDiS (Virtual Campus for Digital Students) project and national responsible on m-commerce, SKILL2E, CBVI, i2Agora, TafCity, ESIL, e-Taster, e-report projects, as well as the national DidaTec project (Training in blended-learning and new educational technologies for university academic staff). She is now leading the UniCampus project with the goal of creating the first Romanian MOOCs. She actively promotes Open Educational Resources (OER), Open Knowledge (OKF) and Massive Open Online Courses (MOOCs) as part of her everyday activities or through her work in different associations or task-force.

Chapter 10
Open Educational Resources in Serbia

Ivan Obradović, Ranka Stanković, Marija Blagojević and Danijela Milošević

1 Case Overview

The educational system in Serbia, in accordance with the Law on the Basis of the Education System (Official Gazette of RS, No. 68/2015), comprises the following levels:

1. Preschool education and upbringing;
2. Primary education and upbringing;
3. Secondary education;
4. Tertiary education.

These levels of education are carried out in:

Preschool institutions (up to 7 years of age);

Primary schools:

(a) Regular primary schools,
(b) Primary schools for the adult education,
(c) Primary music or ballet schools and
(d) Primary schools for students with developmental disorders;

I. Obradović · R. Stanković
University of Belgrade, Faculty of Mining and Geology, Đušina 7, 11000 Belgrade, Serbia
e-mail: ivan.obradovic@rgf.bg.ac.rs

R. Stanković
e-mail: ranka.stankovic@rgf.bg.ac.rs

M. Blagojević (✉) · D. Milošević
University of Kragujevac, Faculty of Technical Sciences Čačak, Svetog Save 65, 32 000 Čačak, Serbia
e-mail: marija.blagojevic@ftn.kg.ac.rs

D. Milošević
e-mail: danijela.milosevic@ftn.kg.ac.rs

© Springer Nature Singapore Pte Ltd. 2020
R. Huang et al. (eds.), *Current State of Open Educational Resources
in the "Belt and Road" Countries*, Lecture Notes in Educational Technology,
https://doi.org/10.1007/978-981-15-3040-1_10

Secondary schools:

(a) Gymnasiums (general and specialized),
(b) Secondary vocational schools (SVS),
(c) Mixed or combined schools (gymnasiums and vocational or art schools),
(d) Art schools,
(e) Secondary schools for the adult education and
(f) Secondary schools for students with developmental disorders or disabilities;

Tertiary education institutions:

(a) Universities,
(b) Faculties and art academies within universities,
(c) Academies of Professional Studies,
(d) Colleges and
(e) The Colleges of Professional Studies.

Educational institutions were until recently predominantly public, that is, state-owned, but the number of private educational institutions at all levels is rapidly growing, especially at the preschool and tertiary level. Primary education in Serbia is mandatory and available for free of charge in public elementary schools. Secondary and tertiary education is free in public schools and universities (although for a limited number of students), but it is not mandatory. All citizens have access to higher education under equal conditions (Papic et al. 2016).

According to the Statistical Office of the Republic of Serbia (https://www.stat.gov.rs/en-US), in 2019, there were 445 (162 public and 283 private) preschool institutions with 218,567 children enrolled. According to the same source, at the beginning of the school year 2018/19, there were 3319 regular elementary schools with a total of 527,834 students, 506 secondary schools (454 public and 52 private), attended by 252,108 students, and 41 public schools/departments for students with disabilities, attended by 1993 students. As for the tertiary education, 27,801 students were enrolled in the first year of study at 7 accredited public universities, 6,728 at accredited private universities, 10,239 at public high schools, and 1,582 at private high schools.

2   Current Situation of OER

The infrastructure related to OERs in Serbia is comprised of several portals, offering possibilities for publishing OERs and featuring various types of OERs. This section offers a review of these portals.

2.1 Infrastructure

The BAEKTEL Portal

The BAEKTEL portal for indexing of OER and other supporting TEL content including audio, video, and written text materials, published by partners involved in the Tempus BAEKTEL (Blending Academic and Entrepreneurial Knowledge in Technology Enhanced Learning), provides searching capabilities for any type of published content. It includes:

- BAEKTEL Metadata Portal (BMP) with metadata for all published OER within BAEKTEL network.
- Terminological web application for management, browse, and search of terminological resources.
- Web services for linguistic support (query expansion, information retrieval, OER indexing, etc.)
- Annotation of selected resources
- OER repository on local edX platform.

The BAEKTEL OER framework supports publishing of resources of partners in BAEKTEL project (baektel.eu) institutions, but can also integrate OERs that are not created by partner institutions, regardless of the place where they are stored. Those resources only have to be registered and described in the central metadata repository.

The aim of the BAEKTEL Metadata Portal is to provide structured access to information on open education resources within the BAEKTEL network.

To OER creators, the Portal provides OER metadata management, and to learners, metadata search and direct access to learning resources, such as courses, training materials, guidelines, case studies, best practices, etc., available in any media, which can support education.

The BAEKTEL metadata platform development is based on the open-source Digital Asset Management (DAM) system ResourceSpace, relying on PHP backend, MySQL database, and the GD Graphics Library (https://www.resourcespace.org/).

The Platform provides intelligent search ordering by scoring resources against keywords on the basis of user search activity, preselected groups of resources, resource access level permissions by user group, multilinguality, allowing the user to change the language, with most major languages supported, automatic thumbnail creation for resources, multiple file upload, possibility for geolocation search, adaptation of metadata.

The main purpose of the metadata portal is to describe courses created on edX (edx.baektel.eu) portal. Except courses, different downloadable resources, in different formats, can be uploaded and described. On the other side, this portal helps users to find resources of interest, and it provides easy access to courses. There are three different user roles on site:

1. Administrator—creates accounts, controls resource upload, manages the portal
2. Teacher—describes course created on edx portal
3. Learner—search described courses and download uploaded resources.

The upload of resources and descriptions of either uploaded resources or other courses on the Portal is enabled only for authorized users with teacher role, so those users must have an account. Only users with accounts can use the Portal as teachers.

A metadata schema was designed that consists of data elements drawn from existing standards for metadata creation, which enables description and sharing of learning in a common way and, therefore, allowing increasing accessibility of the resources from other OER portals.

The metadata model was defined based on DC (Dublin Core) and with the addition of some elements from LOM (Learning Object Metadata). The selected metadata set is designed to describe the resources sufficiently well for the user to be able to locate and access them easily and to facilitate exchange with other OER systems (see Fig. 1).

Petlja

The Petlja Foundation[1] was founded with the aim of improving algorithmic literacy in Serbia through OERs. It includes the portal with learning materials for programming and Takprog, an official website with materials from competitions of secondary school students in Serbia in programming.

The BubbleBee Portal was developed by a group of professionals from the Microsoft Development Center in Serbia, Mathematical and Computer Gymnasium,

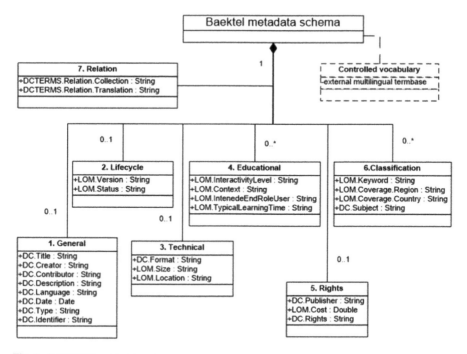

Fig. 1 BAEKTEL metadata scheme

---

[1] https://petlja.org/.

other schools, the Society of Mathematicians of Serbia and the Petnica Research Station. Materials on the BubbleBee portal are freely available, designed for the widest population and approach programming in a simple and interactive way.

Takprog was developed by members of the High School Commission for Programming Competitions of the Society of Mathematicians of Serbia and represents infrastructural support for the maintenance of programming competitions in secondary schools. Now the common infrastructure[2] basis is used for primary and secondary school competitions, as well as for BubbleCup.

OER Serbia

OER Serbia is the portal of the Open Education Initiative, founded by a group of university teachers, and intended for all those who work in education and share the view that knowledge is a common good and that it should be available for everyone (https://oer.rs/).

The portal is developed as a WordPress platform with metadata about resources, links and containing different regulations and various types of information about open education resources.

The aim of the portal of the Open Education Initiative is to contribute to the inclusion of Serbia's educational space in European and global trends in open education. Several university teachers have already made their learning materials freely available on this portal.

Bearing in mind the proximity of the languages used in the Western Balkans region, most of the educational materials that become available through this portal will be able to be used not only within the educational system of Serbia, but also within the educational systems of the region.

Khan Academy Serbia

Khan Academy Serbia[3] has started the translation of Khan Academy instructional videos in 2013, providing interactive exercises, instruction manuals and a personalized learning dashboard that empowers students to learn at their own pace, but also outside the classroom. They are tackling mathematics and computer programming, primarily, while for other languages also history, art history, economics, and others are available. Their mission in mathematics encourages children from kindergarten to tackle mathematical analysis with the most up-to-date adaptive technology that recognizes their advantages and shortcomings in knowledge.

Napon

A significant number of scientific research institutions in Serbia recognized the need to make the results of their research more visible and accessible through different types of repositories and digital archives. The National Open Science Portal—NAPON[4] (Nacionalni Portal Otvorene Nauke) is being implemented within the Erasmus+ project BEOPEN as the future hub of open science in Serbia. As research papers can often serve as educational resources this resource is also considered as part of the

---

[2]https://takprog.petlja.org/.

[3]https://sr.khanacademy.org/.

[4]https://www.open.ac.rs/.

OER infrastructure. The portal will consolidate catalogs of scientific production of Serbian universities and place them on researchers, competent authorities, industry, and society as a whole. Most repositories are based on the free DSpace platform, but there are also examples of self-developed repositories for the specific needs of the institution. Portal map presents links to the currently active repositories in Serbia that meet the requirements related to the standards of machine readability. Adopted institutional policies of open science and institutions that have adopted institutional policies are listed. Guidelines, dictionaries and various types of methodologies related to open science and open data are briefly published.

Among repositories that are registered the following should be highlighted: National Repository of Doctoral Dissertations (https://nardus.mpn.gov.rs/), SCIndeks—Serbian citation index, Repository of newspaper articles with DOI number, https://www.beopen.uns.ac.rs, etc.

Wikimedia Serbia

Wikimedia Serbia was founded in 2005 with the aim to allow free exchange of knowledge and participation in gathering educational content. Within the educational program, they produce content in cooperation with schools and faculties, organize Edu Wiki Camp, Wiki Librarian, Digitization of techno culture.

Wikipedia is located on the Wikimedia Foundation's servers, which also manages a number of other projects, from which we distinguish: Wiktionary—Dictionary and thesaurus, Wikibooks—Free textbooks and manuals, Wikispecies—Directory of species, Wikiversity—Free learning materials and activities.

Authoring tools

Tools for Creating OER are various in use. Some of them are open, some not, but it is obligatory that their output is not in proprietary format, but they do output open file formats.

OBS Studio[5] is free and open-source software for video recording and live streaming. Its powerful API, plugins, and scripts provide further customization and functionality for specific needs. Cross-platform availability and good support gathered large community of users and developers communicating everyday on forums and blogs, improving also wiki pages. Another software from the same category is Debut Screen Recorder Software[6] Within BAEKTEL project booth tools were successfully used to create videos that were later published on YouTube canal and integrated into OER resources.

Main tool for complete production of complex OERs is The Open edX Studio, as a scalable and robust learning software platform, with continuous enhancement and improvement with the latest achievements in learning sciences and instructional design. The Open edX learner platform is driven by our community of developers, technology partners, research teams, and users, but development initiative and support behind edX was by Harvard and MIT in 2012. It is both nonprofit and open-source tool with the mission to increase access to high-quality education for everyone

---

[5]https://obsproject.com/.
[6]https://www.nchsoftware.com/capture/index.html.

and everywhere, enhance teaching and learning on campus and online and advance teaching and learning through research. The Open edX LMS tool has Instructor View where he/she can publish courses, post discussion boards, manage teams and cohorts, edit grades, and communicate with learners. Open edX Studio empowers development utilizing documented and open XML standards (OLX) for import/export of courses, manage course scheduling, course team, and grading policy and access rich 3rd-party tools or add additional building blocks.

Some authors use SlideShare that allows to upload Powerpoint presentations, then embed them in any blog, web page, or online course, marking the content as Creative Commons.

One more option is to use Google Drive to upload Word documents, Excel spreadsheets, and Powerpoint slideshows, which one can then link to—but not embed.

2.2 Policy

Educational policy documents in Serbia scarcely refer to openness in education. OERs are explicitly mentioned only in the Law on Foundations of Educational System, which regulates the preschool, primary and secondary education. Namely, in Article 46a of this Law, a Center for Educational Technology is envisaged within the Institute for Education Quality and Evaluation. With the competence of this Center, Item 4 stipulates that it "provides professional support, develops a methodology and instruments for the development of digital education content, open educational resources and software solutions." However, such a Center has so far not been established.

While this Law that regulates lower levels of education at least recognizes OERs, there is no mention of them in the Law on Higher Education, although there are some references to openness and harmonization with the European educational space. Namely, among the goals of higher education, Article 3, Item 7, states "improvement of the international openness of the higher education system." Article 4, which outlines the principles on which higher education is based, in Item 5 stipulates "openness towards general public and all citizens" and in Item 8 "harmonization with the European system of higher education and enhancement of academic mobility of teaching and non-teaching staff and students." Finally, Article 32 stipulates that the "competent Ministry takes care of the harmonization of the educational system in the Republic with the trends of educational development in Europe."

Other regulations related to education open the possibilities for the development of OERs but need further improvement at the national and institutional level in compliance with OER regulations in Europe.

The Education Development Strategy in Serbia up to 2020, adopted by the Government of Serbia in 2012, criticizes traditional tendencies of the education system for independence from other systems and promotes its openness. It specifically targets openness and accessibility of higher education and provides opportunities for legal regulations for the realization of ideas related to OERs, although it does not mention them explicitly.

Yet another strategic document, the Information Society Development Strategy in Serbia up to 2020, adopted by the Government of Serbia in 2010, fosters application of information technology in education. It emphasizes the development of digital educational content as one of the main goals to be achieved and refers to the introduction of modern concepts of e-learning and open distance learning. However, OERs are not recognized by this document, either.

Given the close relation between Open Access and OERs, given that research results can often serve as educational resources, especially at the level of higher education, it is worth mentioning that the Ministry of Education, Science and Technological Development of the Republic of Serbia adopted an Open Science Platform (https://www.open.ac.rs/). The platform is intended for all participants in scientific and research activities in Serbia, and pertains to the results of research projects and programs financed in whole or in part from the budget of the Republic of Serbia.

2.3 Open License

Open licenses in Serbia are supported and promoted primarily by Creative Commons Serbia (CC-RS), the national Creative Commons (CC) project launched in 2006 with the aim of harmonizing CC licenses with the Serbian language and legislation, promoting open licenses, and providing information on these important instruments for the exchange of creative content (https://creativecommons.org.rs/). National CC standards allow authors and other right holders in Serbia to retain the rights to their work they publish, while at the same time allowing others to use this work under flexible and standardized conditions: "authorship," "non-commercial," "without processing," and "share under the same conditions." Serbian national CC licenses are internationally recognized, according to all rules of the international legal procedure, in 2007, when they officially became an integral part of the CC licensing system. Thus, the validity of national licenses throughout the world has been ensured, and authors and right holders from Serbia have been provided with free licensing of published work under appropriate preselected conditions.

Creative Commons Serbia is a project officially initiated by the Wikimedia Association of Serbia, an independent nongovernmental, nonpartisan, and nonprofit association, founded with the aim of developing free knowledge. Wikimedia Association of Serbia is the official national partner of the Wikimedia Foundation and an institutional member of Creative Commons Global Network.

Creative Commons Serbia aims at achieving the highest level of exchange of creativity and knowledge in Serbia, in accordance with international and national standards and introducing CC licenses into the national legal system.

Creative Commons Serbia is being supported and promoted by a group of individuals comprised of scientific researchers, architects, curators, journalists, and artists, as well as several institutions, such as the Section of librarians of the Association of

Institutes of Serbia, Section of museum librarians of the Association of Museums of Serbia, Youth Center Belgrade, Bureau for Culture and Communication Belgrade, Center for New Media Novi Sad, Independent Journalists Association of Serbia, and the Free Software Network.

It also closely cooperates with the Serbian Academy of Sciences and Arts (SASA institutes, library and gallery, and the Library of the SASA Institute of Technical Sciences), Matica srpska, the oldest cultural-scientific institution of Serbia (MS gallery in Novi Sad), University of Belgrade (Faculty of Mathematics, Faculty of Chemistry, Faculty of Physics, Faculty of Philosophy, University Library "Svetozar Marković"—Department of Scientific Information, University Computer Center), University of Niš (Faculty of Natural Sciences and Mathematics, Teacher's College, University Library "Nikola Tesla"), University of Kragujevac (University Library, Faculty of Philology and Arts), Archaeological Institute Belgrade, National Library of Serbia (Department of Scientific Information, Department of Protection, Conservation and Restoration), Central Institute for Conservation, Library of the Belgrade Polytechnic, Media Center Belgrade, as well as a number of other libraries, museums, galleries, archives, and professional associations.

Although a lot has been done in promoting open licenses, they have not yet been widely accepted by Serbian teachers at all levels of education. One of the problems lies in the fact that educational institutions, in general, still fail to fully recognize the value of open education, and hence do not encourage their teaching staff to use open licenses. Another problem might be the absence of regulations in Serbia pertaining to open licenses. Namely the Law on Copyright and Related Rights, which regulates the protection of a broad spectrum of intellectual property rights, does not have any reference to open licenses and the protection of intellectual property of authors offering educational resources under open licenses. Although open licenses, such as CC licenses, allow considerably more freedom to users of educational resources, they nevertheless impose some restrictions in various degrees. However, the regulations, in the first place the aforementioned Law, do not prescribe any sanctions for the breach of conditions under which an open license has been issued. This is an issue the Serbian legislative system still needs to tackle, hopefully in the nearest future. Until then, the proper use of educational resources released under an open license is left entirely at the discretion of their users.

2.4   Resources

On the **BAEKTEL portal** there are currently 78 items indexed, classified by type as: Lessons (24), Exercises (21), Best Practices and case studies (17), Portal (11), Guidelines and other (5). Detailed statistics by target group is presented in Fig. 2, and can be outlined as follows: Students (29), Learners (20), Employes and others (16), Unclassified (13).

Topics of content (titles and keywords) are visualized by a word cloud in Fig. 3.

Employees, Students		4
Learner		16
Learner, Employees, Students		2
Learner, Manager, Employees, Students		1
Learner, Students		4
Learner, Teacher, Manager, Employees, Students		4
Learner, Teacher, Students		2
Manager,Employees,Students		1
Manager,Supervisor,Employees,Students		1
Students		29
Teacher		1
(blank)		13

Fig. 2 Classification of BAEKTEL portal content by type

Fig. 3 Word cloud of
Baektel portal content
subjects

It can be seen that computer science, modeling, and language technologies are dominant.

OERs are mostly developed as MOOCs using eDX, 18 of them with video content, 34 classified as courses, and 18 as documents, mostly presentations (html and ppt) and pdf documents.

The educational level the OERs are aimed for is presented in Fig. 4.

Petlja portal hosts various materials dedicated to the learning of programming, mostly python, in primary school. Video lectures are on YouTube, classified by school grade. For Grade 6 there are 4 video collections with a total of 28 videos. There is also a collection of 16 Jupyter notebooks for python, Interactive manuals for Python

Higher education	1
Higher education, Lifelong learning	16
Lifelong learning	4
Other	13
School	4
School, Training, Higher education, Lifelong learning	2
School, Training, Higher education, Lifelong learning, Other	3
School,Higher education,Lifelong learning	2
School,Training,Higher education	2
School,Training,Higher education,Lifelong learning	1
Training	1
Training,Higher education,Lifelong learning	17
Training,Higher education,Other	3
(blank)	1
	8

Fig. 4 The educational level the OERs are aimed for

and C#, Graphics programming using Pygame, Collection of algorithmic tasks, and the like.

The Open Education Initiative Portal features 14 OERs selected from other portals, that are evaluated as good quality and might be interesting for a wider audience. Apart from several OERs related to programming and web design, it includes learning materials on Social Network analysis, GIS application in geology, Lexical Analysis in Natural Language Processing, Security in IT, etc.

Khan Academy published mathematics and IT OERs generally for young children. Mathematics OERs are related to Early mathematics, Kindergarten, Arithmetic, followed by Introduction to algebra, Basics of algebra, Algebra I, Basics of geometry. As to materials related to Computer Science and Information technology, they joined the Popular Hour of programming within the Global Movement of Education Week in Computer Science and Code.org. Namely, within a one-hour introduction to computer science and programming small OERs are published.

Portal Napon, as an aggregator for open science repositories in Serbia, integrates at the moment 29 repositories with scientific research papers, reports, and data collections.

2.5   Curriculum and Teaching Methodology

Regarding curriculum and teaching methodology in Serbia, there are two approaches to OER initiative. Some teachers create and publish individual OERs while others develop MOOCs (Massive open online courses). Although there is a high degree

Table 1 OER well-known platforms in Serbia

	Name of platform	Address
1	Open educational resources	https://oer.rs/resursi/
2	Khan Academy Serbia	https://www.youtube.com/user/KhanAcademySerbian
3	Baektel platform	https://edx.baektel.eu/
4	Petlja	https://petlja.org/

of similarity between individual OERs and MOOCs, there are also significant differences. The first difference is (non) variability: one of the main features of the OERs is that they can be changed and combined independently of their authors, while a MOOC does not change, except possibly periodically, by their authors. The second difference is coverage: OORs offer individual teaching materials, and less often curriculum units and courses, while MOOC complete courses with supporting materials. The third difference is the authors' participation: the OOR concept does not provide for the active participation of their authors in their use. The authors place their materials on the Internet for free use, but after that they do not commit to their further maintenance or modification. On the other hand, MOOC includes the active participation of the institution that published them and interact with MOOC users. The last important difference is availability. Unlike the OOR, which are available at any time, MOOC has a start and end date, with a schedule to be followed, including tests and quizzes, as well as evaluations at the end of the course.

The most common MOOC platform in Serbia is edX. Possibilities of Moodle MOOC and edX were compared by Blagojevic and Milosevic (2014). This paper describes MOOC platforms as places where huge number of courses exist in different areas. Most well-known universities use edX platform with possibility of obtaining the certificate. Both mentioned MOOC platforms (edX and Moodle MOOC) provide possibilities of consultation with the teacher, evaluating the acquired knowledge, and all learning materials at one place.

Table 1 gives well-known platforms available in Serbia for OER and accordingly learner/teacher could examine the curriculum and the teaching methodology.

While analyzing given platforms we can conclude that most of them use existing solutions (like YouTube and edX) and smaller number develop their own solutions. Curriculum is usually mapped from blending learning with additional possibilities of OER and MOOC. Teaching methodology is related to specific teaching style of teachers who use OER. It is usually based on specific target group, goals, and teaching materials.

According to Espana-Villegas and Caeiro-Rodriguez (2018), OER includes all types of educational content (complete courses (educational programs), course materials, content modules, learning objects, textbooks, multimedia materials (text, sound, video, images, animations), exams, compilations, periodicals magazines), etc. Same authors define OERs as a "generic denominator that includes courses and curricula," beside other mentioned educational content.

Stefanovic and Milosevic (2017) suggest a holistic approach for the design of open learning software environment and conclude that in the OER field there is a need for specific methodology.

Zancanaro (2015) conclude that collaborative learning and collaborative production is most dominant in OER implementation. Also, the same author provides activities in methodology of OER production which include adaptation of OER, digitalization of materials, defining models and frameworks, repository implementation, surveys of the OER perception, experiences.

For successful OER implementation it is not enough to create excellent OER pedagogical materials. The curricula and teaching methodology which include OER should be carefully planned. According to Kaufman and Campana (2019), teachers could even use "an old technology" like printed course, but in an appropriate way it could be successfully adopted to teaching needs in the same level as electronic educational materials.

2.6 Outcome

Implementation of OER in Serbia already produced some valuable outcomes, which affect several target groups. A very important outcome is partnership in developing, implementing, and using OERs. Within the BAEKTEL project educational institutions in Serbia cooperated with several partners from regional and EU educational institutions and industry in order to develop quality OERs. This partnership gave a successful example for further cooperation in the OER domain. Sharing and reuse of OER could also be a measure of outcome. As Serbia is a country with few years' experience in OER implementation, some BAEKTEL OERs were reused from partner institutions in other countries.

The outcome of OER initiative in Serbia is visible in several aspects:

– *Teachers develop skills for developing, publishing, and applying OERs and MOOCs in the teaching process*

With development of OER initiative in Serbia teachers developed knowledge and skills related to OERs. They introduced OERs in the teaching process, as a new way of knowledge transfer with a positive effect on students and other teachers, but also other interested individuals. Through the developing and publishing process teachers also learn about licensing and possibilities in sharing and applying OER.

– *Learners are able to use OER in education or lifelong learning*

Besides traditional teaching/learning process in Serbia, blended learning is also very common. In this kind of learning teachers usually use some of learning management systems in addition to traditional teaching. In recent times, OERs and MOOCs became more popular. Learners can use meta-portals for searching adequate OERs and after that improve their skills and competencies through OERs within the chosen platform.

– *OER initiative becomes more recognized in Serbia*

Thanks to many enthusiastic individuals and groups and also through implemented projects OER initiative in Serbia is very active. Platforms with metadata and also with OER are established and the number of teachers and learners who use them is growing. The next step of OER initiative in Serbia is OER recognition in official university regulative.

Quantitative outcome could be given according to metadata portals in Serbia:

meta.baektel.eu: 78 open educational resources. OERs on the platform are developed by universities and industry partners and they are all used by interested individuals.

Some of open educational resources (14) are published under https://oer.rs/resursi/.

The outcome could be presented as part of logical model provided by the William and Flora Hewlett foundation (Fig. 5).

All mentioned outcomes are necessary for achieving two main goals: mainstream adoption and educational effectiveness.

Fig. 5 Outcomes and goals (William and Flora Hewlett foundation)

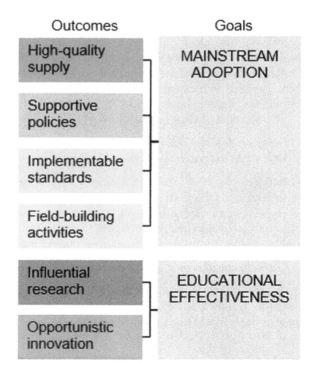

2.7   Stakeholders

While more and more authors in Serbia develop open educational resources, the level of awareness and involvement of stakeholders in the use and adaptation of OERs is not at a high level. There are many benefits from OERs in educational institutions, for students and teachers. Both groups are aware of the significant potential for improving their knowledge and skills while developing or using OERs.

Teachers usually develop OERs bearing in mind a specific target group. But, an OER is always "open," so the content finds another interested target group beside the initially planned. This kind of OERs for specific target groups are sometimes inadequate or not well pedagogically adjusted to all stakeholders. In order to make the developed OER adequate to wider community, the process of OER development should be well planned and done in collaboration with industry, wider community, and some specific subjects who are interested in using the resources.

In Serbia the same stakeholder groups are recognized as in McGill et al. (2008):

- The global community
- The national community
- Educational Institutions
- Subject communities (including employers and professional bodies)
- Individuals supporting learning and teaching
- Learners.

Global community is recognized in Serbia as the starting point for developing and publishing OERs as a good pool of best practice examples. With raise of OER in Serbia the global community has become a stakeholder for created OERs.

National community is organized through the well-known initiatives like Serbia's Open Education Initiative (oer.rs). The Initiative provides a platform for open educational resources, which could be interesting for different stakeholders. OERs are developed in Serbian language and their content covers different fields. The main goal is to allow teachers to offer their teaching materials at all levels of education to their colleagues, students and students for free use, reuse, processing, combination, and further distribution, with open licenses.

Educational institutions are currently the main stakeholder in Serbia for open educational resources. At the same time, educational institutions are mainly OER developers. Students and teachers develop and use the resources in order to increase knowledge and skills. The most common platform in Serbia is: meta.baektel.eu, oer.rs, https://petlja.org/…

Subject communities in Serbia are mostly related to industry companies, which are strongly connected to educational institutions and collaborate with teachers and/or students. In analyzing the current OERs in the aforementioned platforms, it could be noticed that the petroleum company NIS Company (nis.eu) took part in developing OERs in order to connect industry with educational institutions and provide blending learning. Also, OER development is recognized at the university level. At most Universities in Serbia groups for open science are formed. Almost all Ph.D. thesis from 2016 and some of earlier thesis are available through an open platform under one of Creative Commons licenses. Also, Universities in Serbia have an open platform for scientific work of researchers.

Individuals supporting learning and teaching

Regarding individual support of open learning and teaching in Serbia, it is still based on the enthusiasm of teachers and students. In recent times the concept of OER has been recognized as a very important part of teaching process through many initiatives, working groups…

Learners

Learners as initial target group for OER give valuable feedback about OER quality and improvement of current state. Also, former students as current employees in industry are new creators of OERs that affect blending learning based on cooperation between academic and entrepreneurial institutions.

2.8 Impact

There are many efforts in Serbia to broaden the impact of OER initiatives. Number of OER increases rapidly, but users still belong to a group of enthusiasts or well-educated self-learners. OER impact could be also analyzed according to given stakeholders groups given in Sect. 2.7.

OER impact on global community is related to file sharing, reuse and appropriate licensing of materials. Serbian educational institutions and also industry subjects made a big effort to develop and use OERs in order to provide new skills and knowledge. Within the BAEKTEL project (baketel.eu) they provided a platform with metadata of published OERs, which gives the possibility for searching and indexing all Serbian OERs within the global community. Also, some of the created OERs are translated into English, so that they might have produced an impact on users abroad.

OER impact on national community in Serbia is still in progress. OER initiative (oer.rs) with realized projects and enthusiastic teachers and students gives an excellent base for further development of OER and their effect on teaching and learning process. National community includes educational and industry institutions and also users which collaborate in order to improve OER development and sharing. Many implemented projects related to OER gave valuable results to Serbian community. Students and interested individuals are able to practice lifelong learning with open educational resources, and teachers can improve their own experience in developing open materials.

OER impact on educational institutions is obvious in every university in Serbia. Also, many schools are included in the process of developing OERs. BAEKTEL project gave valuable results related to a platform for metadata and OER publishing. Interested educational institutions can develop their own platform or use the existing one. The next step at the university level is recognizing the process of developing and publishing OERs in rulebooks for promoting university professors.

OER impact on subject communities is related to opening and sharing their own knowledge and skills through OER publishing. Employees could develop the skills that improve their presentation as authors and promotes their institution. In Serbia, subject communities in the process of developing and publishing OERs usually cooperate with higher education institutions. In the process of collaboration, teachers and students have the possibility to get insight into the industry process, while the company gets scientific knowledge from educational institutions and state of the art information in the domain field.

OER impact on individuals supporting learning and teaching in Serbia is related to knowledge and skills of individuals in the domain of creating and publishing OER and learning through OER. Individuals who create OERs usually learn some new methodology in the process (for example creating MOOC courses) and get skills related to licensing of materials.

OER impact on learners

Learners improve learning skills through open educational resources and new technology that support OERs (MOOC courses, for example). Also, learners in Serbia use the portal with metadata for searching OERs (meta.baektel.eu).

3 Discussion and Conclusion

The most important reason for harnessing OER is the fact that openly licensed educational resources have an exceptional potential to contribute to the improvement of the quality and effectiveness of education. Apart from responding to the demand for access to ICT infrastructure, educational institutions are also required to improve the teaching and learning environment (development and enhancement of curricula, program and course design, planning of contact hours, elaboration of quality teaching and learning materials, effective assessment) while managing the associated costs through increased use of resource-based learning (Butcher 2011). The transformative educational potential of OER revolves around three related prospects which are applicable in Serbia:

1. Increasing the availability of high quality, relevant learning resources can contribute to more productive learners and educators. Since OER eliminates all restrictions regarding copying resources, it can decrease the cost of accessing educational materials. In many systems, royalty payments for textbooks and other educational materials represent a substantial proportion of the overall cost, while procedures of obtaining permission to use copyrighted material can also be very time-consuming and expensive.

2. One of many mechanisms for creating roles for students as active participants in educational processes is provided by the principle of allowing adaptation of materials. Students learn best not by merely passively reading and absorbing, but by doing and creating. Content licences that encourage students' activity and creation through the reuse and adaptation of that content can make an important contribution to creating a more effective learning environment (Butcher 2011).

3. OER has the potential to build capacity by providing institutions and educators with access, at low or no cost, to resources they need in order to advance their skills in producing teaching and learning materials, as well as by implementing the necessary instructional design to allow for an integration of such materials into high-quality programs of learning (Butcher 2011).

Deliberate openness, therefore, acknowledges that:

- Investment in creating effective educational environments is crucial for good education.
- The key to a productive system is to build on common intellectual capital, rather than reproducing similar efforts.
- All things being equal, collaboration will increase the quality.
- Since education is a contextualized practice, it is vital to make adaptations of materials imported from different settings easy (where this is required), which should be encouraged rather than restricted (Butcher 2011).

OER initiatives and open licenses options provide many benefits for educational institutions, individuals, and commercial organizations (Falconer et al. 2013). These benefits are recognized in Serbia also:

- Offer a vast variety of freely available resources for both learners and teachers.
- Do not limit the ways of adapting and reusing these resources to suit the user's context.
- Let teachers and learners see a range of alternative methods for extending and enriching the curriculum.
- Encourage the practice of sharing, improving the quality, and lowering the cost of curriculum development.

Provided information in the previous subsections gives full rights to conclude in several affirmative directions, regarding OER in Serbia:

- Outcomes regarding initiatives and number of OER and also teachers/learners included in open education gives the opportunity for further successful OER development and implementation.
- Licenses for open education are introduced and supported but need additional activities to be widely adopted.
- Impact on stakeholder groups is evident and future OER implementation will give bigger impact on every group.

Acknowledgements The work presented here was supported by the Ministry of Education and Science of the Republic of Serbia (Project III 44006 and Project III 41007).

References

Blagojevic, M., & Milosevic, D. (2014). *Massive open online courses: EdX vs Moodle MOOC.* In 5th International Conference on Information Society and technology, Kopaonik, March 8–11, 2015. (pp. 346–351).

Butcher, N. (2011). *A Basic Guide to Open Educational Resources (OER).* https://www.oerafrica.org/resource/basic-guide-open-educational-resources-oer.

España Villegas, C.B., & Caeiro Rodriguez, M. (2018). *Open Education with OER (OPEN EDUCATIONAL RESOURCES) Ecosystem.* In OE Global Conference.

Falconer, I., McGill L., Littlejohn A., Boursinou E. (2013). Overview and Analysis of Practices with Open Educational Resources in Adult Education in Europe. https://ftp.jrc.es/EURdoc/JRC85471.pdf.

Kaufman, R., & Campana, A. (2019). OER: lessons from the field. *UKSG Insights, 32*(1), 15. https://doi.org/10.1629/uksg.464.

McGill, L., Currier, S., Duncan, S., Douglas, P. (2008). Good intentions: improving the evidence base in support of sharing learning materials. https://repository.jisc.ac.uk/265/1/goodintentionspublic.pdf.

Obradović, I., Stanković, R., Prodanović, J., & Kitanović, O. (2013). A Tel Platform Blending Academic and Entrepreneurial Knowledge. In *Proceedings of The Fourth International Conference on e-Learning (eLearning-2013).* Belgrade, Serbia.

Papić, M., Papić, Ž., Kuzmanović, B., & Aleksić, V. (2016). Educational system in Serbia, Management and education, Vol. XII(3) pp. 22–28.

Stanković, R., Obradović, I., Kitanović, O., Prodanović, J., & Ilić, V. (2011). An approach to implementation of blended learning in a university setting. In *Proceedings of the Second International Conference on e-Learning, eLearning 2011* (pp. 61–66).

Stanković, R., Obradović, I., Kitanović, O., & Kolonja, L. (2012). Building Terminological Resources in an e-Learning Environment. In *Proceedings of The Fourth International Conference on e-Learning (eLearning-2012)* (pp. 114–119). Belgrade, Serbia.

Stefanovic N., & Milosevic D. (2017) Innovative OER model for technology-enhanced academic and entrepreneurial learning. In: M. Jemni, M.K. Khribi (Eds.), *Open Education: from OERs to MOOCs.* Lecture Notes in Educational Technology. Springer, Berlin, Heidelberg.

The William and Flora Hewlett Foundation, Open educational resources-Breaking the Lockbox on Education (2013). https://hewlett.org/wp-content/uploads/2016/08/OER%20White%20Paper%20Nov%2022013%202013%20Final_0.pdf.

Zancanaro, A. (2015). Produção de recursos educacionais abertos com foco na disseminação do conhecimento: uma proposta de framework, 2015.

Dr. Ivan Obradović is a retired full professor of Mathematics and Informatics at the University of Belgrade. He was one of the founders of the University of Belgrade Information Center and its Director from 2005 to 2012, and Director of the University Center for e-Learning and Distance Education from 2014 to 2016. Professor Obradović has published four books and more than 100 scientific papers related to applications of artificial intelligence methods and tools, development of language resources and tools, open educational resources and e-learning application in HE. He participated in numerous domestic and international projects, including BAEKTEL, a project aimed at developing OERs in a cooperation of universities and industrial companies. Since his retirement at the University his is actively participating in the activities of the Language Resources and Technologies Society (JERTEH), of which he was one of the founders. He is the initiator of the Open Education Initiative Serbia, which is intended for all those who work in education and share the view that knowledge is a common good and that it should be available for everyone.

Ranka Stanković is associate professor at University of Belgrade, Faculty of Mining and Geology, where she is teaching several courses related to informatics and geoinformatics. She received her Master's degree in 2000 and Ph.D. 2009 at the Department for Computer science, Faculty of Mathematics University of Belgrade. Professor Stanković is interested in e-learning, open education, semantic web, information systems, database modelling, geoinformation management and artificial intelligence. Her current research is focused on building custom components that incorporate knowledge from various language and lexical resources. She is head of Computer Centre for the Mining department, Chairman of Technical comity A037 Terminology in Institute for Standardisation of Serbia and vice president of Language Resources and Technologies Society (JERTEH). She actively participated in BAEKTEL Tempus project in building and exploitation and learning platform. She published more than 100 papers in journals and proceedings of scientific conferences, most of them in the area of human language technologies and more than 15 related to TEL.

Marija Blagojević Associate Professor at the Faculty of Technical Sciences in Čačak, University of Kragujevac at the Department of Information technology. Born in 1984. M.Sc. in Technics and Informatics in 2007. Ph.D. in technical sciences in 2014. Current research interest: data mining, artificial neural networks, e-learning, programming… Eleven years' experience in teaching and research activities. Author or coauthor of more than 80 research paper. Reviewer for many scientific journals. Project and study programs reviewer. Member of partner university for Tempus project 544,482-TEMPUS-1–2013-1-IT-TEMPUS-JPHES. Participant in four Erasmus mobilities. Member of Commission for self-evaluation at faculty. Member of the organizational committee of several conferences. Participant in national and international project and project coordinator for one project.

Danijela Milošević is full professor and dean at the Faculty of Technical Sciences in Čačak. She belongs to the Department of Information Technologies. She graduated at Military Technical Faculty in Zagreb, Croatia, and received M.Sc. and Ph.D. degrees at the University of Belgrade. Her expertise includes distance learning, intelligent tutoring systems, adaptive user modeling and Semantic Web. She teaches traditional, online and blended IT courses. She was coordinator of the regional Tempus project DL@WEB for improving the quality of distance learning in higher education institutions in the Western Balkans and responsible for the development of accreditation standards for study programs for distance learning. Also, she coordinated WUS MSDP project "M.Sc. in eLearning: e-moderating Module" at the Faculty of Technical Sciences Čačak. She holds certificates for training on Quality assurance in Higher Education by EFQUEL - European Foundation for Quality in e-Learning. She is the president of Balkan Distance Education Network BADEN, and editor in chief of BADEN Newsletter aiming to disseminate and exchange the knowledge and experiences across the Western Balkan region.

Chapter 11
Open Educational Resources in South Africa

Tony Mays

1 Case Overview

South Africa has a long and complex history with the notion of open education. In both the colonial and the apartheid eras, access to quality educational opportunities was hugely uneven, an unfortunate legacy that endures in some ways to the present time, and it is therefore not surprising that calls to open access to quality education for all were central to the liberation movement (African National Congress, 1994). While there has been progress since 1994, addressing concerns about access and success in education at both schooling and tertiary levels remain central to building a uniquely South African democracy (Christie, 2008; Council on Higher Education, 2016). Hence this chapter is about the ongoing process of opening education, and the role that OER can play, rather than assuming that South Africa has arrived at a state where education can be said already to be open.

The chapter explores the evolution of understandings about openness in the policy context from the first post-democracy education policy framework in 1994 (Department of Education, 1994) through to the draft open learning policy framework (Department of Higher Education and Training, 2017) discussed in a national workshop in 2017. It will also detail South Africa's policy engagement with open educational resources (OER) in this period (South Africa is signatory to both the Cape Town and Paris Declarations).

T. Mays (✉)
Unit for Distance Education, Faculty of Education, University of Pretoria, Groenkloof Campus, Letlotlo Building, Office 2-64, Pretoria, Republic of South Africa
e-mail: tony.mays@up.ac.za
URL: http://www.up.ac.za

University of Pretoria, Cnr George Storrar Drive and Leyds Street, Groenkloof, Pretoria, Republic of South Africa

Unit for Distance Education, Faculty of Education, University of Pretoria, Private Bag X21, Hatfield 0028, Republic of South Africa

© Springer Nature Singapore Pte Ltd. 2020
R. Huang et al. (eds.), *Current State of Open Educational Resources in the "Belt and Road" Countries*, Lecture Notes in Educational Technology,
https://doi.org/10.1007/978-981-15-3040-1_11

The chapter then explores the infrastructural support available to open access to education generally and to mainstream the use of OER in particular. It unpacks the evolution of open, distance and e-learning (ODeL) in South Africa in both the public and private sectors, as well as the current developments in access to connectivity through national interventions such as the Tertiary Education and Research Network (TENET) and through the expansion of mobile and fiber networks.

The discussion then moves to the emerging new copyright legislation in the country and the extent to which it accommodates open licensing.

The chapter also showcases selected examples of ways in which openness in general, and OER in particular, are informing curriculum and teaching methodology in select programs and initiatives as well as attempts to find a uniquely South African voice in ODeL provision and OER development and use (Baijnath, 2014; Hülsmann & Shabalala, 2016; Letseka, 2016; Mays, 2017; Prinsloo, 2017; Saide, 2015; Subotzky & Prinsloo, 2011).

Finally, the chapter synthesizes recent studies on the outcomes and impact of open practices, resources and methods in the South African context, identifies gaps in South Africa's current engagement with open education and OER and suggests areas for future focus.

2   Current Situation of OER

In this section we explore the current situation regarding a supporting environment for OER as well as examples of actual engagement with OER.

2.1   Infrastructure

Although OER are not necessarily accessed and shared only as digital files, increasingly this is in fact the case and for some kinds of OER, such as audio and video resources, obviously the only way to engage. Therefore access to ICT is an important consideration in opening access to and use of OER. According to the most recent report from the Independent Communications Authority of South Africa (ICASA), 87% of households had access to a cellular phone only, approximately 10% had access to both cellular and landline telephone but only 3.5% had access to neither in 2016. However, household internet access was somewhat lower at about 59.3% with Gauteng and the Western Cape at 72.2% and 68.5%, respectively, and Limpopo with the lowest level of access at 42.4%. The internet was accessed by 53.9% of households using mobile devices, while access through other means was considerably lower: at home (9.5%), at work (15.8%) or at internet café or educational institution (9.8%). However, smart phone subscriptions have grown dramatically from an estimated 24,340,341 in 2016 to 42,094,018 in 2017 and internet bandwidth grew correspondingly in this period with 99% of population areas now able to access 3G and 77% LTE/4G in 2017 (ICASA, 2018). It seems likely then that in South Africa access to OER would primarily be via a mobile device.

However, the cost of mobile data relative to annual salaries, while decreasing, remains high (Hülsmann, 2016) and this likely militates against accessing data-intensive OER such as long, high-definition video, for example, and explains the very large difference between the poorest and the most affluent population sub-groups in accessing the internet (DTPS, 2016, p. 28). For this reason, ODeL institutions such as Unisa and the University of Pretoria's Unit for Distance Education often still provide printed learning resources and/or digital resources on flashdrives (or increasingly digital files downloadable from a learning management system to a flashdrive) for use off-line. As in the rest of the world, however, higher education provision in particular is progressively moving online, and that move requires that teachers make at least some learning resources available, which may in turn foster an increased engagement with OER as a means to an end for teachers trained as disciplinary experts rather than learning resource developers (Mays, 2016). An appropriate policy framework could support such a move.

2.2 Policy

In 2016, the Department of Telecommunications and Postal Services (DTPS) published the *National Integrated ICT Policy White Paper* (DTPS, 2016). The policy reflects a belief in the potential of ICT to contribute to socio-economic transformation and states:

> The core philosophy informing all of the revised policies introduced in this White Paper is a move towards facilitating "openness" – open access, open Internet and open Government. (DTPS, 2016, p. 4)

A specific role is seen for ICT in addressing the poor quality of schooling:

> E-learning and innovative use of ICTs in the education sector can assist in addressing inequalities in education in schools across South Africa, and facilitate ongoing improvement of educator skills. (DTPS, 2016, p. 8)

Of specific interest for the current discussion, the policy recognizes the need to respect intellectual property rights but at the same time promote open access and make the following commitment:

> Government will therefore explore measures aimed at introducing a creative commons licensing framework. (DTPS, 2016, p. 145)

The 2016 ICT White Paper represents an important contribution to an alignment of policy in recognizing the potential of open educational practices, informing open, distance and e-learning provision and mainstreaming the use of OER; a conversation that has evolved in South Africa over a number of years (Mays, 2017).

South Africa's post-1994 first White Paper on Education and Training of 1995 began by making an important distinction between open learning and distance education. Open learning, it was stated, was a set of principles that should apply to **any** educational program:

> Open learning is an approach which combines the principles of learner-centredness, lifelong learning, flexibility of learning provision, the removal of barriers to access learning, the recognition of credit for prior learning experience, the provision of learner support, the construction of learning programmes in the expectation that learners can succeed, and the maintenance of rigorous quality assurance over the design of learning materials and support systems. (Department of Education, 1995)

Nonetheless, it is the University of South Africa (Unisa), South Africa's dedicated distance education provider, and one of the world's mega-universities, which has embraced the notion of openness as central to its vision and mission. In 2008, Unisa adopted the following understanding of "open distance learning" (ODL) which continues to underpin its emerging curriculum practices:

> Open distance learning is a multi-dimensional system aimed at bridging the time, geographical, economic, social and communication distance between: student and institution, student and lecturers/tutors, students and courseware, and student and peers. Open distance learning focuses on removing barriers to access learning, flexibility of learning provision, supporting students and constructing learning programmes with the expectation that students can succeed. (Unisa, 2008, p. 2)

In seeking to give effect to this understanding, the Unisa ODL policy (Unisa, 2008, p. 4) committed the institution to curricula that:

- "have academic integrity and are responsive to the vision and mission of Unisa, national educational imperatives, and societal and employment needs;
- are aligned with the student profiles;
- articulate clear exit level outcomes;
- design teaching, learning and assessment strategies to meet these outcomes;
- emerge from a curriculum design conducted by a team involving academics, curriculum and course designers, student support specialists, student counsellors, language specialists, tutors, relevant external stakeholders and, where possible, representatives of current and past students;
- place the student at the center of the entire learning process from the moment the student intends registering through to graduation, and continuing on through to its alumni who play a vital role in evaluating impact and as ambassadors for the institution;
- use evaluation strategies that assure the quality of the learning process and suggest improvements placing particular emphasis on student feedback; and
- ensuring support for students throughout their period of study".

More recently, Unisa has adopted Open Distance e-Learning (ODeL) as its business model, seeking to make greater use of technology to mediate ODL provision including greater use of digital resources and OER (Rammutloa, 2013).

The 2010/11—2014/15 Strategic Plan of the DHET supported the development of open learning opportunities as part of the post-school system with the intention of connecting education institutions and curricula to emerging networks and information resources; as well as to promote innovation and opportunities for lifelong learning.

One of the major initiatives of the DHET was the release of the *Green Paper on Post School Education and Training* in 2011 which recognized and acknowledged the need to create an integrated, coherent post-school education and training system to, among other imperatives, address the vulnerabilities of a growing number of young people not in employment, education or training. This large group includes those who have a very poorly attained matric, those who have dropped out of school before completing grade 12 and those with less than a grade 9. After public comment, the *White Paper for Post-School Education and Training* (DHET, 2013a) was published and is the policy currently providing direction to the sector.

In a separate chapter of the White Paper entitled *Opening learning through diverse modes of provision*, commitments are made to broadening the models of educational provision to provide easier access to meaningful opportunities to people throughout their lives. It emphasizes the importance of creating networks of providers and learning centers to open up educational opportunity, as well as the necessity to create an enabling ICT infrastructure. The *Draft Framework for the Provision of Distance Education for Universities*, released for comment in 2012, and published as a formal policy in 2014 (DHET, 2014) also sees distance education as part of this wider open learning system, provided the quality thereof can be enhanced.

Developed in parallel, an *Open Learning in Post School Education and Training Concept Note* (DHET, 2013b) recognized that open learning should be embedded in, enhance and expand the current education and training system more broadly. During the course of 2017, the DHET subsequently published an *Open Learning Policy Framework for Post-School Education and Training* for public comment. The policy framework advocates making "high quality, shared teaching and learning and resources available as open educational resources" and to establishing an enabling framework and a national set of repositories to serve the system (DHET, 2017, p. 28) and there has already been some development in this regard.

2.3 Open License

In South Africa, intellectual property and copyright issues are governed by the Copyright Act No. 98 of 1978 (as amended) and its Regulations. Realizing the need to revisit copyright issues in a digital era, the Department of Trade and Industry (DoTI) tabled a Copyright Amendment Bill in 2016 (DoTI, 2016) and an explanatory summary thereof in 2017 (DoTI, 2017). Of interest for this chapter, the proposed revisions recognize the possibilities of different kinds of licensing and provide a liberal understanding of "fair use", particularly in relation to education. The revised copyright bill has, however, come under fierce criticism for being too vague about what constitutes free and fair use (Desai, 2019).

South Africa is a signatory to various international intellectual property agreements, for example, the Berne Convention and the Agreement on Trade-Related Aspects of Intellectual Property Rights (TRIPS). South Africa has also signed the World Intellectual Property Organization (WIPO)'s two Internet Treaties but has not yet acceded to them. South Africa has also supported both the Cape Town and Paris Declarations on open licensing.

Although other forms of open licensing such as GNU General Public License exist, the most commonly used form used, at least in the Global South, is the Creative Commons (www.creativecommons.org) (Arinto, Hodgkinson-Williams, King, Cartmill, & Willmers, 2017). This is also the case in South Africa: where individuals and institutions share openly licensed content, it is usually through the application of a Creative Commons license; the most commonly used being CCBY, CCBYSA and CCBYSANC.

2.4   Resources

Many developing countries in the Global South are exploring the potential of OER, partly in response to the high costs of imported textbooks but also to respond to the need for more contextually, culturally and linguistically appropriate resources, but currently the OER available are mostly in English and there is need for more OER in a greater variety of other languages (Arinto et al., 2017).

Within South Africa, universities publish all successful Masters and Doctoral studies online in open access repositories (see, e.g., https://repository.up.ac.za/handle/2263/31741).

However, there are a number of initiatives which focus specifically on OER. These include, but are not necessarily limited to, the following examples:

- OER Africa
- African Storybook
- DBE workbooks
- TESSA
- Siyavula
- AfriVIP
- OpenUCT
- Unisa Open.

OER Africa

OER Africa (https://www.oerafrica.org/) is an initiative of an NGO called Saide, based in Johannesburg. The OER Africa website provides access to resources to support understanding of OER, examples of OER courseware (in Agriculture, Foundation studies, Health and Teacher Education), research, case studies and policies as well as news on what is happening in OER in the higher education sector in Africa.

African Storybook

African Storybook (https://www.africanstorybook.org/) is another Saide initiative. It provides a platform through which to read, make and use African storybooks for young readers in multiple languages in multiple countries, including South Africa. A Reader App for the website can be downloaded from Apple App Store as well as Google Play.

Department of Basic Education Workbooks

The Department of Basic Education (which has responsibility for the provision of public schooling in South Africa) has developed a series of workbooks, in all 11 official languages, for Grades 1–9 of the school curriculum. The workbooks, as well as additional support resources such as past examination papers, can be accessed from https://www. education.gov.za/Curriculum/LearningandTeachingSupportMaterials(LTSM)/ Workbooks/2018Workbook2.aspx). Developed in full color, the workbooks are very large PDF files which take some time to download but otherwise can be used and distributed freely provided that they may not be sold.

TESSA

Teacher Education Sub-Saharan Africa (TESSA) (see https://www.tessafrica.net/) is a network of teachers and teacher educators stretching across Sub-Saharan Africa. At the heart of the network is a bank of open educational resources (OER), linked to the school curriculum, and designed to support teachers and teacher educators in developing active approaches to learning. The network is coordinated by The Open University, UK. South Africa is one of the countries which has participated in the TESSA network (see https://www.open.edu/openlearncreate/course/view.php? id=2055).

Siyavula

Siyavula (https://www.siyavula.com/) is a website which provides access to online open textbooks linked to the South Africa senior secondary school curriculum in mathematics and science in Grades 10, 11 and 12. For an additional small fee, users can also access additional assessment instruments and support.

AfriVIP

Access is provided to Veterinary Open Educational Resources contextualized for South and Southern Africa through the AfriVIP portal (https://www.afrivip.org/) which is hosted by the University of Pretoria. The portal is targeted not only at veterinary and para-veterinary professionals and students but also at farmers, agri-businesses, governments, NGOs and other key stakeholders seeking and sharing veterinary sciences information, educational knowledge and content and research findings in Africa.

OpenUCT

The University of Cape Town (UCT) was one of the early adopters of OER in South Africa. Its portal, which can be accessed at (https://open.uct.ac.za/), offers access to resources related to a number of communities including higher education development, commerce, engineering and the built environment, health sciences, humanities, law, science, the graduate school of business and others.

Unisa Open
The Unisa Open site (https://www.unisa.ac.za/sites/corporate/default/Unisa-Open) provides guidelines on the nature of OER and where to find them as well as access to a collection of Unisa documents which support OER use, examples of resources (full courses and learning objects) that have been created by Unisa and which are openly licensed as well as to the Unisa institutional repository which contains theses and dissertations, research articles, conference papers and other items.

South Africa has also seen national initiatives to support the collaborative development of OER for programs which address national training needs. For example, between 2006 and 2008, the then single Department of Education led an initiative working with individuals, NGOs, teacher unions and 17 higher education providers, with funding support from private foundations, to develop a set of OER for the training of current and aspirant school principals (the Advanced Certificate in School Management and Leadership—for an overview see https://www.education.gov.za/Portals/0/Implementation%20guidelines.pdf?ver=2009-10-14-130624-897). At the time of writing, a similar process was underway to develop national openly licensed learning resources to support an Advanced Diploma in School Leadership and Management as well as an Advanced Diploma in Technical and Vocational Teaching aligned with the new teacher education qualifications framework (DHET, 2015).

2.5 Curriculum and Teaching Methodology

Although there is growing interest in the integration of OER into curricula and teaching methods, this is often not followed through systematically in institutional policies and practices (Mays, 2017).

Mays (ibid.) goes on to explain how much further and higher education provision in Africa, in terms of both the curriculum and the management of implementation, remains heavily influenced by past colonial practices (Coetzee & Roux, 2002; Higgs, Vakalisa, Mda, & Assie-Lumumba, 2000; Ngugi, 2011; Nsamenang & Tchombe, 2011) and this has resulted in debates in South Africa regarding decolonizing the curriculum (Heleta, 2016; Le Grange, 2016).

This raises questions about the extent to which what we teach, how we teach it and how we manage our programs and relate with one another can or should reflect our context—centralizing African/South African concerns, contributions and approaches.

This in turn raises issues for both the design of the curriculum as well as the management of implementation regarding issues such as multi-lingualism, recognition of indigenous knowledge, contextually- and culturally-informed work and learning practices in South African and global contexts.

In 2004, UNESCO published a position paper on "Higher education in a Globalized Society", in which it adopted the following understanding of the notion of globalization: "the flow of technology, economy, knowledge, people, values and ideas … across borders. Globalization affects each country in a different way due to each nation's individual history, traditions, cultures, resources and priorities" (Knight & De Witt, as cited in UNESCO, 2004, p. 6). The position paper noted the multifarious effects of globalization on higher education and argued that an appropriate response for UNESCO was to participate in the development of normative frameworks, to promote and engage with regional conventions on higher education and debates surrounding the recognition of qualifications within and across borders, and to promote and participate in global fora related to quality assurance, accreditation and the recognition of qualifications. South Africa is involved in such processes at a regional level through its involvement in initiatives in the South African Development Community such as the development of appropriate regional (SADC, 2012) and institutional (Makoe, 2018) ODL policy frameworks.

Writing for UNESCO, Altbach, Reisberg, and Rumbley (2009) identify globalization and internationalization as remaining one of the key trends affecting contemporary higher education and training, noting the growing dominance of English as the language of scientific communication; increasing moves toward the development of regional qualifications frameworks to facilitate portability; and the growing dominance of a few mostly wealthy, English-medium universities in the developed world in setting higher education agendas (in some parts of the world, national policies actively encourage such high-profile universities to establish local campuses). There is, therefore, a growing tension between a curriculum that retains and celebrates local culture and autonomy and curriculum practices premised on being an active participant in the global higher education arena which has seen a continued marginalization of non-English medium universities generally, and of those in developing countries in particular.

In this regard, and closer to home, Le Grange (2006, p. 370) notes the extensive discussion in recent years of the concept of the "African" university and points to the work of Horsthemke who, after noting the sterility of the debate between Afrocentrists and Afrosceptics on this issue, argues for an approach based on "Afrorealism"—recognizing that there is no single identity such as "the African University", but that universities in Africa face a number of common challenges, should be part of an "enabling, internationally competitive tertiary (as well as technical and practical) education system" and should "feed back into the community" (Horsthemke, 2006, p. 464).

While Bangura (2005, p. 13) suggests adopting an approach informed by "Ubuntugogy" (pedagogy informed by the principles of Ubuntu), Higgs and Moeketsi (2011) further problematize the issue, noting the diversity of perspectives on what constitutes both African in general and African philosophy in particular, emphasizing the importance of recognizing human agency.

More recently, Luckett (2011, p. 1) argues the need for the curriculum to "offer students subject positions that transcend and subsume the old Western or African identities", while Kanu (2014) argues the need for both a universal and a particular character in conceptualizing an African philosophical perspective, and Letseka (2016) argues that such perspectives should infuse our entire teaching and learning experience, not just what is taught but also how it is taught and assessed and how staff relate to one another, to students and to the wider community.

Logically, then we would expect teachers in South and Southern Africa to use the space created by open licensing to adapt resources developed elsewhere for a better alignment to local needs, languages and cultures. While there is some evidence of this, as discussed under the section on Resources, it is far from being a mainstream practice.

In fact, recent research points to the following key weaknesses in the meaningful integration of OER:

1. The dependence on copying of existing OER and the corollary failure to localize;
2. The adaptation of OER, but with inconsistent curation and rehosting of derivative works on publicly available platforms or in repositories, limiting access to the derivative OER;
3. Limited circulation of derivative OER due, in part, to the absence of a communication strategy;
4. Inconsistent quality assurance processes; and
5. A weak feedback loop for continuous improvement of the original or derivative work (Hodgkinson-Williams, Arinto, Cartmill, & King, 2017).

In seeking to understand the factors impacting engagement with OER at three South African universities, research suggests a number of inter-related issues need first to be addressed. These include:

- Access to appropriate infrastructure in the form of computers, internet and electricity;
- Permission to use or create OER as determined by the institutional IP policy;
- Awareness of OER, what they are and how they differ from other educational resources;
- Capacity to find, use, create and/or upload OER, whether personally or with support;
- Availability of relevant OER of requisite quality; and
- Volition to adopt OER on personal, social and institutional levels (Cox & Trotter, 2017).

There is also a clear synergy between OER and distance education provision, given that the provision of quality resources for independent learning is one of the two key legs, along with decentralized learner support, for successful distance education practice. An example of a recent case study that makes this link within an African context is provided by Barlow-Zambodla and Ferreira (2012). Their case study illustrates several quality criteria proposed by the National Association for Distance Education and Open Learning in South Africa (see www.nadeosa.org.za) and published in book form as Welch and Reed (2005). It demonstrates the benefits and challenges of offering a rural, community-based, open and distance learning program targeted at improving household food security. The program explored in the case study incorporated OER and has been published as OER for others to adapt and use.

Although on the face of it there seems to be a clear logic in integrating OER in an ODeL context, an e-learning context or even a "flipped classroom" context, since the provision of learning resources is integral in each case, adoption of such an innovation is by no means simple. Reflecting on the Unisa experience of integrating OER De Hart, Chetty, and Archer (2015), found Rogers' "Diffusion of Innovation" model a useful lens. They note that Rogers proposes that four main elements influence the spread of a new idea such as mainstreaming OER: the innovation itself, communication channels, time and a social system. Rogers also identifies five main stages: knowledge/awareness, persuasion/interest, decision/evaluation, implementation/trial and confirmation/adoption. The researchers found that while knowledge about OER was quite high within Unisa, actual take-up was dependent on other factors such as efficient ICT infrastructure, supportive policy, and training and support related to intellectual property issues.

In a similar study among the members of the Washington Community and Technical College System Chae and Jenkins (2015), found that there were often compelling motivations for integrating OER, such as cost-savings for students, possibilities for more responsive instruction, increased collaboration, increased reflection on practice and convenience of use. However, there were also several contextual challenges to take-up, including lack of time, an uninviting institutional climate, lack of technology and skills, uncertainty about Intellectual Property Rights (IPR), copyright and policy issues, difficulty in finding and selecting appropriate resources and differences in course specifications. The report summarizes the kinds of support needed which are consistent with earlier findings. More generally, Mays (2016) argues for a more systematic process to support disciplinary experts with the unfamiliar practice of curriculum and materials development, and the integration of engagement with OER as part of such processes rather than as a separate activity.

In undertaking new research, it is standard practice to survey the literature to ascertain what has already been done to work out how a unique contribution might be made. A similar process is well established in the field of distance provision where it may be possible to find existing resources that could be adopted or adapted, instead of creating all the learning resources ab initio at great expense (COL, 2005; Mays, 2014; Randell, 2006, 2015). Glennie, Harley, and Butcher (2012, p. 287) point to the extensive literature on resource-based learning, which can be drawn upon in this regard.

2.6 Outcome

Access to affordable, high-quality and contextually relevant learning resources remains central to realizing meaningful access to higher education. Recent discussion charts, the complexity of this issue over three decades in South Africa concluding:

Although currently fragmented in South Africa, in both policy and practices, OER presents an obvious opportunity in a system that needs less costly, more flexible, and legal solutions. If the current trends hold, solutions will likely emerge from partnerships between government, universities, educational NGOs, and the commercial sector, and ideally will produce effective digital delivery systems that accommodate the vast range of underserved paths through South African higher education. (Gray & Czerniewicz, 2018, p. 148)

One of the arguments for use of OER is to reduce the costs for parents, learners and/or the state on the purchase of commercially produced textbooks, and this is also an issue in the schooling sector where supply chain issues have also resulted in numerous problems in recent years. However, in South Africa, where the provision of learning and teaching support materials is a provincial competence for public schooling, the data available is not sufficiently detailed to be able to make a case for or against cost-savings through the use of OER (Goodier, 2017). Systems therefore need to be created to track costs and cost-savings.

It seems self-evident that learners who have access to appropriate learning resources will fare better than those who do not, so it is difficult to argue that OER by virtue of being OER can impact positively on student performance: the key issue is whether the resources availed to learners are appropriate for the purpose, and then if they are, it seems there is evidence of positive impact (Cooney, 2017; Grewe & Preston Davis, 2017), but only provided the other contextual factors impacting learner performance are also addressed (Holborn, 2013; Visser, Juan, & Feza, 2015).

In another study, King (2017) explored the role that postgraduate students might play in integrating OER into teaching and learning resources, concluding that they are best suited to support curation, metadata and copy-right clearance and that involvement in co-authorship for pedagogical improvement is much more difficult and probably requires students to be involved in co-teaching the course and in co-developing its materials from the start.

2.7   Stakeholders

As noted in the preceding discussion above, both the Departments of Basic Education and Higher Education and Training have a key role to play in creating an enabling and supportive policy framework, and more recently also the Department of Telecommunications and Postal Services.

Institutions within the education sector also have key roles to play with some institutions, such as the University of Cape Town being early adopters of OER.

In the context of civil society, both Saide (www.saide.org.za) and Nadeosa (www.nadeosa.org.za) have and continue to play key roles in advocating use of OER as a part of a larger strategy toward opening quality education provision.

As noted in the discussion in Sect. 2.3, with respect to the development of OER to address national education and training priorities, we are able to achieve more when different role-players collaborate to address a shared vision and set of objectives.

Both external and internal funders also have an important role to play in supporting the creation, adaption and use of OER. For example, the Hewlett Foundation has supported much of Saide's work in OER Africa and Comic Relief its work in African Storybook. Both the Shuttleworth and Zenex Foundations have supported South African initiatives to develop training materials for current and aspirant school principals as OER.

2.8 Impact

Although there is growing interest in the potential of OER, and examples of practice in using OER, it remains the case that engagement with OER is not yet a mainstream practice.

3 Discussion and Conclusion

As noted by Mays (2017), a commitment to integrating OER, as a matter of course, into increasingly prevalent resource- and activity-based flexible modes of provision needs to be reflected in national and institutional strategic plans and supporting policy frameworks, especially in the areas of intellectual property rights, human resource management, ICT policy, infrastructure and support and quality assurance mechanisms (among other things to ensure equivalent quality of provision across different modalities) (OER Africa, 2012).

With a clear strategic and policy framework within which to work, it is important to identify and develop an appropriate business model to enable and support the intention set out in policy. A key component of the business model must then be costing and budgeting that reflects the features of ODeL provision, including budget for recurring openly-licensed learning resource development and review as well as integrated support (Hülsmann, 2016; Kanuka & Brooks, 2010; Rumble, 1997, 2004, 2012; Simpson, 2013).

When OER are to be employed as part of a drive toward a wider resource-based and ODeL strategy, it is important to give attention to developing the appropriate systems and sub-systems to support that move (Moore & Kearsley, 2012).

It is further suggested that central to forward planning should be adoption of what (Downes, 2007) and (Ehlers, 2011) refer to as an "open ecology", which might be depicted as follows:

Figure 1 illustrates the notion that an institution's strategic plan should continue to be informed by its vision, mission and values but suggests that the adoption of more open educational practices, in which collaboration and the sharing of intellectual property is encouraged, is entirely consistent with these beliefs and values and supportive of expanded provision of open, distance and e-learning, which embraces

Fig. 1 Proposed   OER
open-ecology model

ODeL

OEP

Vision and
mission

a wide range of more flexible forms of provision to suit different learning needs and target audiences.

In such a context, the development and review of learning resources becomes a mainstream practice, part of every academic's job description, and with support from the library in finding appropriate OER (Salem, 2016), it should be possible to make it standard practice that in developing new courses, a search for existing OER that might be adopted and adapted is always a first step in the materials development process.

However, the learning resources are only one part of a complex whole. We need to think much more systemically about the nature of appropriate education provision in a digital era and the challenges of the associated change (CHE, 2014; Fullan & Langworthy, 2014; Mehaffy, 2012; The World Bank, 2016).

A recent report by Inamorato dos Santos, Punie, and Castaño-Muñoz (2016) suggests that there are ten cross-cutting dimensions that will support the opening of educational opportunities: six are considered core and relate to being more open about content, pedagogy, recognition, collaboration, research and access; four are considered transversal by making the first six possible and comprise leadership, strategy, quality and technology. This reinforces the notion of a need to consider engagement with OER from a wider systems perspective and not in isolation.

In short, within South Africa there is growing interest in the use of OER and growing evidence of interest being taken up into practice. However, there is need for more contextual research into the incidence, effectiveness and impact of this engagement. While several instances of OER use have been identified in the discussion, engagement with OER is not yet a mainstream practice and there remains some skepticism or even resistance to such engagement. National policy, however, may begin to shift attitudes, as increasingly there is an expectation that resources developed in whole or in part using public funds should be openly licensed.

Acknowledgements If you wish to acknowledge persons who contributed or sponsoring agencies, do so here in this optional section.

References

African National Congress. (1994). *A policy framework for education and training*. Johannesburg: ANC Education Desk.

Altbach, P. G., Reisberg, L., & Rumbley, L. E. (2009). *Trends in global higher education: Tracking an academic revolution.* A report prepared for the UNESCO 2009 world conference on higher education. Paris: UNESCO.

Arinto, P. B., Hodgkinson-Williams, C., King, T., Cartmill, T., & Willmers, M. (2017). Research on open educational resources for development in the Global South: Project landscape. In C. Hodgkinson-Williams & P. B. Arinto (Eds.), *Adoption and impact of OER in the Global South* (pp. 3–26). Cape Town and Ottawa: African Minds, International Development Research Centre, Research on Open Educational Resources for Development.

Baijnath, N. (2014). Curricular innovation and digitisation at a mega university in the developing world—The UNISA 'signature course' project. *Journal of Learning for Development (JL4D), 1*(1).

Bangura, A. K. (2005). Ubuntugogy: An Africa educational paradigm that transcends pedagogy, andragogy, ergonagy and heautagogy. *Journal of Third World Studies, xx11*(2), 13–54.

Barlow-Zambodla, A., & Ferreira, F. (2012). *Good practice in community engagement: A case study of household food security in Eastern Cape*. Retrieved from https://www.nadeosa.org.za/documents/HFS.pdf.

Chae, B., & Jenkins, M. (2015). *A qualitative investigation of faculty Open Educational Resource usage in the Washington Community and Technical College System: Models for support and implementation*. Retrieved from https://oerknowledgecloud.org/sites/oerknowledgecloud.org/files/FINAL_OER_USE_WA_CTC.

Christie, P. (2008). *Changing schools in South Africa: Opening the doors of learning*. Sandton: Heinemann Publishers.

Coetzee, P. H., & Roux, A. P. J. (Eds.). (2002). *Philosophy from Africa: A text with readings* (2nd ed.). Southern Africa: Oxford University Press.

Commonwealth of Learning. (2005). *Creating learning materials for open and distance learning: A handbook for authors and instructional designers*. Retrieved from https://www.col.org/resources/creating-learning-materials-open-and-distance-learning-handbook-authors-instructional.

Cooney, C. (2017). What impacts do OER have on students? Students share their experiences with a health psychology OER at New York City College of Technology. *International Review of Research in Open and Distributed Learning (IRRODL), 18*(4), 155–178.

Council on Higher Education. (2014). *Distance higher education programmes in a digital era: Good practice guide*. Pretoria: CHE.

Council on Higher Education. (2016). *South African higher education reviewed: Two decades of democracy*. Pretoria: CHE.

Cox, G., & Trotter, H. (2017). Factors shaping lecturers' adoption of OER at three South African universities. In C. Hodgkinson-Williams & P. B. Arinto (Eds.), *Adoption and impact of OER in the Global South* (pp. 287–348). Cape Town & Ottawa: African Minds, International Development Research Centre, Research on Open Educational Resources for Development.

De Hart, K., Chetty, Y., & Archer, E. (2015). Uptake of OER by staff in distance education in South Africa. *International Review of Research in Open and Distance Learning (IRRODL), 16*(2), 18–45.

Department of Education. (1994). *A policy framework for education and training*. Pretoria: DoE.

Department of Education. (1995). *White paper on education and training, notice 196 of 1996*. Pretoria: DoE.

Department of Higher Education and Training. (2013a). *White paper for post-school education and training: Building an expanded, effective and integrated post-school system*. Pretoria: DHET.

Department of Higher Education and Training. (2013b). *Concept note: Open learning in post school education and training*. Pretoria: DHET.

Department of Higher Education and Training. (2014, July 7). *Policy for the provision of distance education in South African universities in the context of an integrated post-school system. Government Gazette, No. 37811, 7 July 2014*. Pretoria: Government Printer.

Department of Higher Education and Training. (2015). *Revised policy on the minimum requirements for teacher education qualifications*. Retrieved from Pretoria

Department of Higher Education and Training. (2017). *Open learning policy framework for post-school education and training*. Pretoria: DHET.

Department of Telecommunications and Postal Services (DTPS). (2016). *National integrated ICT policy white paper*. Retrieved from Pretoria. https://www.gov.za/sites/default/files/40325_gon1212.pdf.

Department of Trade and Industry. (2016). *Copyright Amendment Bill, Government Gazette No. 40121 of 5 July 2016*. Pretoria: Government Printer.

Department of Trade and Industry. (2017).*Copyright Amendment Bill*. Retrieved from https://libguides.wits.ac.za/ld.php?content_id=32174808.

Desai, R. (2019, April 11). Copyright bill: Don't throw the baby out with the bathwater. *Daily Maverick*. Retrieved from https://www.dailymaverick.co.za/opinionista/2019-04-11-copyright-bill-dont-throw-the-baby-out-with-the-bath-water/.

Downes, S. (2007). Models for sustainable open educational resources. *Interdisciplinary Journal of Knowledge and Learning Objects, 3*, 29–44.

Ehlers, U.-D. (2011). Extending the territory: From open educational resources to open educational practices. *Journal of Open, Flexible, and Distance Learning, 15*(2), 1–10.

Fullan, M., & Langworthy, M. (2014). *A rich seam: How new pedagogies find deep learning*. London: Pearson.

Glennie, J., Harley, K., & Butcher, N. (2012). Conclusion: Reflections on practice. In J. Glennie, K. Harley, N. Butcher, & T. Wyk (Eds.), *Open educational resources and change in higher education: Reflections from practice* (pp. 283–291). Vancouver: COL.

Goodier, S. (2017). Tracking the money for open educational resources in South African basic education: What we don't know. In C. Hodgkinson-Williams & P. B. Arinto (Eds.), *Adoption and impact of OER in the Global South* (pp. 233–250). Cape Town & Ottawa: African Minds, International Development Research Centre, Research on Open Educational Resources for Development.

Gray, E., & Czerniewicz, L. (2018). Access to learning resources in post-apartheid South Africa. In J. Karaganis (Ed.), *Shadow libraries: Access to knowledge in global higher education* (pp. 107–157). Cambridge, MA; London and England: MIT Press.

Grewe, K. E., & Preston Davis, W. (2017). The impact of enrollment in an OER course on student learning outcomes. *International Review of Research in Open and Distributed Learning (IRRODL), 18*(4), Online.

Heleta, S. (2016). Decolonisation of higher education: Dismantling epistemic violence and Eurocentrism in South Africa. *Transformation in Higher Education, 1*(1), 1–8.

Higgs, P., & Moeketsi, R. M. H. (2011). *An African perspective on academic development: The University of South Africa's College of Human Sciences' scholars development programme*. Pretoria: Unisa.

Higgs, P., Vakalisa, N. C. G., Mda, T. V., & Assie-Lumumba, N. (2000). *African voices in education*. Lansdowne: Juta & Co., Ltd.

Hodgkinson-Williams, C., Arinto, P. B., Cartmill, T., & King, T. (2017). Factors influencing open educational practices and OER in the Global South: Meta-synthesis of the ROER4D project. In C. Hodgkinson-Williams & P. B. Arinto (Eds.), *Adoption and impact of OER in the Global South* (pp. 27–68). Cape Town & Ottawa: African Minds, International Development Research Centre, Research on Open Educational Resources for Development.

Holborn, L. (2013). *Education in South Africa: Where did it go wrong?* Retrieved from https://www.ngopulse.org/article/education-south-africa-where-did-it-go-wrong.

Horsthemke, K. (2006). The idea of the African university in the twenty-first century: Some reflections on Afrocentrism and Afroscepticism. *South African Journal of Higher education (SAJHE), 20*(4), 449–465.

Hülsmann, T. (2016). *The impact of ICT on the costs and economics of distance education: A review of the literature.* Vancouver: Commonwealth of Learning.

Hülsmann, T., & Shabalala, L. (2016). Workload and interaction: Unisa's signature courses—A design template for transitioning to online DE? *Distance Education, 37*(2), 224–236. https://doi.org/10.1080/01587919.2016.1191408.

Inamorato dos Santos, A., Punie, Y., & Castaño-Muñoz, J. (2016). *Opening up education: A support framework for higher education institutions.* JRC science for policy report, EUR 27938 EN. Seville, Spain: European Union.

Independent Communications Authority of South Africa (ICASA). (2018). *3rd report on the state of the ICT sector in South Africa.* Johannesburg: ICASA.

Kanu, I. A. (2014). The meaning and nature of African philosophy in a globalising world. *International Journal of Humanities and Social Sciences and Education (IJHSSE), 1*(7), 86–94.

Kanuka, H., & Brooks, C. (2010). Distance education in a post-Fordist time: Negotiating difference. In M. F. Cleveland-Innes & D. R. Garrison (Eds.), *An introduction to distance education: Understanding teaching and learning in a new era* (pp. 69–90). New York and London: Routledge.

King, T. W. (2017). Postgraduate students as OER capacitators. *Open Praxis, 9*(2), 223–234.

Le Grange, L. (2006). The changing landscape of the contemporray university. *South African Journal of Higher Education, 20*(4), 367–371.

Le Grange, L. (2016). Decolonising the university curriculum. *South African Journal of Higher Education, 30*(2), 1–12.

Letseka, M. (Ed.). (2016). *Open Distance Learning (ODL) through the philosophy of Ubuntu.* New York: Nova Science Publishers Inc.

Luckett, K. (2011). Knowledge claims and codes of legitimation: Implications for curriculum recontextualisation in South African higher education. *Africanus, 40*(1), 4–18.

Makoe, M. (2018). Avoiding to fit a square peg into a round hole: A policy framework for operationalising open distance education in dual mode universities. *Distance Education, 39*(2), 159–175.

Mays, T. (2014). Teaching, learning and curriculum resources. In P. du Preez & Reddy, C. (Eds.), *Curriculum studies: Visions and imaginings* (pp. 110–133). Cape Town: Pearson.

Mays, T. (2016). Designing and developing programmes in open, distance and e-learning. *Progressio, 38*(2), 132–150. https://doi.org/10.25159/0256-8853/1025.

Mays, T. (2017). *Utilising open educational resources in support of curriculum transformation at Africa Nazarene University: A participatory action research approach* (DEd). Pretoria: Unisa. Retrieved from https://hdl.handle.net/10500/22619.

Mehaffy, G. L. (2012). *Challenge and change.* Retrieved from https://online.tarleton.edu/fdi/Documents/EDUCAUSE_Mehaffy.pdf.

Moore, M. G., & Kearsley, G. (2012). *Distance education: A systems view of online learning* (3rd ed.). Belmont, CA: Wadsworth, CENGAGE Learning.

Ngugi, C. (2011). OER in Africa's higher education institutions. *Distance Education, 32*(2), 277–287.

Nsamenang, A. B., & Tchombe, T. M. S. (Eds.). (2011). *Handbook of African educational theories and practices: A generative teacher education curriculum.* Bamenda, Cameroon: Human Development Resource Centre (HDRC).

OER Africa. (2012). *Policy development and review toolkit.* Retrieved from https://www.oerafrica.org/policy/PolicyReviewandDevelopmentHome/tabid/914/Default.aspx.

Prinsloo, P. (2017). *Talkin Bout a Revolution: (Re)claiming distance education as a revolutionary, humanising praxis. Keynote address.* Paper presented at the Nadeosa Conference 2017, University of the Free State, South Campus, Bloemfontein.

Rammutloa, M. (2013). *From distance learning and ODL to ODeL: Unisa library's journey to transformation and innovation.* Retrieved from https://uir.unisa.ac.za/handle/10500/12043.

Randell, C. (2006). *Resources for new ways of learning: A manual for developers of learning resources.* Johannesburg: Saide.

Randell, C. (2015). Learning activities and feedback. *Developing curriculum and learning resources: Guidelines for effective practice* (pp. 33–49). Abuja, Nigeria: NCCE & TDP.

Rumble, G. (1997). *Costs and economics of open and distance learning.* London: Kogan Page.

Rumble, G. (Ed.). (2004). *Papers and debates on the economics and costs of distance and online learning.* Oldenburg, Germany: Bibliotheks- und Informationssystem der Universität Oldenburg.

Rumble, G. (2012). Financial management of distance learning in dual-mode institutions. *Open Learning, 27*(1), 37–51.

Saide. (2015). *Course design guide.* Retrieved from https://www.saide.org.za/design-guide/.

Salem, J. A. (2016). Open pathways to student success: Academic library partnerships for open educational resource and affordable course content creation and adoption. *The Journal of Academic Librarianship.* https://doi.org/10.1016/j.acalib.2016.10.003.

Simpson, O. (2013). Student retention in distance education: Are we failing out students? *The Journal of Open, Distance and e-Learning, 28*(2), 105–119.

Southern African Development Community. (2012). *Regional open and distance learning policy framework.* Retrieved from https://www.sadc.int/files/3113/7820/8525/Approved_Regional_ODL_Policy_Framework_June_2012_1.pdf.

Subotzky, G., & Prinsloo, P. (2011). *Enhancing student success in ODL: Unisa's integrated student success and support frameworks and strategies.* Paper presented at the Nadeosa 2011, Johannesburg. https://www.saide.org.za/resources/Nadeosa/Conf_2011/Subotzky%20and%20Prinsloo.pptx.

The World Bank. (2016). *Financing higher education in Africa.* Washington, DC: The International Bank for Reconstruction and Development/The World Bank.

United Nations Educational, S. a. C. O. U. (2004). *Higher education in a globalized society (UNESCO Education Position Paper).* Paris: UNESCO.

University of South Africa. (2008). *Open distance learning policy.* Pretoria: Unisa.

Visser, M., Juan, A., & Feza, N. (2015). Home and school resources as predictors of mathematics performance in South Africa. *South African Journal of Education, 35*(1), 1–10.

Welch, T., & Reed, Y. (Eds.). (2005). *Designing and delivering distance education: Quality criteria and case studies from South Africa.* Johannesburg: Nadeosa.

Tony Mays is the Manager of the Unit for Distance Education, within the Faculty of Education, at the University of Pretoria. He has always played a consultant or support role rather than occupying an academic post. Nonetheless, he has over 30 peer-reviewed publications, over 40 conference presentations, has supervised 6 Masters students to completion and has externally examined 1 Masters and 1 Doctoral candidate. He is also author, co-author and/or editor of more than 190 learning resources, and reviews articles for a number of journals. He is past president, and current long-standing vice-president, of the National Association for Distance Education and Open Learning in South Africa (Nadeosa); Honorary Treasurer of the Distance Education Association of Southern Africa (DEASA) and chair of the biennial conference on Distance Education and Teacher Training in Africa (DETA). He holds a DEd in Curriculum Studies from Unisa. Tony is on LinkedIn https://za.linkedin.com/in/tonyjohnmays at and can also be contacted at: tony@tmas.online.

Chapter 12
Open Educational Resources in Turkey

Secil Tisoglu, Engin Kursun and Kursat Cagiltay

1 Case Overview

The education system in Turkey is formed of two elements as formal and non-formal education as shown in Fig. 1. Formal education consists of five periods in terms of pre-child education, kindergarten, primary education, secondary education, high school and higher education system (associate degree, undergraduate and graduate programs). Similarly, special education also holds five periods of education. Pre-child education covers daycare centers for 0–3 years old children within the structure of the Ministry of Family, Work and Social Service. For kindergarten, two types of education are operated: private agencies for 3–5.5 years of children and public education for 4–5.5 years of children under the Ministry of Education. Twelve years education, which includes primary, secondary and high school education is mandatory since 2012 where each system is affiliated under the Ministry of National Education. Primary education is provided for children with 5.5–10 years of age in formal schools. Children in the age group of 10–14 are supposed to be included in secondary education. For high school, 14–18 years of age children are placed in different types of schools (Science, Anatolian, Social Science, Fine Arts, Sports, Vocational and Technical Schools and Religion High Schools). Except Fine Arts schools, the students are placed in schools based on a national exam. Secondary and high school education

S. Tisoglu (✉)
Education Faculty, Kastamonu University, 37200 Kastamonu, Turkey
e-mail: skaya@kastamonu.edu.tr

E. Kursun
Kazim Karabekir Education Faculty, Ataturk University, 25240 Erzurum, Turkey
e-mail: ekursun@atauni.edu.tr

K. Cagiltay
Education Faculty, Middle East Technical University, 06800 Ankara, Turkey
e-mail: kursat@metu.edu.tr

© Springer Nature Singapore Pte Ltd. 2020
R. Huang et al. (eds.), *Current State of Open Educational Resources in the "Belt and Road" Countries*, Lecture Notes in Educational Technology,
https://doi.org/10.1007/978-981-15-3040-1_12

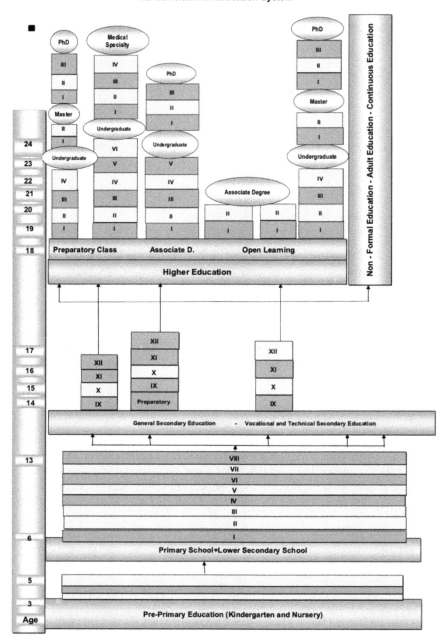

Fig. 1 Turkish National Education System (MEB, 2018)

also consists of open education for the people who could not attend formal education process (Department of Strategy Development, 2017).

Higher education institutions comprise two periods of undergraduate and graduate degrees. Undergraduate programs consist of an associate degree (2 years) and a bachelor's degree (4–6 years) (Some programs requires 5–6 years education like law and medicine schools). Graduate programs are also two types as master's (2–3 years) and doctoral degree (4–6 years). Higher education is also affiliated under the Higher Education Council which is placed within the Ministry of Education (MEB).

Non-formal education provides opportunities for people who couldn't attend the formal education process. In 2016, the registered non-formal education institutions were 28,801 (TurkStat, 2016a). These institutions are formed under four directorates as lifelong learning (public training center, vocational training center, maturation institutions and tourism training center), special education and guidance services (special education and guidance research centers (Science and Art Center for gifted children)), and special education (private courses, special education and rehabilitation center, motor vehicles drivers' course). Moreover, non-formal education also aims to provide lifelong education for learners which is enhanced by the 2009–2013 and 2014–2018 Strategic Reports (Ministry of National Education, 2018).

Regarding the enrollment rate and the quality of education, a report was published by European Commission in 2018 (see https://ec.europa.eu/neighbourhood-enlargement/sites/near/files/20180417-turkey-report.pdf). According to this report, "there has been some progress in the enrolment rate of children, particularly in preschool education where it stands at 52% which remains well below the EU target of 95%. Adult participation in lifelong learning, which stands at 6%, also needs to be increased. Turkey needs to develop a system to reduce early school leaving, which stands at 34%" (European Commission, 2018, p. 89). In the academic year 2015–2016, the schooling rate for children was 95% for primary, 94% for lower secondary, 80% for upper secondary education (TurkStat, 2016b). However, the number of higher education institutions and enrollment rates are on increase, the concerns about the quality of education still remain. "Significant quality differences also persist among Turkey's higher education institutions. Turkey set up a Higher Education Quality Board in charge of quality assessment and assurance. Turkey is however not yet a member of the European Association for Quality Assurance in Higher Education. Education remains at high risk for inappropriate political influence, especially in higher education" (European Commission, 2018, p. 89).

2   Current Situation of OER

The swift advancement in Information and Communication Technologies (ICT) has provided opportunities for improving access, transfer and share of knowledge and information around the world. With this advancement, the idea of "openness" has become more popular. The acquaintance of open education in Turkey formerly began with Open Education Faculty which was founded in 1982 within the body of Anadolu

University in Eskisehir. In the following years, European Commission's policies on Open Access, Bologna Process, UNESCO's EFA reports, EU Horizon 2020 liabilities have guided the open education and access policies in Turkey. It was 2004; a group of young Turkish researchers working in the USA came together under a platform called "Biliminsanı Platformu". In collaboration with researchers from Turkey, Europe and the USA, they decided to initiate the Turkish OCW project where MIT's courses were translated into the Turkish language. Although this project did not continue, it was the first spark of OER movement for developing OER courses in the Turkish language.

This first attempt was followed by studies of open access and the development of OCW platforms (Kursun, Cagiltay, & Can, 2014). The establishment of the Turkish OCW consortium with the leadership of the Turkish Academy of Sciences (TÜBA) led to future collective and full-scale studies. In October 19, 2006, TÜBA sent a letter about the OCW to all university administrations in Turkey and the first meeting was held on March 23, 2007 with the participation of 24 universities, Turkish Academic Network and Information Center (ULAKBIM) under the Scientific and Technological Research Council of Turkey (TÜBITAK), and the State Planning Organization (DPT). A project was held with the contribution of 8 universities to create and develop OERs in different disciplines. This project probably leads to other projects and studies, however, when compared to other countries, Turkey has scored low top-down (policy-led) and moderate bottom-up (community-led) activities so far. Therefore, OER initiatives in Turkey can be categorized into three groups. The first one is the nationwide OER initiative led by the Turkish OCW Consortium within the body of Turkish Academy of Sciences (TÜBA). In this initiative, there was an allocated budget provided by the State Planning Organization (DPT) and quality assurance process employed before publishing courses free to use. Two projects were implemented within this attempt: first, the translation of the courses from different platforms and the creation of Turkish courses. The second one was institutional-based initiatives started by universities. The related universities opened their course materials with their own efforts and facilities. There was no strict quality assurance system. Faculty members were responsible for the quality of course materials. A personal attempt led by individual faculty members is the third type of OER initiatives in Turkey, though the exact number of personal OER initiatives is not known. Some faculty members created their personal websites include their resources and course activities openly (for an example, see https://mustafasozbilir.wordpress.com/derslerim/).

2.1 Infrastructure

Despite the recent good news about the rapid pace of the country's economic development, Turkey still lags behind many countries in GNI (gross national income) levels. The World Bank ranks Turkey in the upper middle-income economies at about $10,903 per capita in 2017 (see https://data.worldbank.org/indicator/NY.GNP.

Internet access of households, 2017

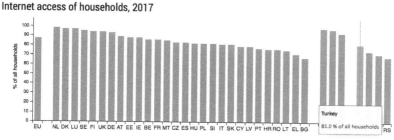

eurostat■

Fig. 2 Internet access in households in Turkey

PCAP.CD?end=2017&locations=TR&start=1967&view=chart). The Internet diffusion also ranks in the upper middle of the countries. Internet access to households in Turkey was shown as 81% (European Commission, 2018). In most countries of the European Union (EU), the numbers of individuals regularly using the Internet (85%) also surpass the number in Turkey. Figure 2 shows the percentages of Internet users in the EU, ages 16–74 in 2017 (Eurostat, 2018). However, based on OECD statistics, access to computers from home was 50% in 2017 as shown in Fig. 3. On the other hand, mobile broadband subscriptions were 72% (OECD, 2017) and the use of the Internet is 80% for males and 66% for females (TurkStat, 2018).

According to the Turkish Information Society Statistics Report, there is a rapid increase in computer and Internet usage in Turkey. However, digital divide between rural and urban areas still continues (Cagiltay, Kara, & Esfer, 2016). As could be seen from Fig. 4, computers and Internet usage in rural areas are lower than urban areas (Eurostat, 2018).

2.1.1   ICT in Higher Education

Though important progress has been achieved worldwide to benefit from new technologies, as acknowledged in the strategic plan of the Turkish Higher Education Council (YÖK), it is difficult to see this development on the Turkish higher education system sufficiently (Higher Education Council of Turkey, 2007). In the report, it is pointed out that "old instructional techniques are dominant in Turkish higher education. Teaching methods based on lecture notes prepared by using limited number

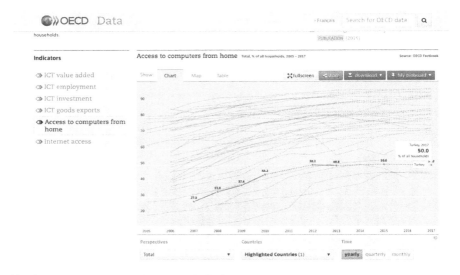

Fig. 3 Access to computers from home in Turkey

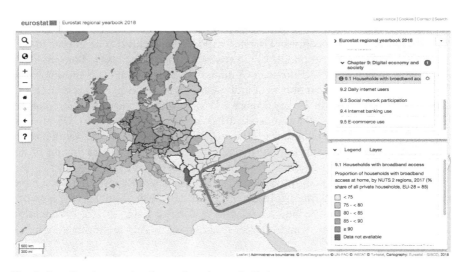

Fig. 4 Broadband access in urban and rural areas in Turkey

of educational resources or made student take notes are widely used in higher education institutions" (p. 185). As presented in the YÖK's strategic report, educational resources are scarce or difficult to access especially in new universities. Moreover, old instructional techniques have still been widely used in courses. The report draws attention to such initiatives as MIT-OCW to support teaching and learning activities in tertiary education. After the open access movement in Turkey, a strategic report in

2012 focused on developing digital and open access resources by collaboration with the universities and TÜBITAK (2012, 2015). In 2013, TÜBITAK announced two new projects of developing academic e-book and e-courses. However, this project did not get enough attention from the institutions.

2.1.2   ICT in K-12

According to the State Planning Organization's Information Society report (2010), there is major progress accomplished in the infrastructure of ICT in schools with the great investment made by the Ministry of National Education (MEB) in recent years (The State Planning Organization, 2009). As of the end of 2009, 27,999 information technology laboratories have been established in schools. Besides this, ICT equipment has been provided for 17,261 primary schools which fail to meet the necessary requirements of establishing ICT infrastructure. All elementary schools and 94% of primary schools have an Internet connection. As of 2009, MEB also established 1,850 Public Internet Access Points (PIAP) which provides citizens with ICT access and ICT competency. Throughout the country, the number of students per computer is 30.8 in primary schools and 25.1 in elementary schools.

In recent years, different projects have been initiated to strengthen ICT infrastructure in schools. Most of the projects have conducted under the supervision of Directorate General of Innovation and Educational Technologies which is a public institution within the Turkish Ministry of National Education to support and search educational technology developments. First project, developing digital resources program was valid for primary and secondary education. 440 e-course and 372 e-resource was developed (Strategic Planning Report, 2015). Second, FATIH Project which stands for as "Movement of Enhancing Opportunities and Improving Technology" which is an important educational investment in the information and communications sector in recent years. The aim of this project is to equip 40,000 schools with latest information and communication technologies. Two phases of the project were completed (84,921 in the first phase and 347,367 in the second phase interactive whiteboard were provided to secondary education and high schools), the third phase is in the process which aims to provide 150,000 interactive whiteboards to primary and other schools (see http://fatihprojesi.meb.gov.tr/etkilesimli-tahta/). Another project led by the General Directorate of Educational Technologies under the MEB is the e-Book project. It is aimed at transferring all primary and elementary books into digital format. Another project TeachUP began in 2017 with the collaboration of Directorate General of Innovation and Educational Technologies to support teachers and prospective teachers' twenty-first-century skills through online courses (MOOCs) and assessment methods (see project website http://teachup.eun.org/about). The last project stands for Future Classroom Lab (FCL) project which the Ministry of National Education involved in 2016. This project aims to provide guidelines, recommendations and resources on how to implement ICT strategies and how to use mobile devices cloud services (see project website http://fcl.eun.org/fcl-regio).

2.2 Policy

The first attempt on the policy practices was held on the 10th Internet Conference at Bahcesehir University in 2005 to unite on a common open access policy. In 2006, Open Access Declaration was prepared and announced after Information Technology Conference (Karasözen, Zan, & Atılgan, 2010). Also, Open Access Advisory Board was formed by the attendance of Turkish Academic Network and Information Center (ULAKBIM), Consortium of Anatolian University Libraries (ANKOS), University and Research Libraries Association (ÜNAK) and Turkish Library Association (TKD) to provide a common ground for the open access policy, to provide collaboration between the policymakers, authorities and institutions and to enlighten the open access applications (Ertürk, 2008). At the same time, in 2005, Open Access and Institutional Repositories Working Group in ANKOS was formed to provide information about the open education and open access practices, to provide guidance on the policy practices and to improve the sustainability for the open education practices in Turkey (Karasözen, Zan, & Atılgan, 2010).

In 2014, YÖK provided Open Access and Institutional Repository policy to form a national open access repository and to compile and publish the scientific papers based on the open access standards (YÖK, 2014). The standards have led to produce and reform the institutions' open access policies and repositories. In 2018, YÖK extended the attempts and they declared to start a new perspective called "open access and open science". They aimed to reform the university's open archives and align them with the universal standards, to encourage the faculty members and universities for open access practices (publications and open educational resources), and to form committees in universities to follow the studies periodically (YÖK, 2018). The major progress of this movement is supported by the collaboration with TÜBITAK that TÜBITAK has declared the open science policy in 2019 which leads to provide a nationwide policy regulations in Turkey (TÜBITAK, 2019). In 2017, the registered open access policies adopted in Turkey based on the Registry of Open Access Repository Mandates and Policies (ROARMAP) is shown in Fig. 5. Therefore, the new regulations could accelerate the policy practices in Turkey.

Moreover, some projects were held by the cooperation of institutions and public/private organizations. MedOANET (Mediterranean Open Access Network), and PASTEUR4OA projects within the supervision of Hacettepe University, a website was created to provide technical and procedural information on how to develop policy practices. In 2015, TÜBİTAK ULAKBIM National Open Science Advisory Committee was formed to provide projects and open access policies and to follow the open access studies in the world. In addition, some institutions provided guidance on how to develop open access practices and policy issues.

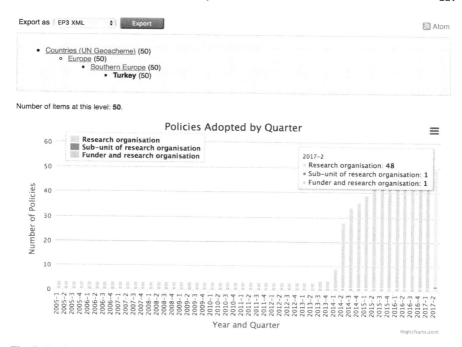

Fig. 5   Registered open access policies in ROARMAP

2.3   Open License

Open license practices in Turkey are shaped under the Creative Commons license. Each institution determines the sharing conditions and provided them under the usage conditions part of the platform. However, the awareness about the license protocols and Creative Commons lags behind the expectancy. Based on the study of Kursun (2011), one of the major challenges for the OER movement was the lack of information about institutional policies on sharing resources. According to the report provided by TÜBITAK, nearly 25% of the participants (672 of 2295 participants) mentioned having concerns about the legal rights and applications of sharing the resources (Basar, 2015).

To increase the awareness of the legal rights and applications of getting and sharing the resources, a website was created as CreativeCommons Türkiye by the Özyeğin University (affiliated institution) and Hacettepe University. The mission of this project is to increase the awareness about open education and open license and to provide a roadmap for how to use and share the resources under the open license. (see the website link through http://creativecommons.org.tr).

2.4 Resources

2.4.1 Open Access Repositories

The first path for the open education movement in Turkey began with the establishment of ANKOS in 2000 (Tonta, 2008) to share the institutions' resources, to provide common license practices and to organize agreements with other consortiums. Since 2000, open access repositories are formed under the institutions and organizations in Turkey. The first repository is provided under the supervision of Ankara University in 2005 (Karasözen, et al., 2010). Moreover, National Thesis Database by YOK (2007) (see https://tez.yok.gov.tr/UlusalTezMerkezi/) and e-thesis repository by Middle East Technical University (METU) (2003) (see http://lib.metu.edu. tr/metu-theses-collection-search) are two examples to transform thesis into digital format and to provide open access for resources within the permission of the authors. Nationwide, by 2017, 76 repositories are registered in OpenDOAR database as seen in Fig. 6.

DergiPark (JournalPark) project is also the data provider of OpenAire and 1.978 journals are accessible through the OpenAire database also. Moreover, with the contribution of ULAKBIM National Open Science Advisory Committee, Turkey Academic Repository was established in 2016 and 62 institutional repositories are active by 2018 (see the website http://arsiv.ulakbim.gov.tr/index).

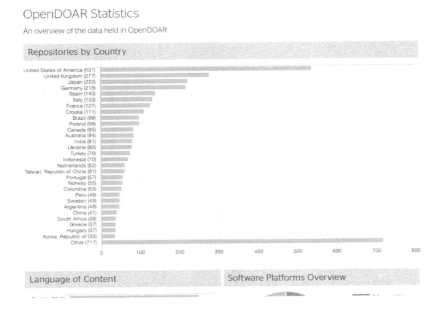

Fig. 6 Open access repositories in Turkey

No.	Name	Type	Software	Country
1.	Adnan Menderes University	Institutional	DSpace	Turkey
2.	Afyon Kocatepe Üniversitesi Açık Erişim Sistemi	Institutional	DSpace	Turkey
3.	Akademik Arşiv	Institutional	DSpace	Turkey
4.	Akdeniz Universitesi Kurumsal Arsivi	Institutional	DSpace	Turkey
5.	Ankara University Archive System	Institutional	Other (MiTOS)	Turkey
6.	Atatürk Üniversitesi Açık Arşivi	Institutional	Other (MiTOS)	Turkey
7.	Atılım University Open Archive System	Institutional	Other (MiTOS)	Turkey
8.	Bartın Üniversitesi Akademik Arşiv Sistemi	Institutional	DSpace	Turkey
9.	Baskent University Institutional Repository	Institutional	DSpace	Turkey
10.	Batman Üniversitesi Akademik Arşiv Sistemi	Institutional	DSpace	Turkey
11.	Beykent University Institutional Repository	Institutional	DSpace	Turkey
12.	Bilecik University	Institutional	DSpace	Turkey
13.	Bilkent University Institutional Repository	Institutional	DSpace	Turkey

Fig. 7 Software used in the open access repositories

Moreover, TÜBITAK provided national document supply through Cahit Arf Information Center (ULAKBIM) that comprises the national academic journals, national academic license and bibliometric analysis (DergiPark, TR Index, EKUAL, UBYT and Bibliometric Analysis). The most used software in the open access repositories in institutions' databases shown in Fig. 7 are DSpace, EPrints, Mitos and Contentdm.

2.4.2 Open Courseware

Open Courseware firstly diffused into educational context by the MIT's OCW project which aims to openly provide course materials. This movements' reflections in Turkey emerged in two directions: nationwide OCW project and the institutions' own OCW platforms.

The first prevalent project was originated to generate a nationwide platform with the collaboration of different organizations: TÜBA, TÜBITAK, DPT and institutions. In the State Planning Organization's (DPT) 2006–2010 Information Society Action Plan (2010), OER movement was pointed as a priority action under action number 89 (DPT, 2009).

TÜBA sent an invitation letter on May 11, 2007 to volunteer universities for their participation to the consortium. On May 25, 2007, the first Turkish OCW Consortium

(UADMK) general meeting was held and the executive board was selected. Although there was slow progress between 2007 and 2009, after the second UADMK general meeting on May 22, 2009 activities related to OER were increased. The number of universities in the Turkish OCW consortium has increased to fifty-seven since its establishment. Figure 6 shows cities where consortium member universities are located. In Istanbul, there are 10 universities which are a member of the Turkish OCW consortium, six of them are private universities and there are also four private and four state universities in Ankara. Although the UADMK has a high number of members (see http://www.acikders.org.tr/mod/page/view.php?id=712), only six of them started their own OCW portals.

In 2009, the DPT provided about 1.2 million USD grant for two-year pilot OER project with the leadership of the Turkish OCW Consortium. In the first year of the project (2010), courses from natural and applied science were developed. In the second year, courses from social sciences were translated to Turkish from other OER initiatives and new courses will be developed in the scope of this project. Interest for the OER is growing in Turkey with the help of institutions like TUBA and DPT.

OCW platforms are mostly provided by institutions. There is a growing number of institutions that shared the course resources online, but few of them have sustained to offer the resources and to update the content of the courses.

METU OCW initiative started officially on April 16, 2008 (Çevik, Gürel, Gürbüz, & Cagiltay, 2010). Now, it is the largest OER initiative in Turkey with 118 courses from 32 departments. METU OCW is also a member institution of International OCW Consortium. Since the language of the instruction at METU is in English, most of the course materials are in the English language, but there are Turkish courses as well. Course materials are provided as texts, presentations, videos and simulations (Simulations are provided for the laboratory courses as well). Besides course materials, there are different kinds of extra materials like videos from METU faculty members or videos of seminars conducted at METU published through the site. The site has been led by the Instructional Technology Support Office (ITS) of METU. This office was established in 2005 under the presidency of the university. Moreover, as part of the OCW project, China Open Resources for Education (CORE) office began to serve a mirror copy of METU OCW.

Ankara University started its work related to OER after the first meeting held in March 2007 within the organization of TUBA. Ankara University is also a member of the International OCW Consortium. The resources are mostly text-based and presentation formats. Ankara University OCW portal is based on Moodle learning management system. The faculty member should commit to preparing their courses based on the standards of the platform. Volunteer faculty members can submit their courses in two ways, either submitting their course materials to the system by signing or applying through e-mail by filling the course application form. In the first method, faculty members create an account on the system and during this step s/he has to provide an e-mail address that belongs to Ankara University (@ankara.edu.tr). Then s/he can upload his/her course materials to the temporary section which is only visible to the faculty member and system administrator. Finally, the course is transferred to the related department section by the system administrator.

One of the important characteristics of the Ankara OCW is that it is the first university that provides academic reward points to faculty members who publish their course materials as an OER (Atılgan, personal communication, September 06, 2010). Although some of the faculty members who need academic points in a short time published their courses on Ankara OCW, this initiative did not make any drastic increase on the number of the courses. Just a few faculty members published their course materials after this incentive.

Hacettepe OCW project (HUADM) has been led by the Digital Media Research and Application Center. There are seven open courses available in the portal under the six departments, Computer Education and Instructional Technology, Electrical and Electronic Engineering and Mathematics. Course materials are generally available in presentation format (pdf, pps and ppt). Courses under the Electric and Electrical Engineering department are comprised of video course materials. These video materials consist of both lecture sessions and problem-solving sessions.

New course applications for HUADM can be done through e-mail. Submitted course materials are organized by the project team. This process has been done in collaboration with the responsible faculty member. The URL for the access of the Hacettepe OCW is http://acikders.hacettepe.edu.tr/index.html.

2.4.3   MOOCs

There are some attempts in Turkey to provide Massive Open Online Course (MOOCs). The first attempt was made by Anadolu University in 2013 but it was not launched because of enrollment rate and lack of support (Erdem-Aydin, 2015). The second attempt was conducted by Koc University by translating some courses in Turkish and creating some courses for Coursera platform in 2014 (Erdem-Aydin, 2015). Third, some profit organizations like Turkcell Digital Academy provided some programs and courses in EdX and their own platforms, and non-profit communities like UniversitePlus offered some courses in collaboration with universities (Aydin, 2017). Moreover, some attempts have been also proceeding that some resources and contents in Khan Academy were translated in Turkish in 2014 and provided under the website (see http://www.khanacademy.org.tr).

On the other hand, the first institutional attempt was conducted by Ataturk University as a non-profit AtademiX platform in 2014 (Bingöl, 2016). By 2018, 12 courses are offered on the website.

In 2014, also another university, Anadolu University, developed the platform Akadema (see the website https://ekampus.anadolu.edu.tr/#). Two types of courses are offered in the platform as structured courses with strict instructional period and non-structured courses that enable to study at self-pace (see Moreover, Yasar University in Izmir provided courses in the website and 21 courses are active by 2018).

The last, BilgeIs project was held under the supervision of METU with the collaborations of different organizations and companies in 2015 which aims to develop and improve the adaptation abilities of employees and employers. 100 courses from

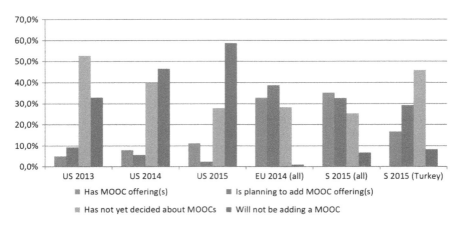

Fig. 8 MOOCs compared to US, EU and Turkey (Aydin, 2016, p. 12)

different professions are aimed to offer online and the materials are formed as videos, texts and simulations (Cagiltay, Esfer, & Celik, 2019).

However, the projects (except Bilgeİş) did not meet the number of initiatives compared to other countries which few attempts struggle to meet the expectations of users. A report in 2016 describes the HE institution's perspectives toward MOOCs which most of them did not have plans to develop a MOOC as could be seen in Fig. 8 (Aydin, 2016).

2.5 Curriculum and Teaching Methodology

There are limited studies on how to integrate OERs into curriculum and to improve the teaching methodologies. Not a nationwide project but one course structure was analyzed based on METU OCW platform.

METU OCW project is significant to integrate OCW process in the university information system. There are different signs of this integration. First of all, some instructors actively use METU OCW portal as a learning management system of their courses. In this way, students can submit their assignments to the course site. Different units of the university allocate their resources for the METU OCW project. For example, the Computer Center of the university provides server and maintenance of OCW METU portal. Faculty members or university students can log in the portal with their METU e-mail account. In this way, students can also upload their assignment to the course page or have the opportunity to discuss issues on forums in the context of OCW courses (Köybaşı-Gürel, Islim, Cagiltay, & Çevik, 2014).

However, there is limited information on how the teachers actively integrate the resources into the course system and how the students actively engage in this process. One of the courses provided in the OCW portal (General Chemistry Laboratory Course) was investigated based on the integration and use of open educational resources through the 2014–2016 academic year (Tisoglu, 2017).

According to this study, the results showed that the formation of the resources did not trigger the use and integration of the resources into the educational system. Related with the use and integration of the OERs, the policy practices, the components and activities in the classroom setting and usage behaviors were found related to providing a complete picture of the phenomenon. The issues were analyzed in three categories (human factor, instructional and administrative level) based on the system theory. The lack of policy practices, personal problems and academic concerns of the teachers, adaptation problems to new technologies, the quality of the materials and their association with the grading systems, the optional profile of the resources were analyzed as the main barriers to integrate the resources into the curriculum. The OERs had somewhat minimal effect on the teaching process for teaching assistants and for students in the experimentation process.

Another study was conducted nationwide (Kursun, Cagiltay, & Can, 2014) which could envision the barriers to create, share and integrate the resources actively into the formal education system. Data were collected from 1637 faculty members from 56 universities in Turkey. According to the results of this study, the greatest barrier for faculty members is having/expecting problems about protecting the intellectual property rights of their own materials ($M = 4.23$, SD $= 1.67$). The other five major barriers with the highest overall means scores are: having/expecting problems about clearing intellectual property rights of someone else' materials ($M = 4.20$, SD $= 1.50$) reluctance of faculty members about sharing their course materials ($M = 4.01$, SD $= 1.41$) lack of necessary incentives about sharing course materials ($M = 4.00$, SD $= 1.66$) increase in plagiarism with freely publishing course materials through the Internet ($M = 3.85$, SD $= 1.65$) lack of institutional policies about sharing course materials ($M = 4.59$, SD $= 1.69$). According to this study, barriers can be categorized into four main themes. These are intellectual property rights, institutional, technical and personal barriers. As for instructors' perceptions of technical infrastructure in their universities ($M = 2.93$, SD $= 1.70$), they think that they have the necessary technical infrastructure at their universities. Items that go under the technical barriers theme have the lowest mean scores. From results, it can be said that most of the instructors perceive that they have required competencies for developing course materials in a digital environment ($M = 2.51$, SD $= 1.57$). Also, most of the instructors do not have problems with accessing the required hardware (computer, scanner etc.) ($M = 2.29$, SD $= 1.54$). That is, we can say that technical equipment is not a critical barrier for instructors. One of the most common barriers mentioned in literature is the lack of time and results show that instructors somewhat agree that they don't have enough time to involve ($M = 3.44$). Results also indicated that instructors' course load is high ($M = 3.52$).

2.6 Outcome

Related with the outcomes of the use and integration of OERs, the limited studies are also valid for the Turkey case. While there are some OCW platforms provided by the universities, the limited published studies for the outcomes lead to problems of making inferences. Regarding the use and awareness of the OERs, three studies were prominent. The first one held by the researcher in TÜBİTAK related to the awareness and satisfaction of open access repositories (Basar, 2015). According to this study, while more than half of the participants were aware of the open education and open access, most of them had concerns about the quality, originality of the resources, license regulations and lack of information about open education practices.

According to another study conducted in METU with 1196 participants, 46.49% of the students ($n = 556$) were aware of the METU OCW platform and the resources and 309 students actively used the system (Islim & Cagiltay, 2016). Among 309 students, 268 of them mentioned that the resources had a positive effect on the lab grades. Another study was conducted between 2014 and 2016 academic year to better understand the current situation of OER use and integration (Tisoglu, 2017). Based on the results of this study, usage behaviors directly affected participants' performances, which encompass academic, cognitive, affective and psychomotor outcomes. However, the students and teaching assistants' use of the resources was not compulsory, thus the academic performance of the students was not solely associated with the use of OERs. Even so, while the resources had a mainly weak effect on students' academic performance, the affective and psychomotor outcomes were found more promising for the OERs. In line with these issues, derived from the expectations, some part of the cognitive domain was highly achieved (procedural knowledge) while much higher tasks were found unsatisfactory.

2.7 Stakeholders

The major funder of the practices of open education in Turkey is TÜBITAK. Beside this council, YÖK, DPT (which engaged under the Ministry of Industry and Technology) and Directorate General of Innovation and Educational Technologies also engaged in ICT projects, OCW initiatives and policy practices. Institutions are also significant to provide projects especially creating and providing OCW platforms. Non-profit organizations also promote activities and conferences especially in open access policies and archives. In Fig. 9, all stakeholders took place in open education initiatives are displayed.

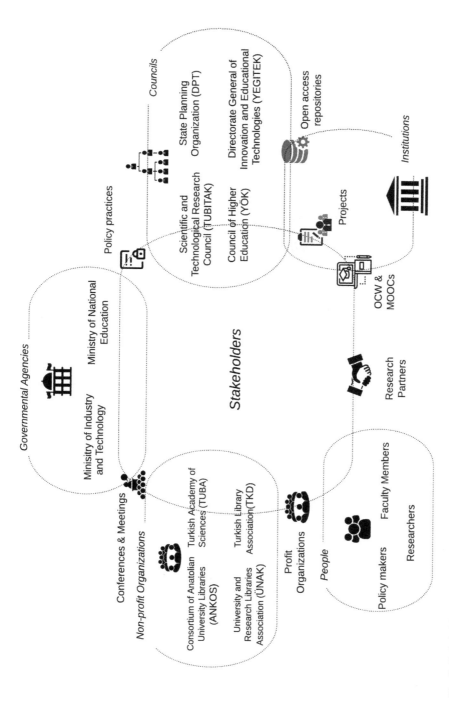

Fig. 9 Stakeholders in open education initiatives in Turkey

2.8 Impact

While the limited studies of drawing a detailed picture for the advancements, practices and outcomes of OERs, policy practices, open access movements, institutional repositories and the international and nationwide projects, and open access symposiums and meetings increase the awareness and triggers the new developments for the OER movement in Turkey. The possible impact of OERs is presented through three paths as the impact on educational developments, improvement of the higher education system and foreign policies of Turkey.

2.8.1 Educational Developments

OER movement helps higher education institutions in Turkey to keep up with the educational developments in other universities around the world. In Organization for Economic Co-operation and Development's (OECD) report, titled Giving Knowledge for Free, four main forces that impact higher education institutions in the coming decade were mentioned: globalization, demography, changing governance and technology. It is important to use these forces for the improvement of Turkish universities and they should get along their steps well with changing world conditions. The collaboration of the universities toward this purpose is crucial in this aspect. OER movement should be implemented in Turkish universities after careful analyses to get maximum benefits from its promises. Through the international projects, EC 2020 liabilities enable the policymakers, organizations and institutions to generate open access policies, repositories and open educational resources. In addition, now most of the universities open up their resources and materials and encourage the faculty members to adapt the new developments of open educational resources.

2.8.2 Improvement of Current Higher Education System

The OER movement helps the improvement of the current higher education system in Turkey by making educational resources more accessible. As stated above, though important progress has been achieved worldwide to benefit from new technologies, as acknowledged in the strategic plan of the Turkish Higher Education Council (2007), it is difficult to see this development on the Turkish higher education system sufficiently (Higher Education Council of Turkey, 2007). As mentioned before, instructional technology needs a paradigm change to focus on new forms of education. Also in the report, it is underlined that there should be a change from instructor-centered approach to student-centered approach. In this sense, OER movement may provide opportunities for Turkish tertiary education since it is likely to accelerate changes in traditional teaching and the evolution of more independent learners (OECD, 2007). As mentioned above, open access is generally achieved by most institutions but the type of materials are not diverse. However, the integration of the OCW platforms to LMS in some institutions provides a comprehensive system for instructional environments.

2.8.3 Positive Impact on Foreign Policies of Turkey

OER movement may have a positive impact on the foreign policies of Turkey. This movement is likely to help higher educational institutions to integrate into Bologna process by accelerating content development through different projects which provided resources on how to produce and use of OERs (OLCOS project, see https://olcos.org/english/cooperations/index.htm). In addition to that, the impact of Turkey on Turkish speaking countries (i.e. Azerbaijan, Turkmenistan, Uzbekistan etc.) can be expanded by opening educational resources in the Turkish language. In this way, people in these countries can find a chance to access educational content in Turkish Universities, so this can be seen as a promotion of Turkish Universities. So, Turkish Universities might attract more students from such countries. Moreover, according to Ministry of Foreign Affairs, there are approximately 6,5 million Turkish citizens who are living abroad where a great portion (around 5,5 million) are living in the European Union member countries, which one of the main problems encountered by the expatriate Turkish community is education (Ministry of Foreign Affairs 2011). Therefore, OER movement might provide opportunities for the expatriate Turkish community abroad by providing materials and resources in their mother-tongues as well as considering the cultural and historical heritage of our country.

3 Discussion and Conclusion

Two initiatives have affected to focus on the open education practices in Turkey. First, the attempt to create platforms to share the course materials as MITs OCW project by the leadership of TÜBA. Second, open access practices since 2005 and the YOK's and TUBITAK's projects which object to open up the resources under the platforms. However, Turkey did not catch the open access developments simultaneously with the world (Karasözen, et al., 2010).

The first initiative gained much attention from universities and faculty members but in practice, the development of course materials is not actively in progress and some institutions currently try to enhance their platforms by their funds and resources. The policies on how to share, collaborate, remix and reuse the resources which lead to awareness on how to use creative commons maintain a challenge to offer the resources. Moreover, teachers faced challenges of developing the content and the lack of guidance and the inequality of the resources among the university's OCW platforms (Al & Madran, 2013). Besides this, the eagerness of faculty members to share the resources is not promising that convincing the faculty members mostly achieved by personal communications and explanations (Kurşun, 2011). This problem was also faced in TÜBITAK's two projects namely academic e-book and academic e-course in 2014. The application to these projects was under the expected that 7 projects for e-book and 8 projects for e-course were supported and funded. Another challenge faced regarding OCW is the lack of common policy practices to apply. Lack of infrastructure and the faculty members' positions, this practice did not correspond to the new practices on OCW platforms. Also, the value of these practices should be added to foster the faculty members to share the resources.

The most faced challenges with regard to open education practices are the shift to the new pedagogical approaches and learning environments. Moreover, the signs of the integration process of OERs into educational contexts are vague to make inferences. The resources provided under OCW platforms are unfortunately *content focused* rather than *learning focused*. Teaching with the new technological developments is valid but the course materials and resources displayed the limited type of resources are provided through the platforms.

The outcomes of the studies related to the OERs points to an increase in awareness of open access, OERs and open access journals, however, the initiatives stay standalone regarding the faculty members to share the resources and to apply license regulations. The license protocol problems seem to be one of the major barriers to change the faculty members' perception and sharing the resources (Şen-Baysal, Cakir, & Toplu, 2015). The attempts to provide a platform to advertise the Creative Commons, this practice needs to be more recognizable nationwide.

The policy practices of open access practices display a more sustainable process by the contribution of YÖK, TÜBITAK, private and public commission and conferences. Most of the universities, organizations began to offer their resources in their open archives which enable them to catch the trends on open access in the world (Cimen, 2012). Most of the universities provide open archives and open access journals increase access to publicly available scientific research. Different profit and non-profit platforms (MOOCs) and websites provided bilingual language (Turkish and English) emerged to foster the lifelong learning but in the future, these initiatives move beyond the early organizations and adopters to the new stakeholders and to provide more applicable and unified strategies and policies for a sustainable open education movement.

In summary, since 2004, some actions have taken place beginning with the translation of MIT's courses to Turkish course resources and have proceeded to the development of OCW platforms, MOOCs and open access repositories. Also, institutions, organizations and councils took actions with participating in some nationwide and international projects which helped to embrace the open educational practices in Turkey. Specifically, the attempts for open access (journals, libraries etc.) stimulated the awareness of open resources and open access policy. However, the practices remain isolated to establish a full-scale awareness for open education. The concerns about policy practices, sharing regulations and the lack of information about creative commons are challenges still faced by faculty members where the policy practices and frameworks fail to enlighten how to integrate the OERs to curriculum and educational activities. Few universities achieved to provide the course materials and they have sustained to enrich the courses, on the other hand, others still struggled to provide their resources. The financial issues, traditional perspectives in education probably inhibit the integration of new developments in education, thus in the future, the institutions should take the role to provide opportunities for faculty members to share the resources and to improve technical issues to develop a platform for the resources. Open education could be meaningful by integrating them into the formal education system. Moreover, policy practices of open education should be reshaped by institutions to align with the curriculum, activities and programs. Governmental agencies and councils could provide more projects to encourage open education practices in Turkey.

References

Al, U., & Madran, O. (2013). An overview to open courseware: An example of the Turkish Academy of Sciences. *Bilgi Dünyası, 14*(1), 1–16.

Aydin, C. H. (2016). Current status of the MOOC movement in the world and reaction of the Turkish higher education institutions. *Higher education Online: MOOCs the European way* (pp. 1–27).

Aydin, C. H. (2017). Current status of the MOOC movement in the world and reaction of the Turkish Higher Education Institutions. *Open Praxis, 9*(1), 59–78.

Basar, F. (2015). Açık Erişim Farkındalık ve Memnuniyet Anketi Sonuç Raporu. TUBİTAK ULAKBIM. https://ulakbim.tubitak.gov.tr/sites/images/Ulakbim/acik_erisim_anket_raporu_aralik_2015.pdf.

Bingöl, I. (2016). *Investigation of factors affecting students' success and completion according to participant types in massive open online courses.* Retrieved from National Thesis Database.

Cagiltay, K., Esfer, S., & Celik, B. (2019). Insights into a Nationwide pdMOOC portal. In K. Zhang, C. J. Bonk, T. C. Reeves, & T. H. Reynolds (Eds.), *MOOCs and open education in the global south* (pp. 130–140). New York: Routledge.

Cagiltay, K., Kara, E., & Esfer, S. (2016). Türkiye'de Aktif İnternet Kullanım Eğilimleri: 2004–2014 Dönemi. Inet-tr Conference, TED University, Turkey.

Çevik, R., Gürel, N., Gürbüz, T., & Cagiltay, K. (2010, February). Orta Doğu Teknik Üniversitesi Açık Ders Malzemeleri Projesi Deneyimleri, Akademik Bilişim, Muğla, Turkey.

Cimen, E. (2012). Future of resource sharing in Turkey: Can open access be an alternative? *Interlending & Document Supply, 40*(3), 144–149.

Department of Strategy Development. (2017). *Turkish education system.* Retrieved from http://sgb.meb.gov.tr/eurydice/kitaplar/Turk_Egitim_Sistemi_2017/TES_2017.pdf.

Erdem-Aydin, I. (2015). Preferences and willingness for participating MOOCS in Turkish. *The Turkish Online Journal of Educational Technology, 14*(2).

Ertürk, K. L. (2008). *Türkgiye'de Bilimsel Gelişim: Bir Açık Erişim Modeli Önerisi* (Doctoral dissertation). Retrieved from BBY Thesis Archive, Hacettepe University, Ankara.

European Commission. (2018, April). *Commission staff working document Turkey 2018 report.* Retrieved from https://ec.europa.eu/neighbourhood-enlargement/sites/near/files/20180417-turkey-report.pdf.

Eurostat. (2018). *Households with broadband access.* Retrieved from http://ec.europa.eu/eurostat/statistical-atlas/gis/viewer/?mids=BKGCNT,C09M01,CNTOVL&o=1,1,0.7&ch=C04,SCT,C09&center=45.24697,32.40735,3&lcis=C09M01&.

Higher Education Council of Turkey (YÖK). (2007, February). *Turkey's higher education strategy.* Retrieved from http://www.yok.gov.tr/documents/10279/30217/yok_strateji_kitabi/27077070-cb13-4870-aba1-6742db37696b.

Islim, O. F., & Cagiltay, K. (2016). The impact of OER on instructional effectiveness: A case study. *EURASIA Journal of Mathematics, Science and Technology Education, 12*(3), 559–567.

234   S. Tisoglu et al.

Karasözen, B., Zan, B. U., & Atılgan, D. (2010). Open access in Turkey and comparison with other countries. *Türk Kütüphaneciliği, 24*(2), 235–257.
Köybaşı-Gürel, N., Islim, O. F., Cagiltay, K., & Çevik, R. (2014, April). Use of OpenCourseWare from the viewpoint of Undergraduate students: Case of OER for Physics Laboratory Experiments, OCWC Global 2014: Open Education for a Cultural World, Ljubljana, Slovenia.
Kursun, E. (2011). *An investigation of incentives, barriers and values about the OER movement in Turkish universities: Implications for policy framework* (Doctoral dissertation). Retrieved from Middle East Technical University E-thesis database, Ankara.
Kursun, E., Cagiltay, K., & Can, G. (2014). An investigation of faculty perspectives on barriers, incentives, and benefits of the OER movement in Turkey. *International Review of Research in Open and Distance Learning, 15*(6).
Ministry of Foreign Affairs. (2011). *The expatriate Turkish citizens.* Retrieved from http://www.mfa.gov.tr/the-expatriate-turkish-citizens.en.mfa.
Ministry of National Education (MEB). (2018). *National education statistics, formal education 2017/'18.* Retrieved from https://sgb.meb.gov.tr/meb_iys_dosyalar/2018_09/06123056_meb_istatistikleri_orgun_egitim_2017_2018.pdf.
OECD. (2007). Giving knowledge for free: The emergence of open educational resources. *OECD Publishing.* https://doi.org/10.1787/9789264032125-en.
OECD. (2017). *Access to computers from home.* https://data.oecd.org/ict/access-to-computers-from-home.htm.
OLCOS. (2007). *The Open eLearning Content Observatory Services project.* https://olcos.org/english/about/index.htm.
Şen-Baysal, A., Çakır, H., & Toplu, H. (2015). The evaluation of open educational resources and the application areas of Turkey. *Türk Kütüphaneciliği, 29*(3), 461–498.
The State Planning Organization (DPT). (2009, March). *Bilgi Toplumu Stratejisi Eylem Planı (2006–2010). Değerlendirme Raporu No:3* [Information society strategy action plan (2006–2010). Evaluation Report No: 3]. Retrieved from http://www.bilgitoplumu.gov.tr/Documents/1/BT_Strateji/Diger/090500_BTS-Degerlendirme_III.pdf.
Tisoglu, S. (2017). *Exploring the use of open educational resources in chemistry laboratory course context: A case study* (Doctoral dissertation). Retrieved from Middle East Technical University E-thesis database, Ankara.
Tonta, Y. (2008). Open access and institutional repositories: The Turkish landscape. In D. Bayır (Ed.), *Turkish libraries in transition: new opportunities and challenges* (pp. 27–47). İstanbul: Turkish Librarians' Association.
Turkstat. (2016a). *Number of registered non-formal institutions.* Retrieved from http://www.tuik.gov.tr/PreTablo.do?alt_id=1018.
Turkstat. (2016b). *Education statistics of schooling rate for children.* Retrieved from http://www.tuik.gov.tr/PreTablo.do?alt_id=1018.
Turkstat. (2018). *Information society statistics.* Retrieved from http://www.tuik.gov.tr/PreTablo.do?alt_id=1028.
TÜBITAK. (2012). *Evaluation of developments report from 24th meeting.* Retrieved from http://www.tubitak.gov.tr/tubitak_content_files//BTYPD/BTYK/btyk24/BTYK_24_gelismeler_web.pdf.
TÜBITAK. (2015). *Evaluation of developments report from 28th meeting.* Retrieved from https://www.tubitak.gov.tr/sites/default/files/btyk28_gelismeler.pdf.
TÜBITAK. (2019). *TÜBITAK Open science policy.* Retrieved from http://www.tubitak.gov.tr/sites/default/files/tubitak_acik_bilim_politikasi_190316.pdf.
YÖK. (2014). *Yüksek Öğretim Açık Erişim ve Kurumsal Arşiv Politikası.* Retrieved from http://www.yok.gov.tr/documents/7166509/7180015/Kurumsal+Arşiv.pdf/b5332da8-de7b-4730-bca3-a53e546d1c58.
YÖK. (2018). *Open access and open science.* Retrieved from https://www.yok.gov.tr/Sayfalar/Haberler/acik-erisim-ve-acik-bilim-calismalarina-baslandi.aspx.

Assist. Prof. Dr. Secil Tisoglu earned her Ph.D. from Middle East Technical University and she attended Florida State University as visiting scholar for one year. She currently works at Kastamonu University in Department of Educational Science and her research interests are open educational resources, educational games, technology enhanced learning, and internet safety.

Assoc. Prof. Dr. Engin Kursun earned his Ph.D. from Middle East Technical University and he attended Open University, UK as visiting scholar for six months. He currently works at Ataturk University in Department of Computer Education and Instructional Technology. He is the director and stakeholder of many national and international projects also. His research interests are open educational resources, human computer interaction, mobile learning and internet safety.

Prof. Dr. Kursat Cagiltay earned his double Ph.D. from IST Department and Cognitive Science Program with a minor in Information Science in Indiana University. He is the director of many national and international projects regarding different aspects of educational and information technology. His academic interests are Cognitive Aspects of Human Learning System, Technology Enhanced Learning and STEAM Education, Educational Technology in Special Education, Human-Computer-Interaction, Human Performance Technology, Electronic Games and Simulations, Educational Neuroscience and Neurotechnology, Distance Education and OER/OCW, Social Informatics, Telecommunications and the Internet. Please see http://users.metu.edu.tr/kursat/.

Part III
Conclusion

Chapter 13
Open Educational Resources in the Belt and Road Countries: Conclusions and Future Directions

Ahmed Tlili, Ting-Wen Chang, Ronghuai Huang and Daniel Burgos

1 Introduction

The development of open educational resources (OER) has been considered one of the most important developments in educational practices worldwide (OECD, 2007). This new way of learning and knowledge transfer has been introduced in the Western world since the inception of the new millennium. Due to its positive impact on learning experiences and outcomes, it has drawn the attention of many countries and organizations (Tlili, Huang, Chang, Nascimbeni, & Burgos, 2019). Therefore, the present book chapter summarizes the current state of OER in all the presented 11 countries and conducts a comparative study between them to draw conclusions on what is still missing in order to facilitate OER adoption in the Belt and Road region. Specifically, this chapter discusses each dimension in a separate section and then draws conclusions for the reader.

2 Current Situation

2.1 Infrastructure and Stakeholders

As shown in Table 1, OER adoption requires a solid infrastructure that can have different components, including software, hardware, and resources. Specifically, the presence of these elements is investigated in Table 1. If an element is present in a

A. Tlili (✉) · T.-W. Chang · R. Huang
Smart Learning Institute of Beijing Normal University, Beijing, China
e-mail: ahmed.tlili23@yahoo.com

D. Burgos
UNIR iTED, Universidad Internacional de La Rioja (UNIR), 26006 Logroño, Spain

© Springer Nature Singapore Pte Ltd. 2020
R. Huang et al. (eds.), *Current State of Open Educational Resources in the "Belt and Road" Countries*, Lecture Notes in Educational Technology,
https://doi.org/10.1007/978-981-15-3040-1_13

Table 1 OER infrastructure in the Belt and Road countries

Countries	Authoring tools	MOOC providers	Cloud computing	National OER repositories	Open curriculum	Inclusive open learning
South Korea	✓	✓	✓	×	×	×
Italy	✓	✓	✓	×	×	×
Austria	✓	✓	✓	×	×	×
Turkey	✓	✓	✓	×	×	×
Serbia	✓	✓	✓	×	×	×
Estonia	✓	✓	✓	×	×	×
Morocco	✓	✓	✓	×	×	×
South Africa	✓	✓	✓	×	×	×
Romania	✓	✓	✓	×	×	×
Palestine	✓	✓	✓	×	×	×
China	✓	✓	✓	×	×	×
Mongolia	✓	✓	✓	×	×	×

country, the cell has a sign; otherwise, it has a × sign. Various observations can be made from the table.

Authoring tools. All countries have different kinds of authoring tools that are essential for producing OER. Particularly, most of these countries use international authoring tools, but no national authoring tools are provided by these countries.

MOOC providers. Since the beginning of the OER movement, several massive open online courses (MOOCs) were introduced in different countries in different forms. Most of them are semi-formally online according to the OER definition (i.e., these MOOCs are open, but most of them are not under an open license).

Cloud computing. All Belt and Road countries share reliable and solid infrastructure, which allows easy access to OER, including cloud computing and online databases.

National OER repositories. Most Belt and Road countries access international OER repositories; however, they lack national repositories.

Open curriculum. All countries still use OER in a very simple way, with students getting to access open resources that are not well structured and organized to create open curriculums that can be used on a national level.

Inclusive open learning. OER is a big prospect for revolutionizing and reshaping the educational practice in all its aspects. However, it is found that inclusive OER use in the Belt and Road countries is still in its infancy. For instance, no case study has reported on the use of OER by students with disabilities or to enhance the learning process in rural education.

When OER was first introduced, many people were suspicious about its practicality, pedagogical validation, and integration into formal education. Consequently,

Table 2 The involved stakeholders in OER adoption

Stakeholders	Role
Teachers	Using OER for teaching
Students	Accessing OER to study and learn new skills/knowledge
Researchers	Conducting research on OER practices
Technologists	Developing infrastructure to support accessing OER
Governments	Launching new OER projects to support OER adoption in their countries
Innovators	Providing funds for sustainable OER projects

the number of stakeholders involved in OER was limited. However, gradually, OER has been incorporated into various practices, businesses, institutions, and policies. In the countries considered, several OER stakeholders were reported, as shown in Table 2.

2.2   Policy

Based on the case studies presented in this book, it is seen that OER policies and initiatives were launched by governments, educational institutions (universities and schools), or private enterprises. In all the countries mentioned, OER started as micro practices, subsequently gained widespread attention, and were then seen as an important part of national learning strategies in the countries' futuristic plans. As a result, governments incorporated OER into several policies, such as Austria's Report on Education 2016: Digital Roadmap 2016, Open Educational Resources by the Federal Ministry of Education (MBM, 2017b), and Digital Learning Tools. Similarly, Estonia and other countries passed several policies too. For example, Estonia passed The Estonian Lifelong Learning Strategy 2020 and Italy formed the Ministry of Education, University, and Research (MIUR). Specifically, Fig. 1 shows the Belt

Fig. 1 OER adoption in the Belt and Road countries

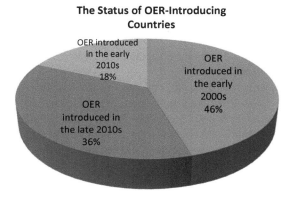

The Status of OER-Introducing Countries

OER introduced in the early 2010s 18%

OER introduced in the early 2000s 46%

OER introduced in the late 2010s 36%

and Road countries' categories based on the dates of introducing OER. For instance, China, Italy, Korea, Austria, Estonia, and Turkey introduced OER resources at the beginning of the 2000s.

2.3   Open License and OER in Learning/Teaching

From the legal perspective, OER should be published under an open license, which defines how other users can use these resources. However, different countries have different academic cultures, rules, and regulations that must be followed in the context of OER (re)use. For instance, Austria uses the Creative Commons license as one of many licenses. Similarly, Estonia uses the Copyright Act and Creative Commons as the licenses for OER. Although these countries use licenses, they still have not installed the latest versions of the basic software, such as Creative Commons 4.0. However, all Belt and Road countries still suffer from copyright issues, which can hinder the full adoption of OER. Therefore, in these countries, further investigation is needed, and copyright awareness must be raised.

Besides, OER is still being used in a very simple way by just accessing open resources. No case study has reported on the use of OER in a structured way in universities or schools to enhance learning outcomes. Researchers are now calling for OER to be applied in innovative ways to achieve new learning methods, including open pedagogies and assessments.

3   Guidelines and Conclusions

The application of OER in educational practices has brought a variety of benefits, such as learning efficacy and cost-efficacy. Particularly, it is seen that the Belt and Road countries have made a good step toward OER adoption by launching several OER pilot projects and programmes. However, it is also observed that several limitations might hinder OER adoption, as follows:

1. Several OER projects have been launched, but they were then stopped due to a lack of funds. Therefore, governments and policymakers should create clear strategies to have sustainable OER models in the Belt and Road countries and worldwide.
2. Copyright is still a common problem that hinders OER adoption in the Belt and Road countries. Therefore, policymakers should raise awareness about open licenses and legal issues of copyright violation.
3. Several national projects are launched to support OER in the Belt and Road countries, but these projects did not focus on developing OER repositories and authoring tools that might facilitate OER development and accessibility. Therefore, national projects should further cover these limitations in the future.

4. OER is being used as a simple resource without the goal of achieving new learning methods in schools and universities, such as open pedagogies and assessments. Furthermore, there is no formal training for teachers and educators regarding OER. Instead, teachers and educators are still using OER based on their own interests and self-regulated strategies. Therefore, all teachers and educators must be trained in the philosophy and practical issues of OER so that the practice can reflect the vision behind OER in education.

5. Further, OER is not part of the formal, accredited curriculum. OER facilities are used as complementary material in the classroom, but no real framework involving formal and nonformal education has been implemented. In doing so, OER would become a powerful ally in fostering quality education both in informal settings and in official academic programmes.

6. OER development to achieve inclusive learning in the Belt and Road countries is still in its early stages. Currently, no case study has reported on involving, for instance, disabled students, rural area students, or students from diverse cultural backgrounds in learning how to use OER. This should be changed as OER has several characteristics, such as openness and free access that allow it to fulfill different needs in different contexts.

References

OECD. (2007). *Giving knowledge for free: The emergence of open educational resources*. https://tinyurl.com/62hjx6.

Tlili, A., Huang, R., Chang, T. W., Nascimbeni, F., & Burgos, D. (2019). Open educational resources and practices in china: A systematic literature review. *Sustainability, 11*(18), 4867.

Dr. Ahmed Tlili is a former Assistant Professor of Educational Technology at the University of Kairouan, Tunisia, where he has supervised over 20 undergraduate students and taught different subjects, such as Human Computer Interaction (HCI), game development, web development, software engineering, and XML. Dr. Tlili is now working as a post-doctoral research fellow at the Smart Learning Institute of Beijing Normal University. He is currently leading projects in the fields of Open Educational Resources (OER) and Edutainment. Dr. Tlili is a member of the IEEE, OER laboratory of Smart Learning Institute, China and the laboratory of Technologies of Information and Communication & Electrical Engineering (LaTICE), Tunisia. His current research interests include open education, learning analytics, game-based learning, distance education, learner modeling, adaptive learning, artificial intelligence in education and educational psychology. Dr. Tlili has published several academic papers in international referred journals and conferences. He has served as a guest editor in the Smart Learning Environments journal, as a local organizing and program committee member in various international conferences, and as a reviewer in several refereed journals. Dr. Tlili is also the co-chair of the IEEE special interest group on Artificial Intelligence and Smart Learning Environments.

Dr. Ting-Wen Chang is the Associate Research Fellow and the Director of International Cooperation Center in Smart Learning Institute of Beijing Normal University (SLIBNU) for doing the research on Smart Learning as well as making many international cooperation projects since

March 2014. As the Director of International Cooperation Center, he has made more than 50 international scholars/experts as well as several overseas institutions for SLIBNU in order to create lots of international cooperation about innovative and the cutting-edge technologies of smart learning. Dr. Chang was the workshop coordinator for some key workshops of SLIBNU, such as in 2017, the 1st Workshop on VR and Immersive Learning in Harvard University, the 4th Annual International Conference "Education & Global Cities: Smart Learning for World Universities" in St. Petersburg, Russia, and the 12th edition of the eLearning Africa Conference in Republic of Mauritius. In September 2017, Dr. Chang has also been responsible for the ME310 Global Project with d.School of Stanford University.

Dr. Ronghuai Huang is currently a Professor in the Faculty of Education and Dean of Smart Learning Institute in Beijing Normal University, the Director of UNESCO International Rural Educational and Training Center and the Director of National Engineering Lab for Cyberlearning and Intelligent Technology. He serves as Vice Chairman of China Association for Educational Technology; Vice Chairman of China Educational Equipment Industry Association; Deputy Director of Collaborative and Innovative Center for Educational Technology; Director of Digital Learning and Public Education Service Center; Director of Professional Teaching and Guiding Committee for Educational Technology; Director of Beijing Key Laboratory for Educational Technology.

Dr. Daniel Burgos is a professor and works as Vice-rector for International Research (UNIR Research, http://research.unir.net), at Universidad Internacional de La Rioja (UNIR, Spain), a young 100% online university with over 34.000 students, and premises in Spain and Latin-America. He also holds a UNESCO Chair on eLearning (http://reserach.unir.net/unesco), and one ICDE Chair in Open Educational Resources (http://www.icde.org). He contributes to research and implementation projects about Educational Technology and Innovation, Open Science and Learning Analytics.